MICROSOFT®
Excel 5.0
by PicTorial

Julie Ying Shang

96. 1.

PicTorial Series

Dennis P. Curtin, Series Editor

Microsoft® Word 6.0 for Windows™ by PicTorial

WordPerfect® 6.0 for Windows™ by PicTorial

Microsoft® Excel 5.0 by PicTorial

Microsoft Access® 2.0 by PicTorial

Windows ™ 3.1 by PicTorial

Essentials of Windows ™ 3.1 by PicTorial

Microsoft® Excel 5.0 by PicTorial

Dennis P. Curtin

Donna M. Matherly

Tallahassee Community College

Prentice Hall
Englewood Cliffs, New Jersey 07632

Library of Congress Cataloging-in-Publication Data

Curtin, Dennis P.
    Microsoft Excel 5.0 by PicTorial / Dennis P. Curtin, Donna M.
Matherly
       p. cm.—(PicTorial series)
      ISBN 0-13-301219-0 (pbk.)
      1. Microsoft Excel (Computer file) 2. Business—Computer pro-
grams. 3. Electronic spreadsheets.
      I. Matherly, Donna M.S. (Donna May Schopmeyer).
      II. Title. III. Series: Curtin, Dennis P., PicTorial series.
      HF5548.4.M523C87   1995   94-43485
      005.369—dc20   CIP

Microsoft and XL design (the Microsoft Excel logo) are registered trademarks, and Windows is a trademark, of Microsoft Corporation in the United States of America and other countries.

Acquisitions editor: Carolyn Henderson
Development editor: Cecil Yarbrough
Marketing manager: Nancy Evans
Director of production and manufacturing: Joanne Jay
Managing editor: Joyce Turner
Screen shots and electronic composition: Cathleen Morin
Illustrations: Warren Fischbach and Freddy Flake
Design director: Linda Fiordilino
Cover art: © David Bishop/Phototake NYC
Manufacturing buyer: Paul Smolenski
Editorial assistant: Jane Avery
Production assistant: Renée Pelletier

© 1995 by Prentice-Hall, Inc.
A Division of Simon & Schuster
Englewood Cliffs, NJ 07632

ISBN 0-13-301219-0

Prentice-Hall International (UK) Limited, *London*
Prentice-Hall of Australia Pty. Limited, *Sydney*
Prentice-Hall of Canada Inc., *Toronto*
Prentice-Hall Hispanoamericana, S.A., *Mexico*
Prentice-Hall of India Private Limited, *New Delhi*
Prentice-Hall of Japan, Inc., *Tokyo*
Simon & Schuster Asia Ptd. Ltd., *Singapore*
Editora Prentice-Hall do Brasil, Ltda., *Rio de Janeiro*

CONTENTS

PREFACE

This text is an introduction to Microsoft Excel, one of the leading spreadsheet programs. Spreadsheets are one of the most common programs used on computers because they allow you to quickly and easily calculate numbers. The applications of programs such as Excel are almost endless, ranging from tasks that can be done just as easily on a calculator, such as adding a column of numbers, to tasks that aren't anywhere near as easy without the power of the computer. For example, you can prepare a single column showing a budget for the month of January and then, just by dragging that column, copy it to calculate the budget for February through December. As powerful as these features are, they pale in comparison to the speed with which you can explore changes. Change a single number anywhere in a budget such as this and instantly, all other numbers that depend on that number also change. For example, you can see how profits are affected if sales or costs rise or fall. Or, if analyzing a home loan, you can instantly see how an increase in interest rates affects the monthly payment on a home or car loan.

This text assumes only limited prior computing experience. Everything you need to know to become a proficient Excel user is presented here. You needn't bring anything else to your learning experience except a willingness to explore a new and exciting way to compute.

■ CONTENTS AND APPROACH

Many people are intimidated by application programs because they seem so complicated. Despite any preconceptions you might have, application programs are easy to learn and use. What makes them seem complicated is the vast number of things they can do. For example, Excel can be automated to do most of your repetitive tasks. However, you don't start learning Excel with this kind of application. You start by using it to analyze small and simple financial problems—and this part is easy. One way to look at learning any application program is to divide its features into four levels: core procedures, performance-enhancing procedures, productivity-enhancing procedures, and task-specific procedures. To learn a new program, you normally master each level before moving on to the next. In this respect it is much like climbing the stairs one step at a time. It is around this step-by-step approach that this text is structured.

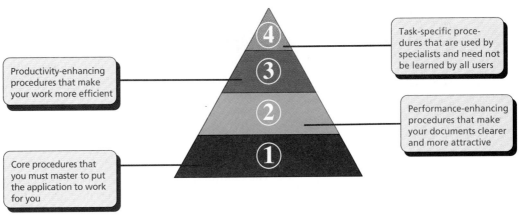

The four levels of features of all application programs

Core procedures are those procedures that you absolutely need to master to make an application useful. These core procedures include opening and saving workbooks, getting around the program, entering and editing data, and making printouts. To master this level of procedures in a program takes a few days at most.

Performance-enhancing features are those that allow you to prepare more sophisticated worksheets. For example, you can save time by entering a function instead of a formula in many situations. Or you can drag items about on the screen to more quickly move or copy them to a new location.

Productivity-enhancing features are those features that speed up your work and make you more efficient. For example, you can customize the application so it works better for you or automate tasks that you perform frequently.

Task-specific procedures are those that you learn only as the need arises. For example, Excel has many features designed for use by professionals in business and finance or by people who prepare papers or reports by extracting data from other programs. Almost no one today knows how to use all of these features of their programs. Some have limited value for most users and are aimed at small segments of the overall user group. These types of procedures are beyond the scope of this text.

■ ORGANIZATION AND COMPUTER ACTIVITIES

This text is organized into pictorial tutorials called *PicTorials*. Each PicTorial begins with objectives and then proceeds step by step through a series of related procedures. The concept behind each procedure is first discussed, and then a *tutorial* guides you in exploring the concept on the computer. At the end of each PicTorial are review questions and a large number of lab exercises that you complete at the computer.

Many textbooks use a projects approach, having you work on a limited set of worksheets as you progress through the text. The problem with this approach is its limitations. How many procedures are required for even a complex worksheet, and how many times need they be repeated? Without practicing procedures, and doing so repeatedly, you don't master them. This text uses a more structured approach that incorporates the following classes of worksheets:

▶ *Tutorial Worksheets* are used in the tutorials in the text. In many cases these are typical business-type worksheets such as checkbook registers, budgets, balance sheets, and income statements. In other cases they are worksheets designed to specifically illustrate a point that is being discussed.

▶ *Procedure Mastery Worksheets*, used in the QuickStep Drills, are designed to reinforce a single procedure though repetitive use. This narrow focus and use of repetition makes you much more familiar with a procedure than a typical worksheet where you might use a number of procedures but use each only once.

▶ *Skill-Building Exercise Worksheets* require more than a single procedure for completion. Many are threaded through the text from the beginning to the end so as you master new procedures, you revise and refine these worksheets. Some of these worksheets have been designed to give practice in worksheet-building while providing interesting or amusing information not related to business. For example, there are worksheets that analyze the foolishness of chain letters, the hidden costs of smoking, and the misleading advertising by state lottery agencies.

▶ *Project Worksheets* are like Exercise Worksheets but are more complex so they require a more thorough understanding of how procedures interact with each other. You are also given less guidance so you have to draw on what you have already learned.

■ KEY FEATURES

Windows is a visually oriented program, so this text uses a visual approach. It features PicTorials in addition to a number of other features designed to make it a better learning tool.

▶ *PicTorials* are heavily illustrated tutorials. The visuals serve two purposes. First, they help explain concepts. Second, they tell you when you are on course as you follow the steps in the tutorials.

▶ *QuickSteps boxes* summarize the steps you use for each procedure. These highlighted boxes are easy to find in each concepts section and make the text an ideal reference manual as well as a teaching tool.

▶ *Pausing for Practice boxes* appear periodically in tutorials when essential procedures have been introduced. They encourage you to stop at key points and practice these procedures until they become second nature.

▶ *Common Wrong Turns boxes* alert you to where many people make mistakes and show you how to avoid them.

▶ *Tips boxes* point out shortcuts and other interesting features about many procedures.

▶ *Looking Back boxes* are used whenever a procedure that has been discussed earlier is essential to completing a new task. These summaries are intended to remind you how to perform a task without your having to refer back in the text for the information.

▶ *Looking Ahead boxes* are used whenever a procedure is unavoidably referred to before it has been discussed in detail. Although this text has been written to make that situation occur infrequently, these boxes should help you avoid confusion by providing a brief description and an assurance that a more detailed discussion will follow.

▶ At the end of each PicTorial you will find a wide variety of true-false, multiple choice, and fill-in-the-blank questions to test how well you have understood the material.

▶ Exercises and Projects at the end of the PicTorials give you the opportunity to practice the procedures you have learned and demonstrate that you have mastered them.

▶ The worksheets used for lab activities are real-world applications. For example, in some places you work on home and car loans, budgets, balance sheets, cash-flow statements, income statements, product pricing, checkbook registers, and many other items you see in business or other areas of your life on a daily basis.

▶ An appendix, "Introducing Windows 3.1," explains important Windows procedures for students who are new to the Windows environment.

■ SUPPLEMENTS

An *Excel Student Resource Disk* and an *Excel Instructor's Manual with Tests*, the latter prepared by this book's co-author, Donna M. Matherly of Tallahassee Community College, are available. The manual contains suggested course outlines for a variety of course lengths and formats, teaching tips and a list of competencies to be attained for each PicTorial, solutions and answers to quizzes and all computer activities, and a complete test bank of over 200 questions.

■ NOTE ON THE STUDENT RESOURCE DISK

The *Excel Student Resource Disk* is provided to instructors for dissemination to their classes in whatever form best suits their laboratory needs. The disk includes all the workbooks needed to complete the lab activities in the text. The text assumes that each student will have the workbooks, which are intended to be copied onto two high-density floppy disks in order to leave room for students to do their own work. Files used in the tutorials and drills are placed on the *Excel Student Resource Disk (Part 1)*, while those used in exercises and projects are placed on the *Excel Student Resource Disk (Part 2)*.

To make the workbooks easy to use as class exercises to be turned in, most of them include a heading that includes a placeholder for the student's name. The heading also includes a date function that automatically calculates the date from the system clock and then updates it in the workbook. When you close a workbook that contains a date function, a dialog box asks whether you want to save your changes—even when you have made no changes. Because saving workbooks on floppy disks can be slow, we suggest that you answer "No" unless you have made changes.

■ NOTE TO THE INSTRUCTOR

Most of the lab activities in this text have a step telling students to print the document. In most cases, these printouts are for your use, not theirs. To reduce paper consumption in your classroom, tell your students to ignore these printing steps unless you ask them specifically to print a document or unless they have a problem they want to show you.

■ NOTE TO STUDENTS AND INSTRUCTORS

We are always happy to hear from users or potential users of the PicTorial Series; it's through such exchanges that improvements are made. If you have any comments or questions, send them to Dennis Curtin by e-mail on the Internet at P00359@PSILINK.COM. (You can use this address when sending e-mail from CompuServe, America Online, or any of the popular commercial services and it will get to him.)

■ ACKNOWLEDGMENTS

We would like to thank all of those people who have worked hard to make this the best possible text.
On the academic end have been the following reviewers:

▶ Cheryl L. Dukarich, Pima Community College

▶ Cynthia Harwell, Pitt Community College

▶ Sally L. Kurz, Coastline Community College

▶ Philip J. Sciame, Dominican College

▶ Katherine F. Vitale, adjunct faculty, Temple University

At the publisher's end Carolyn Henderson and Jane Avery smoothed the way for the authors' efforts, and Cecil Yarbrough edited the text and oversaw its production. Lorraine Patsco, Christy Mahon, and John A. Nestor provided valuable electronic production assistance, and Warren Fischbach and Freddy Flake produced the illustrations. Cathy Morin tested the lab materials, made the screen shots, and did the electronic composition to turn the files into a four-color book.

All of these people, each and every one, took a personal interest in this text; and that interest shows in the work you are now holding. Any shortcomings, are of course the responsibility of the authors and in no way reflect on the professionalism and talent of this fine group.

■ DEDICATION, BY DENNIS CURTIN

This book is dedicated to Quinlan Dougherty, who began his journey through life at the same time this book did and arrived much sooner. Not only was he faster, he's also better!

About the Authors

Dennis Curtin's 25-plus years' business experience in educational publishing provide a rich and unique perspective for his computer applications texts. He has served in executive positions at several companies, including Prentice Hall, where he has been a textbook sales representative, an acquisitions editor, editorial director of the engineering, vocational, and technical division, and editor in chief of the international division. For the past decade he has been primarily a writer of college textbooks on end-user computer applications.

He has been involved with microcomputers since the introduction of the original Apple II and was one of only nine alpha testers of the first version of Lotus 1-2-3, when Lotus Corporation had only a few employees squeezed into a small Kendall Square office. In the years since, he has taught in adult education and corporate training programs, but he readily acknowledges that he has learned most of what he knows about textbooks by working with instructors as an editor and during the writing, reviewing, and revising of his own books.

The primary author and series editor of the COMPASS Series and author of several popular microcomputer concepts texts, he is now spearheading and developing an exciting new series of highly visual Windows applications text called the PicTorial Series, of which this book is a part.

Donna Matherly combines extensive professional experience in computer-related instruction with a strong academic background. Currently an instructor in and coordinator of the Introduction to Computer Literacy course at Tallahassee Community College, Dr. Matherly has previously taught at Indiana University as well as at the secondary level and is active as a trainer and consultant. She is the author of numerous articles related to computer issues, office automation, and business education and has developed instructor-related materials and more than a dozen instructor's manuals for Prentice Hall.

PicTorial 1

Jump-Starting Excel

After completing this PicTorial, you will be able to:

▶ Define the terms *spreadsheet program*, *worksheet*, *workbook*, *model*, and *template*

▶ Load and exit Excel

▶ Describe the Excel screen display and parts of the program

▶ Use menus, toolbar buttons, and dialog boxes to execute commands

▶ Move around a worksheet and enter data

▶ Print a worksheet

▶ Use Excel's on-line Help to get help on procedures

▶ Exit Excel

The programs you use on a computer to do your work are called application programs. Different kinds of application programs do different kinds of tasks. For example, you use spreadsheet application programs such as Excel to work with numbers and word processing application programs such as Word for Windows to work with text.

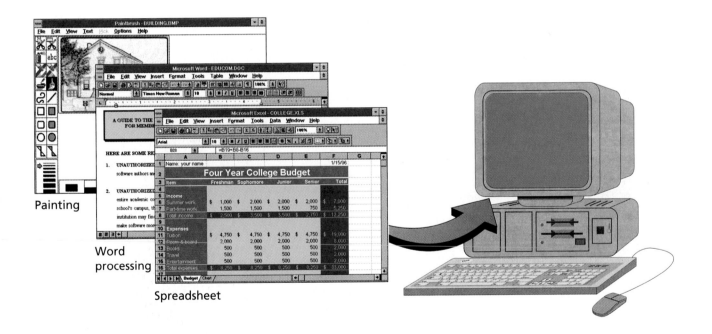

Painting

Word processing

Spreadsheet

Spreadsheets are used to solve and analyze almost any type of problem that involves numbers and calculations. In business, they are used to analyze the performance of products, salespeople, or dealers. They are used to compare costs, prices, and gross margins on individual products in a product line. They are also used to calculate prices, forecast and make budgets for sales, predict expenses and profits, and make cash-flow projections. In the sciences and social sciences they are used to analyze research data. Even in such fields as sports, they are used to analyze performance. Their major advantage is that they allow you to explore a number of alternatives quickly and easily.

One of the primary uses of spreadsheets is to build models to analyze numerical situations and to explore the effects that changes in any assumptions have on their outcome. You use models to simulate real-world situations. Just as a model airplane is tested in a wind tunnel to determine how changing the shape of a wing will affect the airplane's performance, so a model of a situation involving numbers can be tested in a spreadsheet program to determine how changing a part can affect the outcome.

UNDERSTANDING SPREADSHEET TERMINOLOGY

When using a spreadsheet, you should understand five basic terms: *spreadsheet program*, *worksheet* or *sheet*, *workbook*, *model*, and *template*.

A *spreadsheet program* such as Excel is the computer program that you use for financial or other numeric analysis.

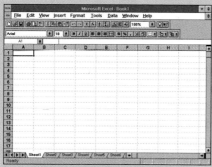

The Excel spreadsheet program's opening screen

A *worksheet* or *sheet* is the arrangement of horizontal rows and vertical columns that appears on the screen. At the intersection of each row and column is a cell into which you can enter text, numbers, or formulas.

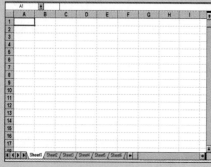

A worksheet

A *workbook* is a collection of worksheets saved together as a single file. When you start Excel or open a new workbook, the workbook contains 16 worksheets.

A *model* is a representation of a real or hypothetical situation that you create on a worksheet to solve a problem or perform an analysis. To create a model, you use three basic types of entries: text, numbers, and formulas.

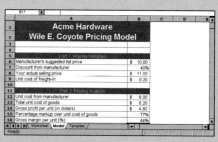

A model

A *template* is a model from which some or all the numbers specific to a situation have been removed, leaving just the descriptive text and formulas. Anyone can then enter new numbers in the labeled cells to get an answer to a problem. In many firms, templates are developed by experts and then distributed to others. For example, the accounting department might develop a template that calculates the price of an item when you know its cost. People who set prices then use the template to calculate them.

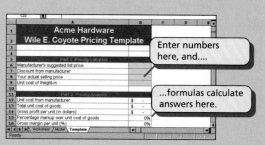

A template

TIP: QUICKSTEPS BOXES

QuickSteps boxes, identified with the sneaker icon, summarize the steps you follow to complete Excel procedures. These boxes can be found throughout this text and serve two purposes:

▶ On your first pass through a section, they highlight the steps you must follow so you can quickly review them before completing the tutorial that follows. You should not actually execute the commands presented in these boxes until after you have completed the tutorial. If you do so, you may not know how to recover from any mistakes you might make. (If you get totally lost, you can always exit Excel and then start it again.)

▶ Later on, when you want to refresh your memory about a procedure, QuickSteps boxes make it easy to locate, review, and follow the numbered steps that accomplish the desired procedure.

Learning how to use a new application program is much like learning how to drive. To drive well, you have to learn the rules of the road and how the car should be maintained for safety and reliability, but you can't wait to get behind the wheel. Once you have taken at least a spin around the block, you have a feel for driving that makes you want to learn more. In this PicTorial, you take Excel for a spin around the block. Just as an experienced driver sat next to you and told you everything to do on your first drive, we'll sit beside you and guide you through your first drive around the block with Excel. The goal here is not to master Excel's many features—those will be covered in greater detail later. Here you should relax and just get a feeling for the program.

TIP: WHAT TO DO IF YOU HAVE TO QUIT

This PicTorial is actually one long tutorial that is meant to be completed in one session. If you have to quit before finishing, here is how to stop and then resume later without losing any work.

To Stop
1. If you haven't saved your work after entering data, skip to Section 1-6, "Saving Workbooks." Follow the instructions for saving your work.
2. Skip to Section 1-10, "Exiting Excel," to exit the Excel application and then exit Windows.

To Resume
1. Restart Excel.
2. Skip to Section 1-2, "Opening Workbooks" and open the workbook *college.xls* as described in that section's tutorial. The workbook will look just as it did when you last saved it.
3. Return to the place in the PicTorial where you quit, and continue from there.

1-1. STARTING EXCEL

To load the Excel application, you must first load Windows and display Program Manager as a window. When Program Manager is displayed as a window, it usually contains other windows known as *group windows* because they contain groups of application icons. (Application icons are what you click to start application programs.) However, some or all of these group windows may be displayed as icons—called *group icons* because they contain groups of related application icons. To open a group icon into a window, you double-click it.

It is easy to customize Windows, so group windows and icons vary widely from system to system. However, your system should have a group window for Excel named *Microsoft Office* or *Excel*. Inside this group window is the application icon named *Microsoft Excel* that starts Excel.

Double-click this application icon to start Excel.

QUICKSTEPS: STARTING EXCEL
1. If the Microsoft Office or Excel group window isn't open, double-click its group icon to open it. In the open window you should be able to see an icon labeled *Microsoft Excel*. This is the icon that starts the Excel application.
2. Double-click the application icon labeled *Microsoft Excel*.

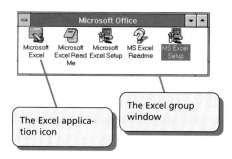

The Excel application icon

The Excel group window

TUTORIAL

In this tutorial you start Excel. Before doing so, be sure Windows is running and Program Manager is displayed as a window.

1. Open the Microsoft Office or Excel group window if it isn't already open. To open it, double-click the group icon normally named *Excel* or *Microsoft Office*.

2. Double-click the application icon labeled *Microsoft Excel* in the group window to start Excel and display its application window, as shown with its parts labeled on page 8. (If Excel does not start with its window maximized, click the Maximize button () in the upper-right corner of its screen.)

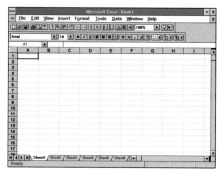

Excel's opening screen

1-2. OPENING WORKBOOKS

When you start Excel, it opens a new workbook automatically (see the margin illustration). But if you are already working in Excel and want to create another new model, you will need to open a new workbook. The title bar of each new workbook that you open reads *Bookx*, where x stands for the number of new workbooks you have opened in the current session. This automatically assigned name is replaced with the name you give to the workbook when you save it.

The New Workbook button

 QUICKSTEPS: OPENING NEW WORKBOOKS
To open a new workbook, do one of the following:
▶ Click the **New Workbook** button on the toolbar.
▶ Pull down the **File** menu and click the **New** command.

To open an existing workbook that was previously saved onto a disk, you use the Open dialog box to specify the drive it's on, the directory it's in, and its filename.

Click the Open button to open an existing workbook.

 QUICKSTEPS: OPENING EXISTING WORKBOOKS
1. Click the **Open** button on the toolbar, or pull down the **File** menu and click the **Open** command to display the Open dialog box.
2. Click the **Drives** box's drop-down arrow (▼) to display a drop-down list of the drives on your system. Click the letter of the drive on which the workbook is stored to select the drive and list it in the **Drives** box.
3. Double-click the file's directory in the **Directories** list to select it and list the files that it contains in the **File Name** list.
4. Use the scroll bar in the **File Name** list to scroll the desired workbook's name into view. Then click it to select it and display its name in the **File Name** text box.

UNDERSTANDING DIALOG BOXES

When you execute some Excel commands, a dialog box is displayed. The elements in the dialog boxes vary but include those shown and described here.

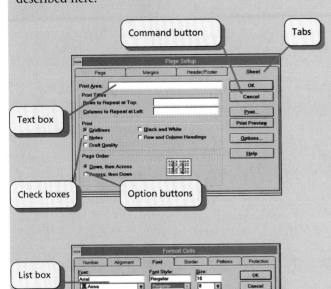

Tabs in some dialog boxes indicate page-like sections on which related settings are grouped together. To see the settings listed under any tab, click the tab to move it to the front of the pack.

Text boxes contain space for typing data. When a text box is empty, you click in it to move the insertion point into it so you can type a new entry or edit an existing one. If you double-click in a text box that already contains an entry, you select that entry, and then typing any character deletes it.

List boxes display a list from which you can choose an item by clicking it. Lists too long to be displayed in the window can be scrolled with the box's scroll bar.

A *drop-down list box* is displayed as a rectangular box listing only the current selection. To display other choices, click the down arrow (↓) to the right of the box.

Command buttons execute commands when you click them. If a button is dimmed, it cannot be chosen from where you are in a procedure.

Option buttons offer mutually exclusive options (only one can be selected at a time). The one that is on contains a black dot (⊙). If you click a button that is off (○), any other related button that is on automatically turns off.

Check boxes offer nonexclusive options (one or more of them can be on at the same time). To turn an option on, click it to display an X in its box (⊠). To turn the option off, click the box to remove the X (☐). If the name of one of the check boxes is dimmed, it can't be chosen from where you are in a procedure.

TIP: THE HOURGLASS

When you open Excel, save workbooks, and at other times when you are using Excel, you will see an hourglass (⌛) appear on the screen. This is Excel's way of telling you it's busy and that you should wait for the hourglass to go away before expecting Excel to do anything else.

TIP: NO ONE SAID THINGS WOULD BE CONSISTENT

Computer terminology is always changing—sometimes on a year-to-year basis. Until recently, it was common to say you were *saving or retrieving a file*. This meant you were saving a letter, memo, or spreadsheet model onto the disk in what was referred to as a file, or that you were retrieving it from the disk into the computer's memory. However, with the introduction of Windows, an attempt has been made to change this language so you say you are *saving or opening a document*. The change in how we express this simple action is not yet complete, and you'll find it spoken and written both ways. To complicate matters slightly, an Excel document is also called a workbook, so you can also say that you are *saving or opening a workbook*. It is this latter style that we use in this text.

PICTORIAL 1   JUMP-STARTING EXCEL XL-5

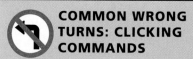

COMMON WRONG TURNS: CLICKING COMMANDS

Many first-time users have trouble choosing commands because they don't point to the right place before clicking. The point of the mouse pointer (⇖) must be over one of the letters in the command when you click. If it is above or below a letter, even by a little bit, you may execute the wrong command or the menu may disappear.

TUTORIAL

In this tutorial you open an existing worksheet supplied to you on the *Excel Student Resource Disk* that accompanies this text. If you do not have that disk, ask your instructor where you can get one. The model you open calculates a budget for fours years at an Ivy League university such as Harvard. Although the numbers may be depressing, the budget is typical of those you would use in business to forecast the relationship between income and expenses over a period of time.

TIP: WHAT YOU NEED TO KNOW ABOUT DISKS AND WORKBOOKS

All of the Excel workbooks used to complete this text are stored on two disks called *Excel Student Resource Disk (Part 1)* and *Excel Student Resource Disk (Part 2)*. Each of these disks has workbooks grouped under directories related to the lab activities in this text: *tutorial, drill, exercise,* and *project*. For example, you will find all of the workbooks used in tutorials in the *tutorial* directory and all of those used for drills in the *drill* directory. As you work your way through this text you will be asked to insert one or the other of these disks to complete lab activities.

Inserting the Student Resource Disk

Getting Ready

1. Insert your *Excel Student Resource Disk (Part 1)* into the floppy disk drive you use to open and save workbooks.

Opening a Workbook Using the Menu

2. Point to the **File** name on the menu bar and click the left mouse button to pull down the menu (see the bottom margin illustration).

3. Point to the **Open** command on the menu and click the left mouse

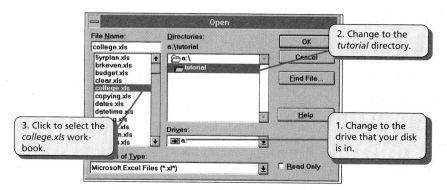

button to display the Open dialog box.

▶ Click the **Drives** box's down arrow (⬇) to display a drop-down list of the drives on your system. Click the letter of the drive you put the disk in to select it and list it in the **Drives** box.

▶ Double-click the *tutorial* directory listed in the **Directories** list to select it and list the files that it contains in the **File Name** list.

▶ Click the *college.xls* filename to select it and display its name in the **File Name** text box. (If necessary, use the scroll bar in the **File Name** list to scroll it into view.)

4. Click the **OK** command button to open the workbook *college.xls*. When the workbook appears on the screen, notice how its name is

The File Menu

listed in the title bar at the top of the window. Click any dark blue cell to display its formula on the formula bar.

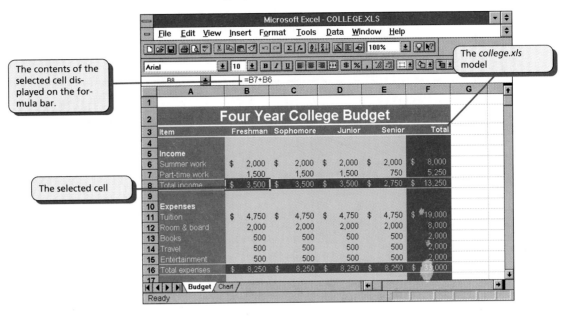

The contents of the selected cell displayed on the formula bar.

The college.xls model

The selected cell

Closing the Workbook

5. Point to the **File** name on the menu bar and click the left mouse button to pull down the menu.

6. Click the **Close** command to close the workbook. (If a dialog box appears, see the Tip box "Meet a Bug.")

Opening the Workbook Again

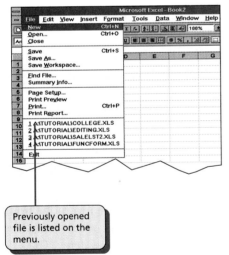

Previously opened file is listed on the menu.

7. Point to the **File** name on the menu bar and click the left mouse button to pull down the menu. You will see the name of the workbook listed at the bottom of the menu. Excel remembers the last four workbooks that you opened. (See the margin illustration.)

8. Click the name *COLLEGE.XLS* to open the workbook.

TIP: MEET A BUG

If a dialog box asks if you want to save your changes when you haven't made any, click the **No** command button to close the workbook without saving it. If this box does appear when you have made no changes, it's what is known as a "bug"—an error in the program.

1-3. EXPLORING EXCEL'S SCREEN DISPLAY

When you start Excel, its window displays a number of elements that make the program fast and efficient to work with. You should become familiar with the names of these elements, many of which are common to all Windows applications.

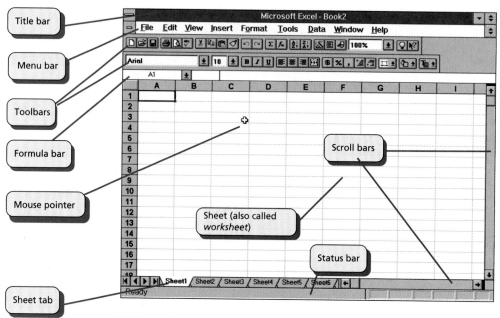

Title bar

Menu bar

Toolbars

Formula bar

Mouse pointer

Sheet tab

Scroll bars

Sheet (also called worksheet)

Status bar

▶ The *title bar* lists the name of the application and any open workbook when the window is maximized, and just the name of the workbook when the window is minimized. Excel's Control-menu box (⊟) is at the left end of the title bar and its Maximize (▲) and Minimize (▼ or Restore (▲▼)) buttons are at the right end.

▶ The *menu bar* lists the names of menus that you can pull down. Each menu contains a list of commands from which you can choose.

▶ The *toolbars* contain buttons that you click to execute commands. When you point to a button, its name is displayed in a small yellow box below the mouse pointer (▷). A description of what it does is displayed on the status bar at the bottom of the screen.

▶ The *formula bar* is used to navigate on the sheet and to see and edit cell contents. This bar is described in detail in the box "Understanding the Formula Bar" on page 9.

▶ The *mouse pointer* takes on the shape of a cross in the worksheet area, but its shape changes when pointing to other areas of the screen.

▶ *Scroll bars* are on the right and bottom sides of the window.

▶ The *sheet* or *worksheet* contains rows and columns that divide it into cells where you enter data and create your models.

▶ The *sheet tabs* at the bottom of the worksheet are used to move from one sheet to another. Sixteen worksheets are open when you start Excel, but how many are displayed depends on your system. (The *college.xls* model displayed on your computer's screen has only two tabs because only two sheets were needed for the model. The remaining sheets were deleted.)

▶ The *status bar* at the bottom of the window displays different information on its two sides. At the left it displays information about a highlighted command or a command in progress. For example, if you point to a button on the toolbar, a description of the button is displayed. The right side indicates the status of keys. For example, when you press NumLock, CapsLock, or Insert (in certain situations) to engage them, *NUM*, *CAPS*, and *OVR* (for *overtype*) are displayed at the right end of the status bar.

UNDERSTANDING THE FORMULA BAR

The formula bar is displayed between the toolbar and the sheet's column headings. It serves a number of functions.

When Not Entering Data

When not entering data, the Name box displays the active cell's address (the cell with the thick border) and its contents (if any) is displayed to the right. You can type a cell's address into the Name box and press Enter↵ to jump to that cell. Or, if you have assigned a name to cells (as you will see later), you can click the Name box's drop-down arrow (↧) to display a list of the names you can jump to.

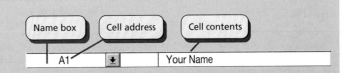

When Entering Data

As soon as you type a character, three new buttons appear on the formula bar. Clicking the Enter button enters the data into the cell. Its just like pressing Enter↵. Clicking the Cancel button cancels the entry. Clicking the Function Wizard button displays dialog boxes that guide you through the process of entering functions.

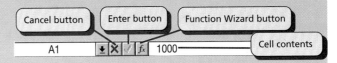

Since you do most of your work on the worksheet, you should also know the names and functions of all of its parts.

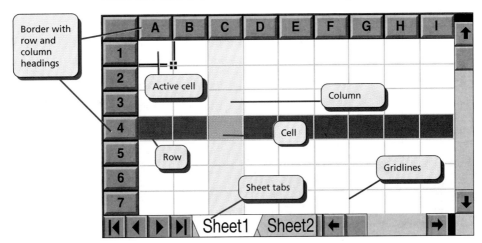

▸ *Gridlines* divide the worksheet into rows, columns, and cells.

▸ The sheet border contains column headings across the top and row headings down the left side.

▸ Columns run vertically down the worksheet and have lettered headings. The first twenty-six columns have the headings A to Z, the next twenty-six AA to AZ, the next twenty-six BA to BZ, and so on up to column IV, the 256th column.

▸ Rows run horizontally across the worksheet and have numbered headings. The headings start with row 1 at the top of the worksheet and end at row 16,384 at the bottom.

▸ *Cells*, into which you enter data, fall at the intersection of each column and row. Cells are referred to by their coordinates, called their *cell reference* or *address*. The reference is given as the column letter followed by the row number. For example, the cell at the intersection of column C and row 4 is cell C4.

▸ The *active cell* is outlined with a heavier border that you can move to another cell by clicking with the mouse or pressing arrow keys. It's into this cell that you enter data when you type on the keyboard. The address of the active cell is always displayed in the Name box at the left end of the formula bar.

UNDERSTANDING CELL ENTRIES

As you progress through this text, here are some of the things you'll see how to enter into the active cell:

▶ *Numbers* can be calculated when referred to by formulas. For example, the principal on a loan may be entered as 10,000 and the interest rate as 10%.

▶ *Dates* and *times* are special kinds of numbers that can also be used in calculations.

▶ *Formulas* calculate numbers entered either into the formulas themselves or into other cells that the formulas refer to. One special type of formula, called a *function*, automatically performs complicated calculations such as mortgage payments.

▶ *Text* is anything you enter that isn't in a form Excel recognizes as a number, date, time, or formula. It is commonly used for titles and as labels for other parts of the worksheet. For example, if a worksheet is used to calculate a loan, it may have a title that reads *Loan Payment Calculator*. Various rows may then have descriptive labels such as *principal, interest, term,* and *monthly payments*.

▶ *Formats* control the way numbers are displayed on the screen and the way text is aligned in a cell. For example, a number entered as 10000 may be formatted so it's displayed as 10,000, $10,000, or $10,000.00.

TUTORIAL

In this tutorial you explore moving the mouse pointer, displaying names of toolbar buttons, and selecting cells.

Exploring the Mouse Pointer

1. Move the mouse pointer around the screen to see how it takes on one of the shapes shown in the box "Understanding the Mouse Pointer."

UNDERSTANDING THE MOUSE POINTER

The mouse pointer changes shape when you point to various elements on the screen.

It is shaped like an arrow (⩍) when pointing to the title bar, toolbar, or menu bar so you can click buttons, menu names, or menu commands to choose them.

It is shaped like an I-beam when inside one of the text boxes on the toolbar or formula bar. When it has this shape, you can click in the text box to move the insertion point there to type a new entry, or to select the current entry so you can edit or replace it.

It is shaped like a large outlined plus sign when in the worksheet area. When it has this shape, you can click cells to select them.

It is shaped like a split double arrow when positioned on the border between column or row headings. When it has this shape, you can drag the mouse to widen or narrow columns and rows.

It is shaped like a small plus sign (✚) when pointing to the small square (called the *fill handle*) in the lower-right corner of the active cell. When it has this shape, you can drag the active cell's outline to copy the contents of the cell to adjoining cells.

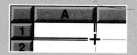

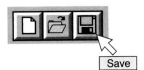

Save

2. Point to any button on the toolbar, and you'll see its name displayed in a small yellow box below the mouse pointer (see the top margin illustration). A description of what the button does is displayed on the status bar at the bottom of the screen.

Exploring Cells

3. Notice which cell is outlined with the heavy border. This is the active cell. Read up the column to find the column letter. Read across the row to find the row number. When combined, these two elements give you the cell's address—for instance, cell A1.

4. Press ←, →, ↑, and ↓ to move the active cell, and watch as its address changes in the Name box at the left end of the formula bar. If the cell has any contents—such as text, a number, or formula—that too is displayed on the formula bar.

1-4. MOVING AROUND A SHEET

When you open Excel, you open a *workbook* that originally contains sixteen sheets—much like pages in an three-ring binder. Each of these sheets has its own tab at the bottom of the screen that you can click to display it. These sheets always remain together when you save and open the workbook—they are all part of the same document or file. This makes workbooks an ideal way to store related information together.

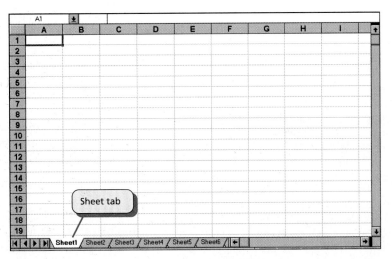

Sheet tab

Only one sheet is active at a time. When you open a workbook, the display screen shows you a small portion of a single worksheet. Normally, only one cell is selected—outlined by a heavy border. This is the *active cell* (see the bottom margin illustration), and any data that you type is entered into it. You can select another cell by clicking it with the mouse or by pressing the arrow keys to move the heavy border so it outlines another cell. You can also move the screen, but not the active cell, with the scroll bars on the right and bottom sides of the window, or by using the Name box on the formula bar, or by using the Go To command. We will look at each of these methods.

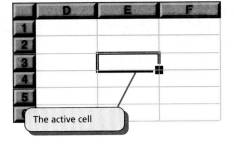

The active cell

CLICKING

The fastest and easiest way to move around a worksheet is to click. Click any cell to make it active.

KEYBOARD COMMANDS

When entering or editing data, it's often faster to change the active cell or scroll the screen from the keyboard than to reach for the mouse. Some keyboard commands move you slowly over short distances, and some move you quickly over long distances. In that respect, these commands are much like the gas pedal in your car. You may want to crawl down the driveway, but you'll want to fly on the freeway.

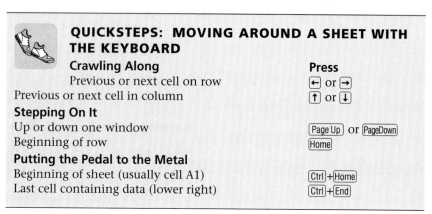

QUICKSTEPS: MOVING AROUND A SHEET WITH THE KEYBOARD

Crawling Along	Press
Previous or next cell on row	← or →
Previous or next cell in column	↑ or ↓
Stepping On It	
Up or down one window	Page Up or PageDown
Beginning of row	Home
Putting the Pedal to the Metal	
Beginning of sheet (usually cell A1)	Ctrl+Home
Last cell containing data (lower right)	Ctrl+End

USING SCROLL BARS

Scroll bars are located on the right and bottom edges of the worksheet so you can use the mouse to scroll through the contents of the sheet.

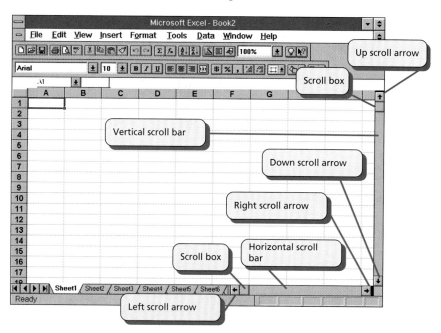

TIP: THE End KEY

The End key is very useful for moving around the worksheet. Using it in combination with other keys allows you to select the first or last cell in a block of data—that is, the cell preceded or followed by a blank cell.

▸ If the worksheet contains data, pressing End (the status bar reads *END*) and then one of the arrow keys selects the next cell followed or preceded by a blank cell. If the sheet contains no data in the direction of the arrow key you press, it selects the first or last cell in the row or column.

▸ If the worksheet contains data, press End and then Home to select the cell in the lower-right corner of the working area of the model. If the sheet contains no data, it selects cell A1.

The scroll bar you use to move the sheet up and down is called the *vertical scroll bar*. The one you use to move the sheet side to side is called the *horizontal scroll bar*.

▸ The vertical scroll bar contains three basic elements: the *up scroll arrow* (↑), the *down scroll arrow* (↓), and the *scroll box* (□).

▸ The horizontal scroll bar also contains three basic elements: the *left scroll arrow* (←), the *right scroll arrow* (→), and the *scroll box* (□).

You scroll through a sheet by clicking the scroll arrows or by dragging the scroll box. The scroll box also serves another function. Its position on the scroll bar tells you where you are in a the window's contents. For example, if it is at the top of the scroll bar, you are at the top of the area of the worksheet that contains data. If it is in the middle of the scroll bar, you are in the middle of the area containing data. If it is at the bottom end of the scroll bar, you are at the bottom of the area containing data. You can move quickly to any part of a sheet's contents (such as the middle) by dragging the box to that part of the horizontal or vertical scroll bar.

When you use the scroll bars to scroll the sheet, the active cell doesn't change as it does when you press keys to scroll the screen. In fact, you can even scroll the active cell off the screen and out of view.

QUICKSTEPS: MOVING AROUND A WORKSHEET WITH THE SCROLL BARS

▶ To move the worksheet up or down one row, click the up (⬆) or down (⬇) scroll arrow.

▶ To move the worksheet left or right one column, click the left (⬅) or right (➡) scroll arrow .

▶ To scroll the worksheet continuously, point to any scroll arrow and hold down the mouse button.

▶ To scroll the worksheet a screen at a time, click above or below the vertical scroll box (☐) or to the left or right of the horizontal scroll box.

▶ To scroll to a specific point in a sheet, drag the scroll box (☐) and release it.

USING THE NAME BOX

The Name box at the left end of the formula bar always displays the address of the active cell. To jump to a specific cell, click the Name box to select the current address listed there, type a new cell address (for example, C10 or F54), and press ⏎Enter⏎ (see the upper margin illustration).

USING THE GO TO COMMAND

To jump to a specific cell, pull down the **Edit** menu and click the **Go To** command to display the Go To dialog box. Type the address of the cell that you want to jump to into the **Reference** text box, and then click the **OK** command button (see the lower margin illustration).

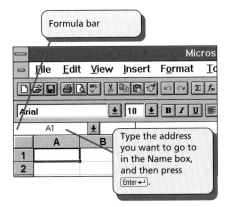

The Name Box

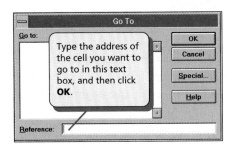

The Go To Dialog Box

TUTORIAL

In this tutorial you explore selecting cells, scrolling the worksheet, and displaying other worksheets.

Selecting by Clicking

1. Click one of the red cells with white text in it to select the cell and display its contents on the formula bar. These cells contain text.

2. Click one of the light blue cells to select it and display its contents on the formula bar. These cells contain numbers.

3. Click one of the dark blue cells with white text to select it and display its contents on the formula bar. Some of these cells contain formulas. For example, if you click cell B8, you'll see the formula

=*B7+B6* on the formula bar. This formula adds the number in cell B6 to the one in cell B7. Some of these cells contain a special type of formula called a function. For example, if you click cell B16, you'll see the function =*SUM(B11:B15)* on the formula bar. This function adds (sums) the contents of all cells between cells B11 and B15.

UNDERSTANDING THE SUM FUNCTION

Spreadsheets are widely used because you can enter formulas in them that calculate numbers entered into other cells. You can also enter functions—think of them as condensed formulas. For example, in this model, there is a SUM function in cell B16 that adds, or sums, all of the cells to which it refers. In this case the =*SUM(B11:B15)* function adds cells B11 and B15 and all of those between them. Entering this function is faster and easier than entering the equivalent formula, =*B11+B12+B13+B14+B15*. You'll see more SUM functions as you progress through this text, so just remember that they add the cells specified in parentheses. The colon that separates the cell references is simply Excel's way of saying *through*, as in "B11 *through* B15."

Using Keyboard Commands

4. Use the commands described in the QuickSteps box *Moving Around a Sheet with the Keyboard* on page 12 to move around the worksheet. (Keys connected with plus signs (+) are to be pressed together. For example, to use the Ctrl+Home command, hold down Ctrl and then press Home as if you were typing a character.)

Using the Name Box

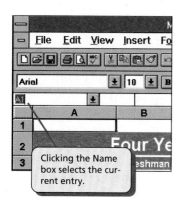

Clicking the Name box selects the current entry.

5. Click the Name box on the formula bar and the current entry is highlighted (see the margin illustration). Type **T50** and press Enter to jump to that cell.

6. Click the Name box, type **A1** and press Enter to jump to that cell.

Using the End Key

7. Click cell G1 to select it, press End so the status bar reads *END*, then press → to select cell IV1—the last cell on the row.

8. Press End, then press ↓ to move to the cell in the lower-right corner of the sheet.

9. Press End, then press ← to move to the last cell in the first column of the sheet.

10. Press End, then press ↑ to move to the first cell in column A containing data.

Using the Scroll Bar

COMMON WRONG TURNS: DRAGGING SCROLL BOX DOESN'T WORK

If you drag the scroll box left or right off the scroll bar when you release the mouse button, the scroll box jumps back to where it was when you started. To be sure the screen scrolls the way you want, release the mouse button only when you can see the outline of the scroll box on the scroll bar.

---

11. Point to the up scroll arrow (↑) on the vertical scroll bar and hold down the left mouse button until the scroll box reaches the top of the scroll bar. This indicates that you are at the beginning of the sheet.

12. Point to the scroll box (☐) on the vertical scroll bar, hold down the left mouse button, and drag the scroll box to the bottom of the scroll bar. Then release the mouse button to move to the end of the sheet.

13. Practice scrolling the worksheet contents up and down a line at a time by clicking the up (↑) and down (↓) scroll arrows on the vertical scroll bar.

14. Practice clicking the scroll bar above and below the scroll box (▭) to scroll the worksheet a screen at a time.

Displaying Another Sheet

15. Click the sheet tab at the bottom of the worksheet labeled *Chart* to display a chart created from the data on the first sheet. (To resize the chart to fit the display screen, pull down the **V**iew menu and click the **Sized with Window** command.)

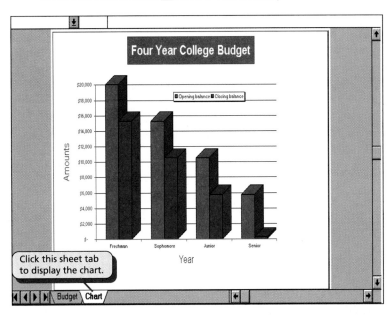

Click this sheet tab to display the chart.

16. Click the sheet tab labeled *Budget* to return to the first sheet.

PAUSING FOR PRACTICE

Practice using the scroll bar until you have mastered the three basic procedures: clicking the arrows and the scroll bar, pointing to the arrows and holding down the left button, and dragging the scroll box.

1-5. ENTERING DATA

You enter data on a worksheet by selecting a cell and typing it in. The data is displayed on the formula bar as you type it. You complete the entry by pressing [Enter ↵] or by clicking the Enter box (☑) on the formula bar (see the margin illustration).

▶ Pressing [Enter ↵] completes the entry and automatically selects the cell below.

▶ Clicking the Enter box (☑) completes the entry and leaves the same cell selected.

If the cell already contains an entry, typing a new entry over it and then pressing [Enter ↵] or clicking the Enter box (☑) on the formula bar replaces the original entry.

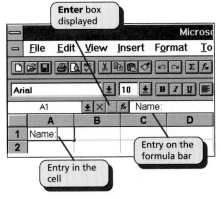

The Worksheet as you enter data

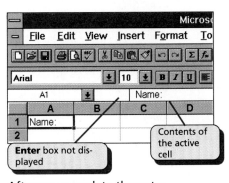

After you complete the entry

TUTORIAL

In this tutorial you enter data into a worksheet. You also explore the true power of a spreadsheet program by changing numbers and seeing new results calculated instantly, a feature called *what-if* or *sensitivity analysis*.

Entering Your Name

1. Click cell A1 to make it the active cell, type **Name:** and press $\boxed{\text{Spacebar}}$, and then type your name. As you do so, the text you type appears both in cell A1 and on the formula bar. (If your text is longer than the cell, it extends into the next cell to the right. This wouldn't happen if that cell contained data.)

2. Press $\boxed{\text{Enter}\leftarrow}$ to complete the entry and automatically select cell A2.

Entering the Date

3. Click cell F1 to make it the active cell and type today's date in the format 1/15/96. As you do so, it appears both in cell F1 and on the formula bar. Click the Enter box ($\boxed{\checkmark}$) on the formula bar to complete the entry.

Exploring What-Ifs

4. Click cell B6 to make it the active cell, then type **1000** and press $\boxed{\text{Enter}\leftarrow}$. The numbers in the *Total income* row below change to reflect the new amount as do those on row 20 and in column F.

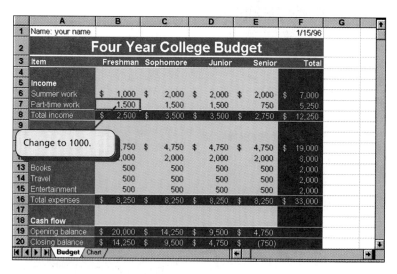

5. With cell B19 the active cell, type **10000** and press $\boxed{\text{Enter}\leftarrow}$. This reduces the opening cash balance, and the closing cash balance below begins to show negative values before college is completed.

COMMON WRONG TURN: MISTAKES WHILE TYPING

If you notice a mistake while typing an entry, press $\boxed{\leftarrow\text{Bksp}}$ to delete it. You can also press $\boxed{\text{F2}}$, then use $\boxed{\leftarrow}$ and $\boxed{\rightarrow}$ to move the insertion point through the entry to the spot where you want to insert or delete characters. Once you have completed the entry by pressing $\boxed{\text{Enter}\leftarrow}$ or by clicking the Enter box ($\boxed{\checkmark}$) on the formula bar, you have to edit the cell's contents in a different way as described in Section 2-3.

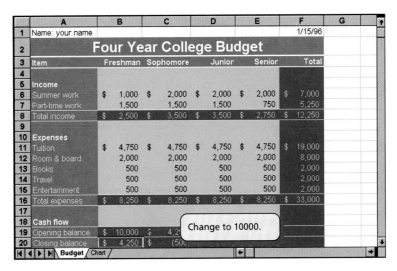

	A	B	C	D	E	F	G
1	Name: your name					1/15/96	
2	**Four Year College Budget**						
3	Item	Freshman	Sophomore	Junior	Senior	Total	
4							
5	Income						
6	Summer work	$ 1,000	$ 2,000	$ 2,000	$ 2,000	$ 7,000	
7	Part-time work	1,500	1,500	1,500	750	5,250	
8	Total income	$ 2,500	$ 3,500	$ 3,500	$ 2,750	$ 12,250	
9							
10	Expenses						
11	Tuition	$ 4,750	$ 4,750	$ 4,750	$ 4,750	$ 19,000	
12	Room & board	2,000	2,000	2,000	2,000	8,000	
13	Books	500	500	500	500	2,000	
14	Travel	500	500	500	500	2,000	
15	Entertainment	500	500	500	500	2,000	
16	Total expenses	$ 8,250	$ 8,250	$ 8,250	$ 8,250	$ 33,000	
17							
18	Cash flow						
19	Opening balance	$ 10,000	$ 4,2				
20	Closing balance	$ 4,250	$ (500				

Change to 10000.

Budget / Chart /

6. Click the tab labeled *Chart*, and you'll see a chart illustrating the opening and closing cash balances for each of the four years of college. Ideally, all of these should be positive numbers.

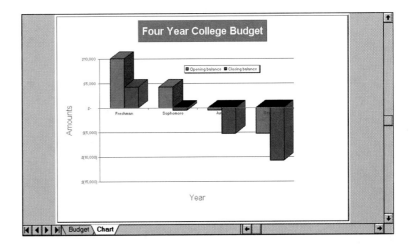

Four Year College Budget

Budget \ **Chart** /

7. Click the tab labeled *Budget* to return to the first sheet.

8. Continue entering numbers in any of the light blue cells to see how easy it is to explore a budget. Try to find a set of numbers that keep the cash flow positive for all four years when the tuition is the same as yours.

1-6. SAVING WORKBOOKS

You should frequently save the workbook you are working on. If you turn off the computer, experience a power failure, encounter hardware problems, or make a mistake, you may lose workbooks that are in the computer's memory. Your workbooks are not safe from these disasters until you save them onto a disk. When preparing a workbook, you should always save it:

▶ Before experimenting with unfamiliar commands

▶ Before making major revisions

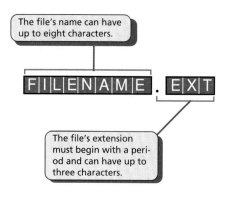

The file's name can have up to eight characters.

FILENAME.EXT

The file's extension must begin with a period and can have up to three characters.

Legal Filename Characters

Legal Character	Example
Letters, uppercase	A–Z
Letters, lowercase	a–z
Numbers	0–9
Underscore	_
Caret	^
Dollar sign	$
Tilde	~
Exclamation point	!
Number sign	#
Percent sign	%
Ampersand	&
Hyphen	-
Braces	{}
Parentheses	()
At sign	@
Grave accent	`

▶ Before printing it (in case something goes wrong during the process)

▶ Before closing it or exiting Excel

On many systems, you save your workbooks onto a hard disk. On others, especially those you share with other students in a computer lab, you save them onto a floppy disk (usually in drive A or B) so that you can take them with you.

When you save a workbook the first time, you must assign it a filename. Excel uses the DOS file-naming conventions. You can assign names to files that have up to eight characters. When you do so, Excel automatically adds a three-character identifying extension that is separated from the name by a period. (Think of this as an eight-character first name separated by a period from a three-character last name.)

The characters that you can use in a filename are called *legal characters.* The characters are listed and illustrated in the table "Legal Filename Characters." If you enter any other character when saving a file, a dialog box will appear telling you *Filename is not valid.*

When you save a workbook the second and subsequent times, you don't have to specify a name again—the version on the screen overwrites the version with the same name on the disk.

QUICKSTEPS: SAVING WORKBOOKS

1. Click the **Save** button on the toolbar, or pull down the **File** menu and click the **Save** command.

   ▶ If you have previously saved the workbook, it is resaved with the same name in the same place.

   ▶ If this is the first time you've saved the workbook, the Save As dialog box appears. If this box appears, continue to Step 2.

2. Click the **Drives** box's drop-down arrow () to display a drop-down list of the drives on your system. Click the letter of the drive on which you want to save the workbook to select the drive and list it in the **Drives** box.

3. Double-click one of the directories listed in the **Directories** list to select it.

4. Double-click in the **File Name** text box, type a filename, and click the **OK** command button to save the workbook.

TIP: SAVING A WORKBOOK UNDER A NEW NAME

There are times when you want to save a workbook under a new name. You may have made a mistake and don't want to overwrite the version on the disk with the new version until you are certain it's OK to do so. Or you may have opened an existing workbook that you want to revise into a new and different one. In cases such as this, you can save the workbook on the screen under a new name by pulling down the **File** menu and clicking the **Save As** command instead of the **Save** command. Then just type a new filename into the **File Name** text box and click the **OK** command button. (If you don't change the name, or if you enter the name of a file already on the disk, and then click **OK**, you are asked *Replace existing 'filename'?*. Click **Yes** to replace it or **No** to cancel the command so you can enter a new name in the **File Name** text box.)

UNDERSTANDING THE SUMMARY INFORMATION DIALOG BOX

When you save a file the first time, a summary information dialog box may appear. Into this box you can enter information about the workbook that helps you locate or identify it later. We do not use this box in the workbooks in this text but you can get information on how to use it or turn it on and off in Excel's on-line Help under the topic *summary information*.

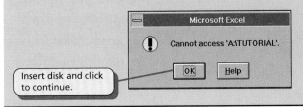

COMMON WRONG TURNS: REMOVING A FLOPPY DISK TOO SOON

When you work on Excel workbooks, Windows creates temporary files on the disk. When saving a workbook to and opening a workbook from a floppy disk, do not remove the disk from the drive until you have quit Excel. If you do, you may see an error message telling you that Excel cannot find the file. If this message appears, reinsert the disk and click the **OK** or **Retry** command button.

TUTORIAL

In this tutorial you save a workbook by clicking a button. This saves the workbook under the same name and in the same directory from which you opened it or in which you previously saved it.

1. Click the **Save** button on the toolbar. (If you don't know which it is, you can point to any button to display its name.) As the workbook is saved, an hourglass (⧗) is displayed, and the status bar keeps you informed of the command's progress.

NOTE: PRINTING CHARTS AND WAITING

You can display the chart sheet on the screen and repeat Step 5 to print it. However, when you print a sheet containing a graphic, it can take some time, especially if others in the class are also sending their worksheets to the same printer. Before printing this chart, you might ask the lab instructor or other students what to expect.

1-7. PRINTING A SHEET

When you want to share a worksheet with others or file a copy for future reference, you usually make a printout. Before you do so, you can preview how the document will look when printed. If you find that you need to make adjustments, you can do so without wasting a sheet of paper.

TUTORIAL

In this tutorial you print out the worksheet on which you have been working. Before you begin, be sure there is a printer connected to your system and that it is on and has paper in it.

1. Click the **Print Preview** button on the toolbar to preview how your model will look when printed. (This can take a while on some systems.)

Click to print.

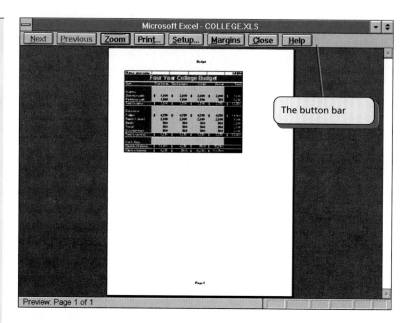

The button bar

Preview: Page 1 of 1

2. Click the **Zoom** command button to enlarge the model.

3. Click the **Close** command button to return to the sheet on which you have been working.

4. Make sure your printer is on, is connected, and has paper in it.

5. Click the **Print** button on the toolbar to print the sheet displayed on the screen.

1-8. CLOSING A WORKBOOK

Once you have saved a workbook, you can close it. This clears the workbook from the screen and removes it from the computer's memory. If you want to work on the workbook again, you open it from the disk on which you saved it.

Once you have finished with a workbook for the time being, you close it. Normally you save a workbook before you close it, but there are occasions when you do not want to save it. For example, if you make a serious mistake, you may not want to overwrite the workbook on the disk with the one on the screen. In cases like this, you close the workbook without saving it. This removes it from the screen and the computer's memory, and it is lost.

**TIP: SAVING WORKBOOKS BEFORE CLOSING
THEM**

Keep in mind that if you close a workbook without first saving it, the workbook is gone forever. Any data that you have entered is lost. When you try to close a workbook without first having saved any changes, a dialog box is displayed.

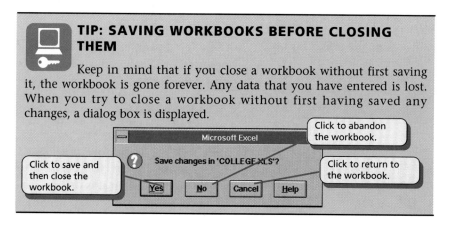

UNDERSTANDING CONTROL-MENU BOXES

Every window, including application windows, workbook windows, dialog boxes, and Help windows, has a Control-menu box (⊟) in the upper-left corner of its screen. The most frequent use of these Control-menu boxes is to quickly close workbook or application windows. To do so, you just double-click the correct Control-menu box. If you look carefully at the Control-menu boxes on the screen, you'll see that the one for an application (⊟) is different from one for a workbook (⊟). When the workbook window is maximized, its Control-menu box appears directly under the application's, so it's easy to click the wrong one.

▶ An application's or Help window's Control-menu box contains a longer dash representing the spacebar (⊟) because you can pull down its Control menu by pressing Alt + Spacebar.

▶ A workbook's Control-menu box contains a character that represents a hyphen (⊟) because you can pull down the menu by pressing Alt + - .

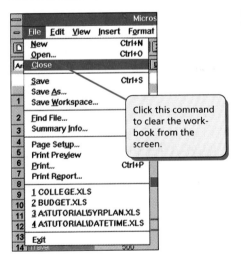

Click this command to clear the workbook from the screen.

TUTORIAL

In this tutorial you close a workbook to remove it from the screen and the computer's memory.

1. Point to the **File** name on the menu bar and click the left mouse button to pull down the menu (see the margin illustration).

2. Point to the **Close** command on the menu and click the left mouse button to close the workbook without saving it. A dialog box asks if you want to save your changes. Since you don't want to save your "what-if" changes, click the **No** command button to close the workbook without saving it.

3. Click the **New Workbook** button on the toolbar to open a new workbook.

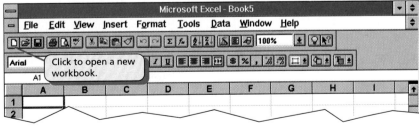

Click to open a new workbook.

1-9. USING ON-LINE HELP

When you are using Excel, you can have tips automatically displayed as you go about your usual tasks, or you can ask for detailed help whenever you want information on a specific procedure.

THE TIPWIZARD

Excel's TipWizard watches how you perform a procedure, and if there is a faster or more efficient way to do it, the **TipWizard** button on the toolbar lights up by changing from white to yellow. To see the suggestion it has to offer, click the button to display current (and new) tips in the TipWizard box just below the toolbar. You can click the up and down scroll arrows at the right end of the TipWizard box to scroll through all tips offered so far in a session. You can also click the **Tip Help** button to the right of the scroll arrows for more detailed help on the displayed tip. If the tip recommends the use of a button on the toolbar, a copy of that button is displayed between the scroll arrows and the **Tip Help** button so you can click it rather than the original button. To hide the TipWizard box, just click the **TipWizard** button again.

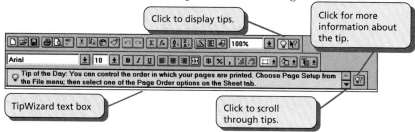

Click to display tips.

Click for more information about the tip.

Tip of the Day: You can control the order in which your pages are printed. Choose Page Setup from the File menu; then select one of the Page Order options on the Sheet tab.

TipWizard text box

Click to scroll through tips.

THE HELP SYSTEM

Excel has extensive *on-line help* available at all times. Once you are in the Help system, you can navigate through topics by clicking underlined terms or command buttons or by searching for specific topics by name. If you display Help in the middle of a command, Help is *context-sensitive*—it describes the procedure you are using and the options you can choose from.

QUICKSTEPS: SEARCHING FOR HELP

1. To display the Search dialog box used to search for specific Help topics, do one of the following:
   ▶ Double-click the **Help** button on the toolbar.
   ▶ Click a **Search** command button on a Help window.
   ▶ Pull down the **Help** menu and click the **Search for Help On** command.

2. Type text into the text box. As you do so, the list in the window below scrolls to the first topic that begins with those letters. To scroll though the list, use the scroll bar on the window.

3. Once you find the topic you want help on, click its name and then click the **Show Topics** command button to list related topics in the lower window.

4. Click any topic listed in the lower window and then click the **Go To** command button to display it.

QUICKSTEPS: USING ON-LINE HELP

Displaying Help

To display help, do one of the following:

▶ Press [F1] at any point in the program.

▶ Pull down the **Help** menu and click any of the listed Help commands.

▶ Double-click the **Help** button on the toolbar to display the Search dialog box described in the "Searching for Help" QuickSteps box.

▶ Click the **Help** button on the toolbar (or press [⇧ Shift]+[F1]), and a question mark is added to the mouse pointer. When you then click anywhere on the screen, the element you click on is explained.

▶ Click a **Help** command button in a dialog box.

Closing Help

To close Help, do one of the following:

▶ Pull down the Help window's **File** menu and click the **Exit** command.

▶ Click the Help window's **Close** or **Cancel** command button.

▶ Double-click the Help windows Control-menu box ([=]).

TUTORIAL

There are many ways to use Excel's on-line Help, and they are essentially the same as those for other Windows applications. In this tutorial you explore how to find on-line Help using the TipWizard and the Help **Search** command.

Turning on TipWizard

1. Click the **TipWizard** button on the toolbar to display the TipWizard box below the toolbar.

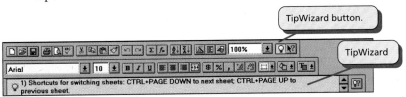

2. Click the scroll up arrow at the right end of the TipWizard box to scroll through any tips that have accumulated during this session. Keep your eye on suggestions made in this box during the remaining steps in this tutorial.

Identifying Items on the Screen

3. Click the **Help** button on the toolbar to add a question mark to the mouse pointer.

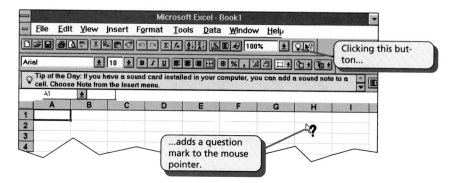

4. Click the **Save** button on the toolbar to display Help on saving workbooks.

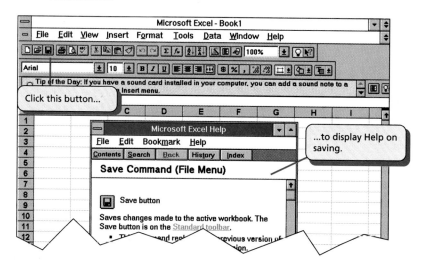

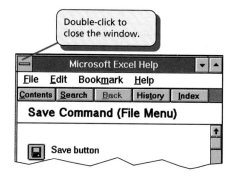

5. After reading the information on saving workbooks, double-click the Help window's Control-menu box (☐) to close the Help window (see the margin illustration).

Searching for Help Topics

6. Double-click the **Help** button on the toolbar to display the Search dialog box. The insertion point is flashing in the text box where you enter the topic you want to search for.

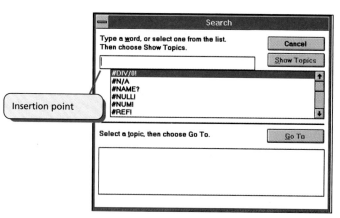

7. Type **help** to display any topics that begin with those letters in the window below.

8. Click the topic *Help, searching for topics* to select it and move it to the text box. Then click the **Show Topics** command button to list related topics in the lower window.

9. Click *Searching Help for a particular topic* in the lower window to select it and then click the **Go To** command button to display Help on that topic. Click the How To window's Maximize button (▲) to enlarge it, and read the Help text.

10. Click the Help window's Minimize button (▼) to reduce it to an icon.

Finishing Up

11. Pull down the Help window's **File** menu and click the **Exit** command to close the Help window.

12. Use the up and down scroll arrows on the TipWizard window to scroll through any tips that might have accumulated during the session. Then click the **TipWizard** button on the toolbar to hide the TipWizard box.

Tip scroll arrows

✋ **PAUSING FOR PRACTICE**

When working with Excel, knowing how to find the information that you need is a very useful skill. Pause here to practice using on-line Help until you feel comfortable navigating the Help system. The Help system is much like a web since you can get to any place from so many others using menu commands, keyboard keys, or toolbar buttons. However, you will always find the same familiar terms such as *Contents*, *Search*, and *Index* that you can use as guides. If you get lost, click the **Contents** command button to return to a list of contents you can access.

1-10. EXITING EXCEL

TIP: SAVING WORKBOOKS BEFORE EXITING EXCEL

Keep in mind that if you exit Excel without saving a workbook, the workbook is gone forever. Any data that you have entered is lost.

When you are finished with Excel, you can exit it. This removes it from the computer's memory and removes its window or icon from the desktop. However, its icon remains in the group window so you can start it again whenever you want to use it.

It is important to quit Excel using the commands designed for this purpose. Although you can exit the program by simply turning off the computer, this is a bad habit to get into because Excel creates temporary files on the disk while you are working, and these are deleted only if you exit correctly. If you quit incorrectly, your workbook may be left damaged.

> **QUICKSTEPS: EXITING EXCEL**
>
> **Fastest**
>
> ▶ Double-click Excel's Control-menu box (⊟). (See the box "Understanding Control-Menu Boxes" on page 21.)
>
> **Menus**
>
> ▶ Click the **File** name on the menu bar to pull it down, then click the **Exit** command.

TUTORIAL

In this tutorial you exit Excel. This removes it from the screen and the computer's memory. However, it will remain displayed as an icon on the desktop should you want to start it again.

Exiting Excel

1. Pull down Excel's **File** menu and click the **Exit** command to close the Excel application.

PicTorial 1 Review Questions

True-False

T / F **1.** You use spreadsheet application programs to work with text.

T / F **2.** Templates are designed to be used again and again by anyone who knows how to enter the numbers to be analyzed.

T / F **3.** An application's Control-menu box contains a long dash, representing the spacebar.

T / F **4.** A worksheet is a collection of workbooks.

T / F **5.** Program Manager contains group icons.

T / F **6.** When in the worksheet area, the mouse pointer takes on the shape of an hourglass.

T / F **7.** A spreadsheet model simulates situations involving numbers.

T / F **8.** The address of the active cell is always displayed in the Name box at the left end of the formula bar.

T / F **9.** Scroll bars contain five basic elements.

T / F **10.** Press [End] to move to the end of the worksheet.

Multiple Choice

1. The _____ command is used to display a worksheet on the screen just the way it will look when printed.

   a. Print Review

   b. Print Preview

c. Workbook Preview

d. File Preview

2. A _____ is the arrangement of horizontal rows and vertical columns that appears on the screen.

   a. Worksheet

   b. Spreadsheet

   c. Workbook

   d. Template

3. In dialog boxes, _____ boxes offer nonexclusive options.

   a. Text

   b. List

   c. Check

   d. Option

4. A _____ is a model from which some or all of the numbers have been removed.

   a. Worksheet

   b. Spreadsheet

   c. Workbook

   d. Template

5. A _____ is the intersection of a column and a row.

   a. Model

   b. Prism

   c. Range

   d. Cell

6. When an Excel window is maximized, the _____ bar lists the names of the application and any open workbook.

   a. Title

   b. Menu

   c. Formula

   d. Status

7. By default, each workbook contains _____ worksheets.

   a. 8

   b. 12

   c. 16

   d. 20

8. The status of NumLock is displayed in the _____ bar.

   a. Title

   b. Menu

   c. Formula

   d. Status

9. In dialog boxes, _____ boxes contain space for typing data.

   a. Text

b. List

c. Check

d. Option

10. In dialog boxes, _____ boxes offer mutually exclusive options.

a. Text

b. List

c. Check

d. Option

 Fill In the Blank

1. _____ divide a worksheet into rows, columns, and cells.

2. The _____ cell is always outlined with a heavy border.

3. To clear a worksheet from the screen, choose the **File**, _____ command.

4. The vertical scroll bar contains three basic elements: _____, _____, and _____.

5. The shape of the mouse pointer appears like a _____ when positioned on the border between column or row headings.

6. To quickly position the active cell in the cell where the lowest row and rightmost column containing data intersect, press _____.

7. If you notice a mistake while typing an entry, press _____ to delete it.

8. _____ buttons execute commands when you click them.

9. To edit an entry, you can press function key _____.

10. The mouse pointer is shaped like a(n) _____ when inside one of the text boxes on the toolbar or formula bar.

PicTorial 1 Lab Activities

▶▶ COMPUTER-BASED TUTORIALS

1-1. Examples and Demos

Excel has built-in examples, practices, and demonstrations you can use to learn more about the program. Here and in the following PicTorials, we suggest lessons you might complete in Excel's *Examples and Demos* section. To complete the suggested activities:

1. Pull down the **Help** menu and click the **Examples and Demos** command to display a list of topics from which you can choose.

2. Click the *Topic* listed in the table "Suggested Examples and Demos to Complete." This opens a window listing subtopics.

3. Click the *Subtopic* listed in the table "Suggested Examples and Demos to Complete" and read the information displayed on the

screen—including any instructions. To explore or quit the lesson, use any of the command buttons described in the box "Understanding Examples and Demos Command Buttons." When finished with one of the Examples and Demos, check it off the list.

Suggested Examples and Demos to Complete	
Topic	Subtopic
❏ Working in Workbooks	How a Workbook Works
❏ Working in Workbooks	Moving Around in a Workbook
❏ Working in Workbooks	Zooming In or Out on a Worksheet
❏ Working in Workbooks	Going to Specific Cells or Ranges
❏ Using Toolbars	Getting Information About a Toolbar Button
❏ Using Toolbars	Displaying, Hiding, and Moving Toolbars
❏ Using Toolbars	Customizing Toolbars
❏ Printing	Previewing a Sheet Before Printing
❏ Printing	Printing

UNDERSTANDING EXAMPLES AND DEMOS COMMAND BUTTONS

Demo demonstrates the procedure.
Practice opens an interactive tutorial in which you practice what you've learned.

Hint lists keystrokes or mouse movements needed to perform the next step.
Show Me performs the next step for you.
Next takes you to the next demonstration or practice screen.
Close closes the subtopic or topic window.

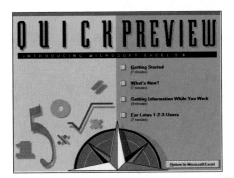

1-2. Quick Preview—Getting Information While You Work

Here you use Excel's Quick Preview feature to take a guided tour of how you get help while working with the program.

1. Pull down the **Help** menu and click the **Quick Preview** command to display its opening screen.

2. Click the Getting Information While You Work button to begin that lesson. Then follow the instructions that appear on the screen. The buttons you click to navigate the preview are described in the box "Understanding Quick Preview Command Buttons."

3. When finished, click the **Return to Microsoft Excel** command button.

UNDERSTANDING QUICK PREVIEW COMMAND BUTTONS

Close returns you to the Quick Preview opening screen.

Next takes you to the next step.
Return to Microsoft Excel closes Quick Preview and returns you to Excel.

▶▶ **SKILL-BUILDING EXERCISES**

1-1. Loading Excel on Your Own System

List the steps here that you use to load Excel so that you have them for future reference.

1. _____
   _____
2. _____
   _____
3. _____
   _____
4. _____
   _____
5. _____
   _____

Documents to Open and Close		
Done	Directory	Filename
❑	*tutorial*	*videos.xls*
❑	*tutorial*	*formula.xls*
❑	*drill*	*bugs.xls*
❑	*drill*	*compsrv.xls*
❑	*exercise*	*congress.xls*
❑	*exercise*	*exchange.xls*

Saving My Name	
Filename	Directory
myname1	*drill*
myname2	*tutorial*
myname3	*exercise*
myname4	*project*

1-2. **Opening, Saving, and Closing Workbooks**

One of the most basic skills you need to master is opening and saving documents in directories on your *Excel Student Resource Disks (Parts 1 and 2)*. As you complete this exercise, and others, in this text, you will have to insert the correct disk.

1. Insert your *Excel Student Resource Disk* with the *tutorial* directory into the floppy disk drive you use to open and save documents.

2. Practice opening and then closing each of the workbooks listed in the table "Documents to Open and Close" using the specified directory and filename (you will have to swap disks to access some directories). After opening each, check it off on the list and then close it.

1-3. **Opening, Saving, and Closing Workbooks**

In this exercise you open a new workbook, enter your name into it, and then save it under a specific filename in a directory on the appropriate *Excel Student Resource Disk*.

1. Insert your *Excel Student Resource Disk* with the *drill* directory into the floppy disk drive you use to open and save documents.

2. Click the **New Workbook** button on the toolbar to open a new workbook.

3. With cell A1 selected, type your name and press [Enter ⏎].

4. Save the workbook as *myname1* in the *drill* directory. (If the Summary Info dialog box appears, just click the **OK** command button.)

5. Close the workbook.

6. Repeat Steps 2 through 5 for three other new workbooks, but change the number at the end of each filename to 2, 3, and 4 and save each in the directory described in the table "Saving My Name" on the appropriate disk.

1-4. **Moving Around a Worksheet**

Moving around the worksheet is simple, but moving quickly to specific places takes some practice. In this exercise you practice using the [End] key to quickly move to the four corners of the worksheet.

1. Open the *explore.xls* workbook stored in the *exercise* directory on the *Excel Student Resource Disk*.

2. Use the [End] key to quickly move to the four corners of the work-

Exploring the Worksheet	
Cell	Words in Cell
A1	_____
A16384	_____
IV16384	_____
IV1	_____
CC100	_____

sheet, and write down the words you find in each cell in the table "Exploring the Worksheet."

3. Use the Name box on the formula bar to quickly jump to cell CC100, and write down the words you find in the cell in the table "Exploring the Worksheet."

4. Use the commands described in the QuickSteps box *Moving Around a Sheet with the Keyboard* on page 12 to move around the worksheet.

5. Use the commands described in the QuickSteps box *Moving Around a Sheet with the Scroll Bars* on page 13 to move around the worksheet.

6. Close the workbook.

1-5. Printing Worksheets

Printing a worksheet is as simple as opening it and clicking a button on the toolbar. In this exercise you print a worksheet that lists all of the files on your *Excel Student Resource Disk*.

1. Open the *filelist.xls* workbook stored in the *exercise* directory on the *Excel Student Resource Disk* and enter your name into cell A1.

2. Use the **Print** button on the toolbar to print the worksheet and file the printout where you can easily find it, because you may want to refer to it at some point. It lists all of the workbooks that you work with throughout this text.

3. Close the document without saving it.

1-6. Using On-Line Help

The best thing about Excel's on-line Help is that it's always available, even long after you've lost the manual. In this exercise you search on-line Help to locate Help on the topics listed in the table "Help Topics to Look Up." Read each topic as you find it and then check it off on the list.

Help Topics to Look Up		
Help Topic	Subtopic	Found
Help, overview	Overview of Using Help to Find the Information you Need	❑
Help, searching	Searching Help for a particular topic	❑
Open command [File menu]	Open command [File Menu]	❑
Save command [File menu]	Save command [File Menu]	❑
Exit command [File menu]	Exit command [File Menu]	❑
screen, parts of	Parts of the Microsoft Excel Screen	❑
undoing, commands	Undoing or repeating a command	❑
editing, cell contents	Editing cell contents	❑
entering, dates	Entering a date or a time	❑
entering, data	Formula Bar	❑
entering, data	Tips for Entering Data	❑
entering, text	Entering text in cells	❑
entering, numbers	Entering numbers in cells	❑
Print command [File menu]	Print command [File Menu]	❑
saving files, tips on	Tips for Working with Files and Documents	❑
starting Microsoft Excel	Overview of Starting and Quitting Microsoft Excel	❑

1-7. Using On-line Help

Click the **Help** button on the toolbar to add a question mark to the mouse pointer. Then click each part of the screen show here and write down the title of the Help screen that is displayed. After reading the Help screen, double-click its Control-menu box to close it.

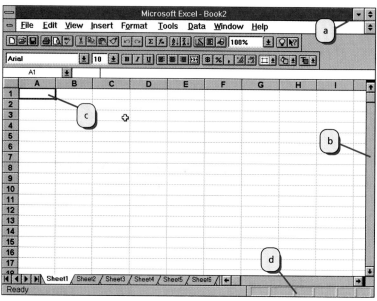

a. Minimize button_____

b. Vertical scroll bar _____

c. Any cell _____

d. Status bar_____

1-8. Describing the Anatomy of the Excel Display

The illustration at the top of the next page shows the Excel display that appears when you first load the application. In the spaces provided, write down the name of each of the lettered elements from the screen on the following page.

a._____

b._____

c._____

d._____

e._____

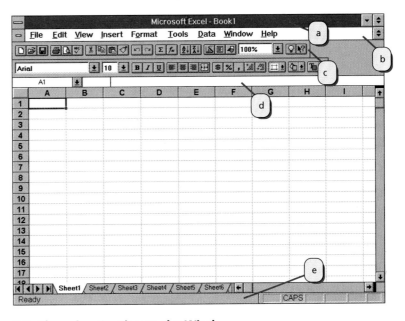

1-9. Throwing Caution to the Winds

In this PicTorial you have already performed almost all of the essential procedures that make spreadsheet programs so powerful. If you are fearless (and there is no reason not to be), you can create models right now! In most classes students fall along a spectrum of fearlessness. At one end of the spectrum are those few who don't hesitate to try new things on their own without even reading about them. At the other end of the spectrum are those who are always afraid of new procedures and who only do those things that are described step by step. The first group makes more mistakes, and gets into bigger jams, but they also learn faster and cover more ground. Here's your chance to see if you belong in the first group. If you get into trouble at any point, or get frustrated, you can always exit Excel and start over. The model you'll enter calculates the total number of cells in the Excel worksheet.

1. Open a new workbook and enter the model shown here. All of the entries are numbers or text except for the formula in cell B8. The asterisk in the formula is Excel's multiplication sign. Just as you might write out 256 × 16384, in Excel you enter the formula as =B6*B7. How large would a worksheet be if it were entirely printed out with each cell 1 inch wide and / inch deep? The size may surprise you. Since each sheet has 256 columns and 16,384 rows, for a total of 4,194,304 cells, its printout would be over 21 feet wide by 341 feet long! Try studying a printout of that in the car on the way to work in the morning.

2. Insert your *Excel Student Resource Disk* into the drive you use to open and save files, and save the workbook as *fearless.xls* in the *exercise* directory.

3. Click the **Print** button on the toolbar to print the document.

4. Pull down the **File** menu and click the **Close** command to clear the workbook from the screen.

	A	B	C	D
1	Name: your name			
2	Filename: fearless			
3	Date: today's date			
4				
5	Number of cells			
6	Width	256		
7	Depth	16384		
8	Total	4194304		

=B6*B7

PicTorial 2

Mastering the Basics

After completing this PicTorial, you will be able to:

▶ Open, save, and close workbooks to any drive or directory

▶ Enter text, numbers, and formulas to create models

▶ Edit cell contents and undo mistakes

▶ Select ranges of cells

▶ Copy the data in cells to other cells

▶ Explain the difference between absolute and relative cell references

▶ Adjust column widths and row heights

There are only a few procedures that you absolutely must know to get value from a program such as Excel, and they are covered in this PicTorial. These procedures include entering text, numbers, and formulas; editing or undoing mistakes; copying data; and adjusting column width.

2-1. ENTERING TEXT AND NUMBERS INTO CELLS

One of the most basic steps in using a spreadsheet is entering text and numbers—often called data. This is a straightforward process, but there are variations and shortcuts that you should be aware of.

ENTERING DATA

You enter data by selecting a cell and typing. (Up to 255 characters are allowed in a cell). As you type, the data is displayed in the cell and on the formula bar. There are three ways to complete an entry:

▶ Press [Enter ↵] to remove the data from the formula bar and automatically select the cell below (the program assumes you are entering data down a column).

▶ Press any of the keys that change the active cell. For example, press [↑], [↓], [←], or [→] to complete the entry and select the next cell in the direction of the arrow you press. When making several entries along a row or up a column, entering data using the appropriate arrow keys saves you a keystroke each time.

▶ Click the Enter box (☑) that appears on the formula bar when you begin entering data in a cell. When you click this box, the same cell remains selected. (The formula bar is discussed in detail in the box "Understanding the Formula Bar" in Section 1-2.)

CANCELING ENTRIES

When entering data, you can cancel the entry before or after you press [Enter ↵] or click the Enter box (☑) to complete the entry.

▶ To cancel the entry before you complete it, press [Esc], click the Cancel box (☒) on the formula bar, or pull down the **Edit** menu and click the **Undo Typing** command.

The Undo button

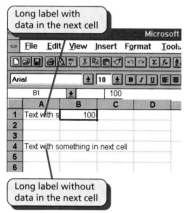

Long label with data in the next cell

Long label without data in the next cell

Text too long to fit in a cell

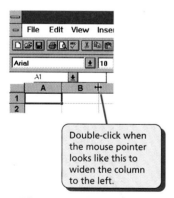

Double-click when the mouse pointer looks like this to widen the column to the left.

Widening a column

▶ To cancel the entry after you have completed it, click the **Undo** button on the toolbar, or pull down the **Edit** menu and click the **Undo Entry** command.

ENTERING TEXT

Text is just like the text in this book or other documents. It can consist of any combination of letters, numbers, or other characters. To enter text, just select the cell, type it in, and press Enter↵. Even if the entry has a number in it (for example, *45 Elm Street*), Excel accepts it as text. If you enter just numbers in a cell and want them treated as text—for example, serial numbers or ZIP codes—precede the number with an apostrophe. Once a number is entered as text, it cannot be used in normal mathematical operations.

If your text is longer than its cell is wide, it overflows into the next cell to the right if that cell is empty. If that cell is not empty, only the characters that fit in the cell being typed in are displayed.

To display all of the text, you can widen the column. The quickest way to do so is to point to the right border of the column heading at the top of the worksheet (the mouse pointer turns into a split double arrow) and double-click.

ENTERING NUMBERS

To enter numbers into a cell, just type them in. They will automatically align with the right edge of the cell. Characters Excel recognizes as numbers include the digits 0 through 9 plus a variety of other characters (see the box "Characters You Can Use in Numbers" in Section 2-5, "Entering Formulas.")

When entering numbers, keep these points in mind:

▶ To enter fractions, precede them with a zero and a space so Excel doesn't consider them to be dates. (Excel treats dates and times in a special way, described in Section 4-5.) For example, if you type **1/2** into a cell, Excel displays it as *2-Jan* since it assumes it's a date. However, if you enter it as **0 1/2** (the space following the 0 is essential), it is displayed as *1/2* in the cell and *0.5* on the formula bar.

▶ You can enter percentages either as decimals or with a percent sign. For example, enter 20 percent either as .2 or 20%.

▶ Numbers can have only one period (decimal point). If you enter more than one period in a cell, the entry is treated as text.

▶ Precede negative numbers with a minus sign (-10) or enclose them in parentheses (10).

▶ When NumLock is engaged, you can enter numbers by typing them on the numeric keypad. When NumLock is engaged, the status bar displays the *NUM* indicator.

> ### 🖥️🔑 TIP: LEADING ZEROS DISAPPEAR
>
> You enter a ZIP code such as 01945 and it is displayed as 1945. This is because Excel treats it as a number and therefore drops any beginning zeros. To enter a number as text, type an apostrophe (') as the first character.

TIP: CONVERTING FROM SCIENTIFIC NOTATION

When a number is too long to be displayed, Excel displays it in scientific notation. Scientific notation is based on powers of 10. The number 1,250,000 can also be expressed as 1.25×10^6. In an Excel cell, this appears as 1.25E+06, where the E separates the exponent (6) from the base (1.25). If the cell is too narrow to show the number even in scientific notation, Excel will fill the cell with a row of number signs (######). In either case, the original number you entered is shown on the formula bar.

SHORTCUTS

When you enter a number into a cell, the cell is automatically formatted with the General number format which displays numbers as precisely as possible. However, you can display a number differently by changing its format. Although formatting numbers is discussed in detail later in this text, there are a few formats you can enter as you enter numbers. For example:

▶ To format the cell using the Currency format ($10.00), enter a dollar sign in front of the number.

▶ To format the cell using the Comma format (1,000), use commas in the number to separate thousands.

▶ To format a number as a percentage, enter the number followed by a percent sign. For example, instead of entering .2, enter 20%. When you enter a percentage as a whole number followed by a percent sign, the program automatically formats the cells using the Percentage format and converts the number in front of the percent sign into a decimal by dividing the number by 100. For example, entering a percentage as 20% is the same as entering it as 0.2 or 20/100.

TUTORIAL

In this tutorial you begin to create a 2-year budget by entering text and numbers. When you have finished this tutorial, your model will look like the one shown in the figure "The Budget—Labels and Numbers."

	A	B	C	D	E
1	Type **Filename:** your name into cell A1 and press **Enter**				
2	Filename: budget.xls				
3	1-Nov-94				
4					
5	2-Year budget				
6	INCOME	FALL	SPRING	FALL	SPRING
7	Bank balance	3,000			
8	Income during semester	1,250	1,250	1,250	1,250
9	College loans	1,000	1,000	1,000	1,000
10	Total				
11					
12	EXPENSES				
13	Tuition	1,000	1,000	1,000	1,000
14	Room & board	1,000	1,000	1,000	1,000
15	Books	200	200	200	200
16	Entertainment	300	300	300	300
17	Travel	500	500	500	500
18	Misc.	200	200	200	200
19	Total				

1. Enter text shown here in cells with light yellow background.

2. Enter numbers shown here in cells with light blue background.

The Budget—Labels and Numbers

Getting Started

1. Open the *budget.xls* workbook stored in the *tutorial* directory on the *Excel Student Resource Disk (Part 1)* and enter your name into cell A1.

Entering Text

2. Enter the text shown in the light yellow cells in the figure "The Budget—Labels and Numbers." Before typing **Total** in cell A10 and cell A19, press ⌷Spacebar⌷ twice to indent the word.

Entering Numbers

3. Enter all of the numbers shown in the light blue cells in the figure "The Budget—Labels and Numbers." When typing numbers with commas between thousands, type the commas in the numbers exactly as shown. This will format the cell to match the entry.

Finishing Up

4. Save, print, and close the workbook.

2-2. EDITING CELL CONTENTS

When you enter data into a cell, it is displayed on the formula bar and you can press ⟨←Bksp⟩ to delete characters. Once you have completed the entry you can edit it either in the cell or on the formula bar.

QUICKSTEPS: EDITING CELL CONTENTS
1. Select the cell to be edited and then do one of the following:
   ▶ Click the formula bar to move the insertion point there so you can edit the entry on the formula bar.
   ▶ Press ⟨F2⟩ or double-click the cell to move the insertion point there so you can edit the entry right in the cell.
2. Edit the entry using the commands described in the box "Understanding Editing Commands."
3. Press ⟨Enter ↵⟩ or click the Enter box (☑) on the formula bar to complete the edit.

UNDERSTANDING EDITING COMMANDS

When the insertion point is in an entry on the formula bar or cell, you can do any of the following.

▶ To move the insertion point through the entry, press ⟨←⟩ or ⟨→⟩. Press ⟨Home⟩ or ⟨End⟩ to move it to the beginning or end of the entry. Press ⟨Ctrl⟩+⟨←⟩ or ⟨Ctrl⟩+⟨→⟩ to move it to the beginning of the previous or next word.

▶ To insert characters at the insertion point, type them in.

▶ To delete characters, press ⟨←Bksp⟩ to delete those to the left of the insertion point and ⟨Delete⟩ to delete those to the right. Hold either of these keys down to delete one character after another.

▶ To switch between insert and overtype modes, press ⟨Insert⟩. In *insert mode* (the default mode), if you type a character into an existing line of characters, the characters to the right move over to make room for the new character. In *overtype mode* (the status bar reads *OVR* when in this mode), any character that you type replaces any character the edit cursor is positioned under.

TUTORIAL

In this tutorial, you open the model shown in the figure "The Unedited Model." You then edited the misspelled entries in column A—some on the formula bar and some in the cell itself.

The Unedited Model

	A	B	C	D	E
1					
2	Edit the cells with				
3	the light yellow				
4	background on the				
5	toolbar. **2-Year Budget**				
6	INCOME	FALL	SPRING	FALL	SPRING
7	Bank balence	$1,500	($3,200)	($4,150)	($5,100)
8	Incom semester	1,250	1,250	1,250	1,250
9	College loans	1,000	1,000	1,000	1,000
10	**Total**	$2,750	($950)	($1,900)	($2,850)
11					
12	EXPENSES				
13	Tuiton · Edit the cells with	$1,000	$1,000	$1,000	$1,000
14	Room · the light blue back-	1,000	1,000	1,000	1,000
15	Books · ground in the cell.	200	200	200	200
16	Entertainment	300	300	300	300
17	Traval	500	500	500	500
18	Misc.	200	200	200	200
19	**Total**	$3,200	$3,200	$3,200	$3,200
20					
21	**Balence**		($3,200)	($4,150)	($5,100)	($6,050)

Getting Started

1. Open the *editing.xls* workbook stored in the *tutorial* directory on the *Excel Student Resource Disk (Part 1)*.

Correcting a Mistake While Entering

2. With cell A1 selected, type **Naame:** just as shown here, with an extra *a*.

3. Press [←Bksp] four times so that the line reads *Na*.

4. Type **me:** and press [Spacebar], then type your name and press [Enter ↵] to enter the new revised label.

Editing Cell Contents on the Formula Bar

5. Correct just the misspelled words or incorrect phrases in the cells with the light yellow background color (see the list "Fixing the Model"). To do so:

   ▸ Click the cell to display its contents on the formula bar.
   ▸ Click the formula bar to move the insertion point there.
   ▸ Use the arrow keys to move the insertion point through the entry, and insert new characters as needed.
   ▸ Use [←Bksp] and [Delete] to delete unwanted characters.
   ▸ When finished, press [Enter ↵] or click the Enter box (☑) on the formula bar to enter the revised entry into the cell.

Editing Cell Contents in the Cell

6. Now correct the misspelled text in the cells with the light blue background color (see the list "Fixing the Model"). To do so:

   ▸ Double-click the cell to move the insertion point there.
   ▸ Use the arrow keys to move the insertion point through the entry, and insert new characters as needed.
   ▸ Use [←Bksp] and [Delete] to delete unwanted characters.
   ▸ When finished, press [Enter ↵] or click the Enter box (☑) on the formula bar to enter the revised entry into the cell.

Fixing the Model

Current Form	Corrected Form
balence	balance
Incom semester	Income during semester
Tuiton	Tuition
Room	Room & board
Traval	Travel
Misc.	Miscellaneous
Balence	Balance

Finishing Up

7. Save, print, and close the workbook.

2-3. UNDOING MISTAKES

If you make a mistake when working with Excel, you can reverse it if you notice it before you have gone further. Only the last command or data entry you have made can be undone.

TUTORIAL

In this tutorial you make a number of deliberate mistakes so you can see how easy it is to undo them.

Getting Started

1. Open the *editing.xls* workbook stored in the *tutorial* directory on the *Excel Student Resource Disk (Part 1)*.

Undoing and Redoing Data Entry with the Menu

2. Click cell A1 to select it, type **Oh no, why did I do this?** and press [Enter ←] to replace the current entry.

3. Pull down the **Edit** menu and click the **Undo Entry** command to restore the original cell contents.

4. Pull down the **Edit** menu and click the **Redo (u) Entry** command to replace the original cell contents with the second entry.

5. Pull down the **Edit** menu and click the **Undo Entry** command to restore the original cell contents.

Undoing and Redoing Data Entry with the Toolbar

6. Click cell A1 to select it, type **Oh no, why did I do this again?** and press [Enter ←] to complete the entry.

7. Click the **Undo** button on the toolbar, and the original cell contents are restored.

8. Click the **Undo** button on the toolbar again to replace the original cell contents with the second entry.

9. Click the **Undo** button on the toolbar a third time to restore the original contents again.

Undoing a Deletion with the Menu

10. Click the heading for column A to select the entire column (the heading is the box with the letter A in it), pull down the **Edit** menu, and click the **Delete** command to delete the column.

11. Pull down the **Edit** menu and click the **Undo Delete** command to restore the deleted column.

Undoing a Deletion with the Toolbar

12. With column A still selected, pull down the **Edit** menu and click the **Redo (u) Delete** command to delete the column again.

13. Click the **Undo** button on the toolbar to restore the deleted column.

QUICKSTEPS: UNDOING MISTAKES
▶ To undo the effect of the last command, click the **Undo** button on the toolbar, or pull down the **Edit** menu and click the **Undo** command (the most recent command is listed following the **Undo** part of the command).

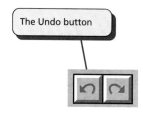
The Undo button

14. Close the workbook without saving your changes.

2-4. UNDERSTANDING FORMULAS

Very few people would use spreadsheet programs if all you could enter were text and numbers. What makes spreadsheets so popular is the ability to enter formulas. The formulas can calculate numbers entered in other cells on the worksheet, on other worksheets, or even other workbooks. This ability makes the spreadsheet a very useful and powerful tool for anyone who works with numbers of any kind.

You can enter formulas into worksheet cells that either calculate numbers directly or refer to cells elsewhere on the worksheet into which you enter numbers or other formulas. The basic rule is that all Excel formulas begin with a equal sign (=).

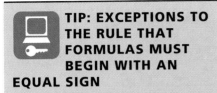

TIP: EXCEPTIONS TO THE RULE THAT FORMULAS MUST BEGIN WITH AN EQUAL SIGN

You can begin a formula with a plus or minus sign, but Excel will add a beginning equal sign when you complete the entry.

OPERATORS—THE BASIC BUILDING BLOCKS

When you enter formulas, certain symbols, called *operators*, tell the program what calculations to perform. These operators are used in conjunction with numbers or cell references to create formulas. The table "Excel Operators" lists some of Excel's operators, and the figure "Operators in Formulas" illustrates some of them.

Excel Operators	
Operator	Use
+	Performs addition
-	Performs subtraction
*	Performs multiplication
/	Performs division
%	Percent (when placed after a value, as in 20%)
^	Raises a number to a specified power

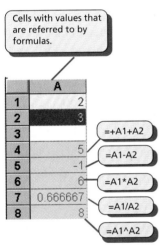

Operators in Formulas

THE ORDER OF OPERATIONS

When you enter formulas that contain more than one operator, the order in which they are evaluated becomes important. Each operator is assigned a priority that determines the sequence in which it is calculated. The table "Order of Operations" on the next page shows these priorities.

▸ Operators with a higher priority are performed first. For example, if you enter the formula =4*2+3, it contains two operators: + (addition) and * (multiplication). Since multiplication has a higher priority, it is performed first, so 4*2 = 8; then addition is performed, so 8+3 = 11.

▸ Operators with the same level of priority are calculated in the order they appear in the formula from left to right. For example, if you enter the formula =5*4/2, it has two operators: * (multiplication) and / (division), which have the same priority. Since calculations are performed from left to right, the answer is 10. First multiplication is performed, so 5*4 = 20; then division is performed, so 20/2 = 10.

You can enter formulas so that calculations occur in the desired sequence, but it is usually easier to use parentheses to control the order of calculations regardless of the priorities assigned to the operators. For example, entering a formula as =4*2+3 calculates an answer of 11. However, the formula =4*(2+3) calculates a different answer since the operations within the parentheses are always performed first. Hence, 2+3 = 5 which is then multiplied by 4 to give 20. If parentheses are nested— for example, 1+(1/(1/2))—the operations are performed from the inner-most parentheses outward; in this formula, the answer would be 3. You can use up to 32 sets of parentheses in any formula.

Order of Operations		
Operator	Description	Priority
-	Negation (as in -10)	Highest
%	Percent	
^	Exponentiation	
* and /	Multiplication and division	
+ and -	Addition and subtraction	Lowest

NUMBERS AND CELL REFERENCES

When you enter formulas, you can use numbers and/or references to other cells. For example, entering the formula =5+10 into a cell displays 15 in the cell because that is the value of 5 and 10 added together. You could also enter the number 5 into cell A1 and the number 10 into cell A2. You can then enter a formula in a third cell that refers to those two cells. For example, the formula =A1+A2 would display 15 because it adds the values in the two cells that it refers to. The formula calculates the values just as if they were entered directly into the formula.

Let's look at an example. Your boss tells you what the sales and costs for the month are and asks you to calculate the monthly profit.

Using only numbers, you enter the formula =100000-20000-18000-57000 into a cell and get the answer 5000 as shown in the figure "A Formula with Only Numbers."

Using cell references, you enter the formula =B1-B2-B3-B4 into cell B5 and get the same answer, 5000 as shown in the figure "A Formula with Cell References."

Just as you finish, your boss comes in and tells you he has some updates for the figures he gave you. Sales are only $99,000 and marketing costs are $18,500. To recalculate using a formula containing numbers, you have to reenter the entire formula as =99000-20000-18500-57000. Using the formula containing cell references, you just type in new numbers for sales and marketing, and the formula automatically calculates the new result.

	A	B
1	Sales	$ 100,000
2	Salaries	20,000
3	Marketing	18,000
4	Manufacturing	57,000
5	Total	$ 5,000

A Formula with Only Numbers

=100000-200000-18000-57000

	A	B
1	Sales	$ 100,000
2	Salaries	20,000
3	Marketing	18,000
4	Manufacturing	57,000
5	Total	$ 5,000

A Formula with Cell References

=B1-B2-B3-B4

TIP: STORED AND DISPLAYED VALUES

Excel stores values calculated by formulas with up to 15 digits of accuracy. However, you can change the way they are displayed by formatting the cells that contain them (formatting is discussed in Sections 3-2 through 3-4). For example, you can calculate pi as 3.14159265358979 and format it to be displayed as 3, 3.1, 3.14, 3.141 and so on. Regardless of how it is formatted, it will be calculated by other formulas using the full value.

TIP: WHY NO FORMULA SHOULD CONTAIN NUMBERS

A strong case can be made for never including numbers in formulas. Here are some of the reasons:

1. Embedding a number in a formula is making an assumption either that it should not or cannot be changed or that changes in it are unimportant to the outcome of the analysis. When exploring the model, you may find it is very sensitive to changes in that number—a phenomenon you would never discover if the number were embedded in a formula.

2. The next time you use the model, you may forget there is a number embedded in a formula and not take it into consideration.

3. When you print a sheet, only the displayed values are normally printed, not the formulas behind them. Anyone else trying to follow your analysis might get lost if numbers are embedded in formulas rather than shown on the printout.

DISPLAYING FORMULAS IN THEIR CELLS

You can press Ctrl+` to display formulas and full values of numbers and then again to hide them. (The ` character is the left single quotation mark located on the key to the left of the 1 key on the alphanumeric keyboard.)

TUTORIAL

In this tutorial you are introduced to formulas by looking at various types in a typical model—shown in the figure "Understanding Formulas." There are formulas that use each of the five most commonly used operators.

	A	B	C	D	E	F	G	H
1	Type **Name: your name** into cell A1 and press **Enter**							
2	Filename: formulas							
3	17-Nov-94							
4								
5		Quantity	Price	Revenue	Cost	Gross margin ($)	Gross margin (%)	
6	Retail sales	1,000	$ 40.00	$ 40,000	$ 20,000	$ 20,000	50%	
7	Wholesale sales	5,000	$ 30.00	$150,000	$100,000	$ 50,000	33%	
8	Total	6,000		190,000	120,000	$ 70,000	37%	
9								
10		Addition	Multiplication	Multiplication using a constant.		Subtraction		
11								
12							Division	
13		Operators						
14								
15		+ Addition						
16		- Subtraction						
17		* Multiplication						
18		/ Division						
19								

Understanding Formulas

Getting Started

1. Open the *formula.xls* workbook stored in the *tutorial* directory on the *Excel Student Resource Disk (Part 1)* and enter your name into cell A1.

Exploring Formulas

2. Select a cell on row 8 that contains a number (except the percentage) to display the cell's formula on the formula bar. These formulas use the addition operator to add the values in the two cells above them.

3. Select cells D6 or D7, and you'll see that these formulas use the multiplication operator to multiply the values in the two cells to their left (price × quantity).

4. Select cells E6 or E7, and you'll see multiplication using a number (a constant) embedded in a formula. These formulas multiply 20 times the quantity sold in column B.

5. Select cells F6 or F7, and you'll see subtraction operators in action. These formulas subtract cost from revenue to calculate gross margin in dollars.

6. Select cells G6, G7, or G8, and you'll see division in action. These formulas divide the gross margin by the sales revenues to calculate gross margins in percentages.

Displaying Formulas

7. Press Ctrl+` to display formulas in the cells instead of their calculated values. You'll notice that columns widen so formulas can be displayed in their entirety. Scroll the screen to see how all of the formulas work.

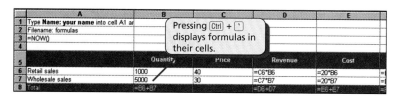

8. Press Ctrl+` again to return to displaying calculated values.

Finishing Up

9. Close the workbook without saving it.

TIP: CLOSING WORKBOOKS

When you close many of the workbooks that accompany this text, a dialog box asks if you want to save your changes even when you haven't made any. This is because these worksheets contain a function in cell A3 that calculates today's date. When you open the workbook, Excel recalculates that function and considers that updating to be a change. Just click the **No** button when the dialog box appears.

2-5. ENTERING FORMULAS

There are two ways to enter formulas: by typing them in or, if they refer to other cells, by selecting the cells they refer to. For a summary of the characters you can use when entering formulas, see the table "Characters You Can Use in Numbers and Formulas on the next page."

TIP: USING EXCEL AS A CALCULATOR

When working with Excel, you can use it as a calculator. Type any formula such as =.5*24.95 but do not press Enter↵. Instead, press F9, and the result of the formula is displayed on the formula bar. You can then press Esc or click the cancel box (☒) to clear it, or press Enter↵ to enter the calculated value into the worksheet.

Characters You Can Use in Numbers and Formulas

Character	Examples	Description
Digits	[0] – [9]	Used for the numbers themselves. For example, to enter 100, type [1][0][0].
Plus sign	[+]	Used to indicate a positive value. Since this is the default you needn't enter it when entering numbers. (In formulas, it is used to indicate addition, as in =2+2, which calculates 4.)
Minus sign	[-]	Used to indicate a negative value. In formulas it is used to indicate subtraction, as in 3-2.
Parentheses	[(] [)]	Used to enclose formulas within formulas, as in =1+(1/2) which calculates 1.5.
Comma	[,]	Used to format an entry so commas are displayed between thousands.
Slash	[/]	Used to indicate division in a formulas, as in 1/2, which calculates .5.
Dollar sign	[$]	Used to format an entry so dollar signs and commas between thousands are displayed.
Percent sign	[%]	Used to format an entry as a percentage. For example, entering 20% is the same as entering .2. However, when entered as 20% it is displayed as 20% and not as .2.
Period	[.]	Used as a decimal point, as in 3.14.
Upper- and lowercase E	[E]	Used to indicate scientific notation (powers of 10), as in 3e2, which is the same as 300.

TYPING FORMULAS

You can type in a formula that refers to another cell, for example, A1*A2. But this formula begins with a letter, so if you type that letter first, the program assumes you are entering text. To enter the formula, you first press = (the equal sign) to enter the formula as =A1*A2.

COMMON WRONG TURNS: THIS ISN'T WHAT I'D HOPED FOR!

When you enter a formula, you may get an error value in the cell rather than the calculated result you expected. Sometimes these error values cascade throughout a worksheet because any cell that refers to a cell with an error value also displays an error value. Error messages in cells always begin with a number sign (#) and end with an exclamation point (!). For example, you might see #NUM!, #REF!, or #VALUE!. If you get one of these error messages, use Excel's Help command to search for topics that begin with #.

SELECTING CELLS TO BUILD FORMULAS

You can create a formula by selecting the cells referred to in it whenever the formula bar is active. For example, you could enter a formula into cell A3 that subtracts the value in cell A2 from the value in cell A1 as follows:

Step 1. With cell A3 selected, press [=] to begin the formula and activate the formula bar.

Step 2. Click cell A1 to select it, and then press [-] (the minus sign). The formula now reads =A1-.

Step 3. Click cell A2 to select it, and the formula now reads =A1-A2.

Step 4. Press [Enter ◄┘] or click the Enter box ([✓]) on the formula bar to enter the formula into cell A3.

Selecting cells is especially useful when working on larger models where the cells you want to refer to are not displayed on the screen. Experienced users almost always build formulas by selecting cells because it is faster, more accurate, and easier than typing.

EDITING FORMULAS

You edit formulas just as you edit text. How you do so depends on whether you want to edit before or after you have clicked the Enter box (☑) on the formula bar or pressed [Enter ↵] to complete the entry.

▶ If you notice a mistake before you complete the entry, press [F2] to edit the entry or press [Esc] and begin over.

▶ If you notice a mistake after you have completed the entry, select the cell to display the formula on the formula bar and edit it there.

You can also edit a formula in its cell. To do so, double-click the cell or select it and press [F2] to display the formula in the cell rather than its calculated result. After editing the formula in the cell, press [Enter ↵] or click the Enter box (☑) on the formula bar to complete the entry

TUTORIAL

In this tutorial, you enter formulas into the budget model on which you have been working. You do so by typing them in and by selecting cells to create them. When finished, your model will look like the figure "The Budget—The Formulas."

The Budget—The Formulas

	A	B	C	D	E
1	Type Filename: your name into cell A1 and press Enter				
2	Filename: budget.xls				
3	20-Dec-93			=B21	
4					
5	2-Year Budget				
6	INCOME	FALL	SPRING	FALL	SPRING
7	Bank balance	$3,000	$2,050		
8	Income during semester	1,250	1,250	1,250	1,250
9	College loans	1,000	1,000	1,000	1,000
10	Total	$5,250			
11	=B7+B8+B9				
12	EXPENSES				
13	Tuition	$1,000	$1,000	$1,000	$1,000
14	Room & board	1,000	1,000	1,000	1,000
15	Books	200	200	200	200
16	Entertainment	300	300	300	300
17	Travel	500	500	500	500
18	Misc.	200	200	200	200
19	Total	$3,200			
20	=B10-B19			=B13+B14+B15+B16+B17+B18	
21	Balance	$2,050			

Getting Started

1. Open the *budget.xls* workbook stored in the *tutorial* directory on the *Excel Student Resource Disk (Part 1)*.

Entering a Formula by Selecting Cells

2. Click cell B10 to select it, and then press [=] to begin a formula. The entry is displayed on the formula bar.

3. Click cell B7, and both the cell and the formula bar display *=B7*.

4. Press [+], and both the cell and the formula bar display *=B7+*.

5. Click cell B8, and both the cell and the formula bar display *=B7+B8*.

6. Press [+], and both the cell and the formula bar display *=B7+B8+*.

7. Click cell B9, and both the cell and the formula bar display *=B7+B8+B9*.

8. Click the Enter box (☑) on the formula bar to enter the formula, and the three cells are added. The formula is displayed on the formula bar when cell B10 is the active cell.

Entering a Formula by Typing

9. Click cell B19 to select it, and then type **=B13+B14+ B15+B16+B17+B18** and press [Enter←]. The formula adds the numbers in the column between cells B13 and B18.

Entering a Formula by Selecting Cells

10. Click cell B21 to select it, and then press [=] to begin a formula. The entry is displayed on the formula bar.

11. Click cell B10, and both the cell and the formula bar display *=B10*.

12. Press [-], and both the cell and the formula bar display *=B10-*.

13. Click cell B19, and both the cell and the formula bar display *=B10-B19*.

14. Click the Enter box (☑) on the formula bar to enter the formula, and the number in cell B19 is subtracted from the number in cell B10. The formula is displayed on the formula when cell B21 is the active cell.

Entering a Formula by Selecting Cells

15. Click cell C7 to select it, press [=], click cell B21, and then click the Enter box (☑) on the formula bar. The reference carries the value in cell B21 to cell C7.

Finishing Up

16. Save, print, and close the workbook.

2-6. SELECTING RANGES OF CELLS

To work with formulas (and use many other procedures), you have to know how to select the cells you want to refer to. Normally, only one cell—the active cell—is selected. As you've seen, you can select another cell by clicking it with the mouse or by pressing the arrow keys to move the heavy border to it.

Although you normally enter data into a single cell, many commands can be applied to a number of cells at once. To do so, you *extend the selection*. When you then execute a command, it affects all of the selected cells.

One way to extend a selection is to point to a cell, hold down the left mouse button, and drag the mouse to highlight adjoining cells.

Another way to extend a selection is to click on row or column headings. Clicking a row heading selects the entire row. Clicking a column heading selects the entire column. Clicking the Select All button, the gray rectangle in the upper-left corner of the worksheet, selects the entire worksheet.

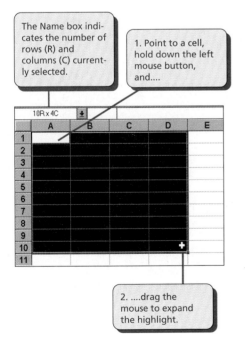

The Name box indicates the number of rows (R) and columns (C) currently selected.

1. Point to a cell, hold down the left mouse button, and....

2. ....drag the mouse to expand the highlight.

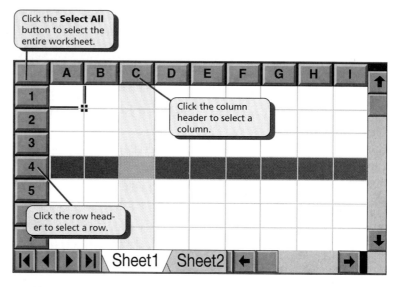

If you point to a row or column heading, hold down the left mouse button, and drag the mouse pointer, you can select adjacent rows or columns.

You can also use the arrow keys to expand the highlight. One way is to hold down ⟨⇧ Shift⟩ while you press the arrow keys (or other keys that move the selected cell). Another way is to press ⟨F8⟩ so the status bar displays *EXT*. Then press the arrow keys (or other keys that move the selected cell) or click anywhere in the sheet to extend the highlight. Press ⟨F8⟩ again to turn *EXT* off.

To select nonadjacent areas, select the first area as you would normally. Then hold down ⟨Ctrl⟩ while you select one or more other areas.

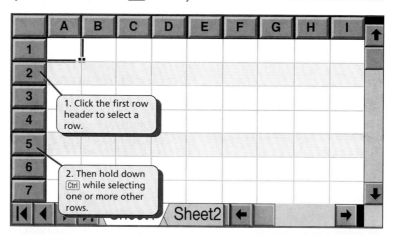

TIP: ENTERING THE SAME DATA INTO SEVERAL CELLS

To enter the same data into several cells, select the cells, type the data, and then press ⟨Ctrl⟩+⟨Enter ↵⟩.

QUICKSTEPS: SELECTING CELLS, ROWS, AND COLUMNS

Selecting Cells, Rows, or Columns

▶ Click a cell to select it.

▶ Click a row or column heading to select the entire row or column.

▶ Click the **Select All** button at the intersection of the row and column headings to select all cells on the worksheet.

Extending a Selection to Other Cells, Rows, or Columns

To extend a selection, do any of the following:

▶ Point to a cell, row heading, or column heading; hold down the left mouse button and drag the highlight to select adjacent cells, rows, or columns. Release the mouse button, and the selected area remains highlighted.

▶ Click one cell, row heading, or column heading to select it. Then hold down ⌜⇧ Shift⌝ and click another cell, row heading, or column heading.

▶ Hold down ⌜⇧ Shift⌝ while you press the arrow keys (or other keys that move the selected cell).

▶ Press ⌜F8⌝, then press the arrow keys (or other keys that move the selected cell) or click anywhere in the sheet to extend the highlight. Press ⌜F8⌝ again to turn *EXT* off and leave the selection highlighted.

Selecting Nonadjacent Areas

▶ Select the first cell, row heading, or column heading as you normally would, then hold down ⌜Ctrl⌝ while you select each of the others.

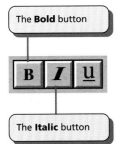

The **Bold** button

The **Italic** button

LOOKING AHEAD: TOOLBAR FORMAT BUTTONS

The toolbar contains three buttons, labeled B, I, and U, that are used to boldface, italicize, or underline data in selected cells. Three other buttons are used to align the contents of cells left, center, or right. These buttons are used in this tutorial so you can see the effects of selecting cells. They are discussed in more detail in Section 3-2.

TUTORIAL

In this tutorial you are introduced to selecting cells, rows, columns, and the entire sheet listing well-known movies now on video. After selecting various areas, you then format them by clicking buttons on the toolbar. Since these buttons are not discussed until later, they are illustrated at the left.

Getting Ready

1. Open the *videos.xls* workbook stored in the *tutorial* directory on the *Excel Student Resource Disk (Part 1)*.

Extending the Selection by Dragging

2. Click cell A5 to select it. Then hold down the left mouse button and drag the highlight to cell E5 and release it. The cells you highlighted remain selected. Notice how the address of the leftmost cell in the range (A5) is listed on the formula bar and that cell is highlighted differently than the other selected cells. This tells you that the cell is the active cell. (See the illustration on the following page.)

3. Click the **Bold** button on the toolbar to boldface the selected area.

4. Click the **Italic** button on the toolbar to also italicize the selected area, then click any cell to remove the highlight.

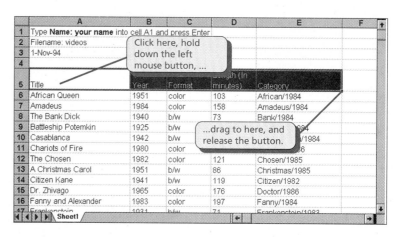

Selecting Columns

5. Click column heading B on the border to select that entire column.

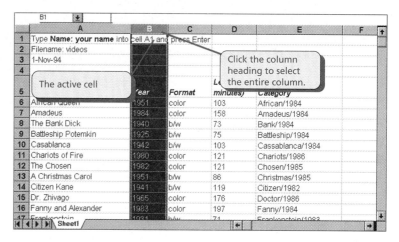

6. Click the **Italic** and **Center** buttons on the toolbar to italicize and center text in the column, then click any cell to remove the highlight.

7. Point to column heading C on the border, hold down the mouse button, and, without releasing it, drag the highlight to the right to select up to column D, then release the mouse button.

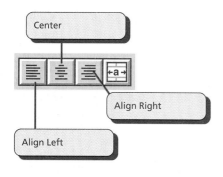

Extending the selection by dragging

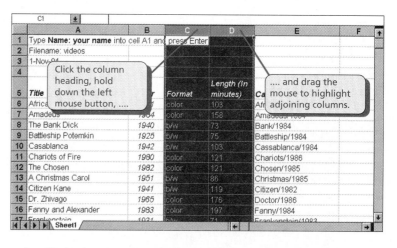

8. Click the **Center** button on the toolbar to center the column entries, then click any cell to remove the highlight.

9. Point to column heading E on the border, click the **Align Right** button on the toolbar to align the text with the right edge of the cells, then click any cell to remove the highlight.

Selecting the Entire Worksheet

10. Click the **Select All** button in the upper-left corner of the border to select the entire worksheet. Notice how cell A1 is listed on the formula bar and that cell is highlighted differently than the other cells. This tells you that cell A1 is the active cell.

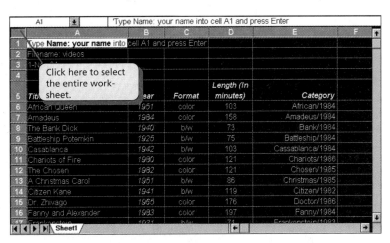

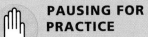

PAUSING FOR PRACTICE

Selecting cells is one of the basic skills you must master to use Excel. Pause here to practice until you have mastered this basic skill.

11. Click any cell to remove the highlight.

Finishing Up

12. Close the workbook without saving your changes.

2-7. FILLING ADJACENT CELLS

Filling copies the contents of selected cells to adjoining cells. This saves you time because you can enter a formula or other data once and then copy it as needed. For example, you can create a monthly budget by entering the necessary formulas in the first monthly column and then copying them to the other monthly columns. To copy data in one cell to adjacent cells, you select the cell or cells that you want to copy and then drag the fill handle, the small square in the lower-right corner of the selected cells. As you do so, an outline highlights the cells that the data will be copied to. When you release the mouse button, the outlined cells are filled with the copied data.

The results you obtain by filling like this depend on what was in the original selected cell or cells.

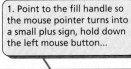

1. Point to the fill handle so the mouse pointer turns into a small plus sign, hold down the left mouse button...

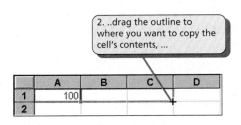

2. ..drag the outline to where you want to copy the cell's contents, ...

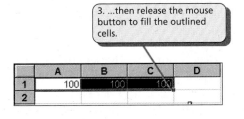

3. ...then release the mouse button to fill the outlined cells.

▶ If the data are formulas, the formulas are copied to the new positions, and any cell references in them adjust automatically.

▶ If the data you copy are values that Excel recognizes as a series of sequential numbers, the series will increment in the range you copy to. For example, copying Jan, January, or 1st Qtr copies to the next cell as Feb, February, or 2nd Qtr. If you want to copy values such as these without incrementing them, hold down Ctrl while you drag the fill handle.

▶ If the data is a single value, such as 1, 10, or 100, it copies as 1, 10, or 100. To have it increment by 1, hold down [Ctrl] while you drag the fill handle.

▶ If you select two cells that already contain an increment, that increment will be repeated. For example, copying cells containing 0 and 10 will create a series 20, 30, 40, and so on.

TUTORIAL

In this tutorial you drag the fill handle on cells to copy formulas to adjacent cells. When you have finished, your model will look like the illustration shown here.

	A	B	C	D	
1	Type Filename: your name into cell A1 and press Enter				Select each cell shown here in red and drag its fill handle to highlight the cells shown here in yellow.
2	Filename: budget.xls				
3	20-Dec-93				
4					
5	2-Year Budget				
6	INCOME	FALL	SPRING	FALL	
7	Bank balance	$3,000	$2,050	$1,100	$150
8	Income during semester	1,250	1,250	1,250	1,250
9	College loans	1,000	1,000	1,000	1,000
10	Total	$5,250	$4,300	$3,350	$2,400
11					
12	EXPENSES				
13	Tuition	$1,000	$1,000	$1,000	$1,000
14	Room & board	1,000	1,000	1,000	1,000
15	Books	200	200	200	200
16	Entertainment	300	300	300	300
17	Travel	500	500	500	500
18	Misc.	200	200	200	200
19	Total	$3,200	$3,200	$3,200	$3,200
20					
21	Balance	$2,050	$1,100	$150	($800)

Getting Started

1. Open the *budget.xls* workbook stored in the *tutorial* directory on the *Excel Student Resource Disk (Part 1)*.

Filling Adjacent Cells

2. Select cell C7 and point to the fill handle on the cell border so the mouse pointer turns into a small plus sign (+). Hold down the left mouse button, drag the fill handle and outline to cell E7, and release the mouse button. The formula is copied to each of the cells you dragged the outline over. (For now they display zeros.)

3. Select cell B10 and point to the fill handle on the cell border so the mouse pointer turns into a small plus sign (+). Hold down the left mouse button, drag the fill handle and outline to cell E10, and release the mouse button. The formula is copied to each of the cells you dragged the outline over.

4. Select cells B19 through B21.

5. Point to the fill handle on the cell border so the mouse pointer turns into a small plus sign (+). Hold down the left mouse button, drag the fill handle and outline to column E, and release the mouse button. The formulas are copied to each of the columns you

QUICKSTEPS: COPYING USING THE CLIPBOARD

1. Select the cells to be copied.

2. Click the **Copy** button on the toolbar, or pull down the **Edit** menu and click the **Copy** command. The selected cells are highlighted by a moving border and the status line reads *Select destination and press ENTER or choose Paste.*

3. Select the cell that will be in the upper-left corner of the range of cells to be pasted in.

4. Press Enter↵, click the **Paste** button on the toolbar, or pull down the **Edit** menu and click the **Paste** command. The cells highlighted by the moving border are copied to the new location. (The moving border around the selected cells disappears if you pressed Enter↵, or when you type any data.)

TIP: COPYING SHORTCUTS

To quickly copy selected cells press Ctrl+Insert to copy them, select the cell in the upper-left corner of where you want them copied to, and press ⇧ Shift+Insert.

QUICKSTEPS: COPYING USING THE SHORTCUT MENU

1. Select the cells to be copied.

2. Click the right mouse button in the selection to display the shortcut menu, and select **Copy**.

3. Click the cell in the upper-left corner of where you want the cells copied with the right mouse button to display the shortcut menu again, and select **Paste**.

dragged the outline over. The formula in each column adjusts to total the cells in the column it is copied to.

Finishing Up

6. Save, print, and close the workbook.

2-8. COPYING DATA

Excel lets you copy data from one location to another in two basic ways. You can drag cells with the mouse, or you can copy data to Windows' Clipboard and then paste it into another location. Using the Clipboard is more flexible than dragging, but dragging is quicker for shorter moves.

To begin copying, you first select the cells you want to copy. You then copy the content of the selected cells to Windows' Clipboard. While the cell content is stored on the Clipboard, you can paste it anywhere in the workbook you copied it from. (You can also paste it into another workbook, or even into another application's document.) When you copy and paste, you choose among menu commands, toolbar buttons, shortcut menu commands, or keyboard shortcuts as the means you use.

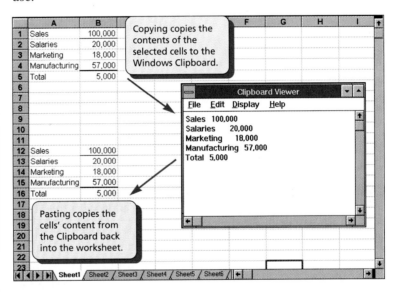

When you copy a range of cells, its content and formats are copied from the original cells to a new location. The data in the cells you copy from is left unchanged. If any cells contain data in the range you copy to, it is overwritten by the copied data.

TIP: PASTING IN MORE THAN ONE LOCATION

When copying, if you use the **Paste** button on the toolbar or the **Paste** command on the **Edit** menu to paste the data, it remains on the Clipboard so you can paste it into a number of locations. If you paste the contents by pressing Enter↵, you clear the Clipboard and cannot paste the cells in another location.

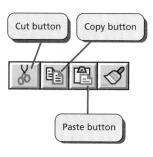

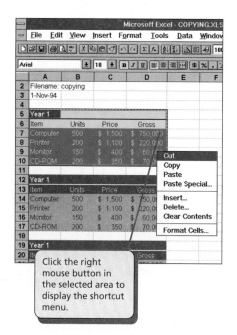

Click the right mouse button in the selected area to display the shortcut menu.

COPYING BY DRAGGING AND DROPPING

To begin copying with dragging and dropping, you first select the cells you want to copy. You then drag a copy of the selected cells to a new position.

To insert copied cells among existing cells so the existing cells move aside to make room for them, hold down both Ctrl+⇧ Shift while you drag and release them. When you point to the area where you want to insert the dragged cells, the mouse pointer turns into a horizontal or vertical "I-beam" shape (I). When vertical, the cells to the right move to the right to make room for the dragged cells. When horizontal, the cells below move down to make room.

TUTORIAL

In this tutorial you are introduced to copying data using menu commands, toolbar buttons, and the shortcut menu.

Getting Started

1. Open the *copying.xls* workbook stored in the *tutorial* directory on the *Excel Student Resource Disk (Part 1)* and enter your name into cell A1.

Copying a Range with Menu Commands

2. Select the range of cells from A5 to D10, pull down the **Edit** menu, and click the **Copy** command.

3. Select cell A12, pull down the **Edit** menu, and click the **Paste** command.

Copying a Range with Toolbar Buttons

4. Select the range of cells from A5 to D17 and click the **Copy** button on the toolbar.

5. Select cell A19 and click the **Paste** button on the toolbar.

Copying a Range with the Shortcut Menu

6. Select the range of cells from A5 to D10. Then point to the selected area, click the right mouse button to display the shortcut menu, and click the **Copy** command.

7. Click cell A26 with the right mouse button to display the shortcut menu again, and click the **Paste** command.

Finishing Up

8. Edit the headings for the four copies so you have models for Years 1 through 4.

9. Save, print, and close, the workbook.

2-9. SPECIFYING ABSOLUTE CELL REFERENCES

If you typed in every formula and function that you needed, you would not have to be concerned about relative and absolute cell references. But they become very important when you enter a formula in one cell and then copy it to others to save time.

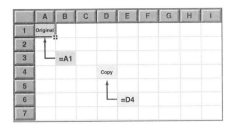

Column and row references are both relative. If the reference is to a cell one column over and two rows up, the copied cell reference will also refer to a cell one column over and two rows up.

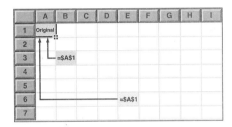

Column and row references are both absolute. No matter where the cell reference is copied, it will always refer to the same cell.

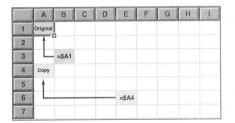

Column reference is absolute but row reference is relative. The copied cell reference will always refer to the same column. However, if the original reference was to a cell two rows up, the copied reference will refer to a cell two rows up.

Column reference is relative but row reference is absolute. The copied cell reference will always refer to the same row. However, if the original reference was to a column one column to the left, the copied reference will refer to a column one column to the left.

When you create formulas, they often refer to other cells in the worksheet. The program does not automatically "remember" the actual cell address that the formula refers to; instead, it remembers the position relative to the cell the formula is entered in—for example, one column to the left and two rows up. No matter where you copy the formula to, it always refers not to the original cell but to whatever cell is one column to the left and two rows up from the cell you copied it to.

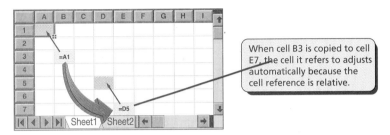

When cell B3 is copied to cell E7, the cell it refers to adjusts automatically because the cell reference is relative.

This automatic adjustment occurs because the reference to the cell is a relative reference; that is, the position of the cell referred to is relative to the position of the formula. All formulas you enter have relative references unless you specify otherwise.

You do not have to keep references to cells relative. You can make them absolute references so that a formula refers to the same cell wherever it is copied on the worksheet. For example, an absolute reference to cell A1 will continue to refer to that cell regardless of where you copy or move it to.

You can also use mixed references, which keep the reference to the row or column relative while making the other reference absolute.

You specify absolute references by typing dollar signs ($) in front of the column or row references.

> **TIP: EDITING ABSOLUTE AND RELATIVE CELL REFERENCES**
>
> When the cell reference is the last one on the formula bar, you can press the F4 key to cycle through the four possible reference combinations. The table "Absolute and Relative Cell References" describes the sequence of choices. Pressing F4 also works when you the formula is displayed on the formula bar for editing (after you press F2 or click the formula bar). Move the insertion point into the cell reference that you want to change, and press F4 to cycle the cell reference through the four possible combinations.

Absolute and Relative Cell References		
Cell Reference	Column	Row
A1	Relative	Relative
$A1	Absolute	Relative
A$1	Relative	Absolute
A1	Absolute	Absolute

TUTORIAL

In this tutorial you use absolute and relative references to copy formulas so they continue to refer to the correct cells in their new locations. The model you use is a five-year plan that is used for forecast profits given certain sales and expenses estimates. The finished model is shown in the figure "The Five-Year Plan."

	A	B	C	D	E	F
1	Name: your name					
2	Filename: 5yrplan					
3	2-Nov-94					
4						
5	Part 1. Variables					
6	Initial sales	$1,000				
7	Sales growth rate	10%				
8	Cost of goods sold	56%				
9						
10	Part 2. Five-Year Plan					
11	Year	1996	1997	1998	1999	2000
12	Sales	1000	1100	1210	1331	1464.1
13	Cost of goods sold	560	616	677.6	745.36	819.896
14	Gross margin	440	484	532.4	585.64	644.204

The Five-Year Plan

Getting Started

1. Open the *5yrplan.xls* workbook stored in the *tutorial* directory on the *Excel Student Resource Disk (Part 1)* and enter your name into cell A1.

2. Enter the numbers in cells B6 through B8. One of them is currency, so enter it as **$1,000**. Two of the numbers are percentages. To enter them, type **10%** and **56%** so they are displayed as percentages.

Entering Formulas

3. In cell B12, enter the formula **=B6** and press [Enter ←] to carry down opening sales from cell B6 in Part 1 of the model.

4. In cell B13, enter the formula **=$B8*B12** and press [Enter ←] to calculate cost of goods using the percent figure in Part 1 of the model.

5. In cell B14, enter the formula **=B12-B13** and press [Enter ←] to subtract cost of goods from sales.

6. In cell C12, enter the formula **=B12+($B7*B12)** and press [Enter ←] to calculate sales by adding last year's sales to 10% of last year's sales for a 10% sales increase. The dollar sign in front of the B7 cell reference will keep the column absolute when the formula is copied.

Copying Formulas

7. Select cells B13 and B14 and drag the fill handle to copy the formulas to column C.

8. Select cells C12 through C14 and drag the fill handle to copy the formula to the next three columns.

Looking At The Copied Formulas

9. Press [Ctrl]+[`] to display formulas in the cells, then scroll the screen to see what happened when formulas with absolute references were

copied. All formulas that refer to cells in the numbers section continue to refer to the same cells after being copied because they had absolute references to column B. All other references to cells refer to the column to their left because they were relative references.

	A	B	C	D	E	
1	Name: your name					
2	Filename: 5yrplan					
3	=NOW()					
4						
5	Part 1. Variables					
6	Initial sales	1000				
7	Sales growth rate	0.1				
8	Cost of goods sold	0.56				
9						
10	Part 2. Five-Year Plan					
11	Year	1996	1997	1998	1999	20
12	Sales	=$B6	=B12+($B7*B12)	=C12+($B7*C12)	=D12+($B7*D12)	=E
13	Cost of goods sold	=$B8*B12	=$B8*C12	=$B8*D12	=$B8*E12	=$
14	Gross margin	=B12-B13	=C12-C13	=D12-D13	=E12-E13	=F

> The copied formulas

10. Press Ctrl+` again to return to displaying calculated values.

Saving the Workbook

11. Click the **Save** button on the toolbar to save the workbook. You are about to make changes in it that you won't want to save.

12. Click the **Print** button on the toolbar to print the worksheet.

Exploring What-Ifs

13. Change the sales growth rate in cell B7 from 10 to 15 percent (type it as 15% or .15). Sales increase in all but the first year by 15 percent instead of the original 10 percent. Cost of goods also increases but remains a constant 56 percent of sales. Gross margins increase because sales are increasing faster than cost of goods.

14. Change the cost of goods percentage in cell B8 from 56 to 60 percent (type it as 60% or .60). Sales stay the same as in the previous what-if but are still higher than in the original example in all but the opening year, where they remain unchanged. Cost of goods also increases and is higher than the original example because it is now 60 percent of sales instead of 56 percent. Gross margins are lower than in the previous what-if but are higher than in the original example. If your goal was to obtain higher gross margins despite increases in cost of goods (perhaps because of increased prices), you have discovered how you can achieve this—increase sales sufficiently to achieve the increase in gross margins despite the increased cost of goods.

Finishing Up

15. Close the workbook without saving your what-if changes.

2-10. ADJUSTING COLUMN WIDTHS AND ROW HEIGHTS

When you first open a workbook, all columns and rows are set to standard widths and heights. However, you can easily change these if you want to. For example, there are times when you may want to widen a column. If you enter text that is longer than the column is wide, all of the text is displayed only if the cell to its right is empty. If the adjoining cell contains data, any text that overflows into that cell is not displayed. The width of columns also affects whether numbers or values calculated by formulas are displayed correctly. If a number is too large to be displayed in a cell, Excel will either:

▸ Display it in scientific notation—for example, display 100,000 as 1.00E+5; or, if the cell is too narrow for that

▸ Fill the cell with number signs (#######).

The width of a column determines how many characters can be displayed in cells within it. Narrow columns let you display more columns on the screen and squeeze more into a printout, so there is an advantage to making columns as narrow as possible. Since column width is always set for an entire column, a column must be set to the width required by the longest entry in the column.

In addition to adjusting column widths and row heights, you can also hide rows and columns so their letters or numbers and their contents are not displayed on the screen or printed out. This is useful when you just want to show summaries of your worksheet ands hide details. It's also useful when there are some entries on the worksheet that you don't want others to see.

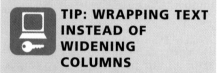

TIP: WRAPPING TEXT INSTEAD OF WIDENING COLUMNS

To fully display text in cells, you can widen a column. However, you can also wrap long text into two or more lines in the same cell. To do so, select the cell, pull down the **Format** menu, and click the **Cells** command to display the Format Cells dialog box. Click the *Alignment* tab, click the **Wrap Text** check box to turn it on (⊠), and then click the **OK** command button.

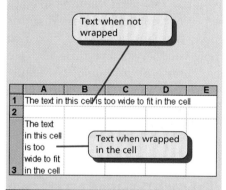

QUICKSTEPS: ADJUSTING COLUMN WIDTHS AND ROW HEIGHTS
Clicking

1. Point to the right column heading border or the lower row heading border, and the mouse pointer turns into a split double arrow. (You can also select more than one column or row, and point to any of their borders.)

2. Double-click to set the width of the columns or height of the rows so they automatically adjust to the size of the entry (or to reset a column or row to the default width or height.)

Dragging

1. Point to any row or column heading border, and the mouse pointer turns into a split double arrow. (You can also select more than one column or row, and point to any of their borders.)

2. Hold down the left mouse button, drag the columns or rows wider or narrower, and then release the mouse button.

Menus

1. Select any range of cells spanning the rows or columns to be changed, or use the row or column headings to select the entire rows or columns.

2. Pull down the **Format** menu and click the **Row** or **Column** command to cascade the menu.

3. Choose any of the settings described in the box "Understanding Row and Column Menu Selections."

UNDERSTANDING ROW AND COLUMN MENU SELECTIONS

When you pull down the **Format** menu and click the **Row** or **Column** command to cascade the menu you have the following choices:

Row Commands

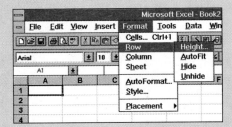

Height displays a dialog box into which you can type a row height in points (each point is 1/72 of an inch, and you can enter a number from 0 to 409—0 will hide the row).

AutoFit adjusts the height of selected rows to a size related to that of the largest type size used on the rows.

Hide hides the selected row(s) and removes its number from the border.

Unhide unhides any hidden rows in the selected range. To use this command, select the rows on both sides of the hidden rows.

Column Commands

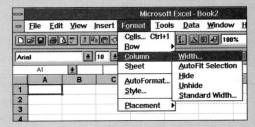

Width displays a dialog box into which you can type a column width in characters (from 0 to 255).

AutoFit Selection adjusts the width of selected columns to display the longest entry currently in the column.

Hide hides the selected column(s) and removes its number from the border.

Unhide unhides any hidden columns in the selected range. To use this command, select the columns on both sides of the hidden columns.

Standard Width displays the Standard Width dialog box so you can either:

▶ Click the **OK** command button to return selected columns to the standard width.

▶ Enter a column width (0 to 255—0 will hide the column) and click the **OK** command button to change the width of all columns on the worksheet that you have not previously adjusted.

TUTORIAL

In this tutorial you are introduced to changing column widths using the menu and by dragging their borders. You then see how to hide and unhide cell contents. The worksheet you use contains a GPA model that calculates grade point averages. (Ignore the misspellings in the model for now; you'll fix those in a later PicTorial with Excel's built-in spelling checker.)

Getting Started

1. Open the *gpa.xls* workbook stored in the *tutorial* directory on the *Excel Student Resource Disk (Part 1)*. Do not enter your name in cell A1 yet.

Changing Column Widths With Menu Commands

2. Select columns A through E by dragging the mouse pointer over the column headings to select the entire columns.

3. Pull down the **Format** menu, click the **Column** command to cascade the menu, and then click the **AutoFit Selection** command. This adjusts all column widths to fit their contents. Notice how column A is now much too wide because the entry in cell A1 is long and its length was used to calculate the width of the column. Since the text in the heading will flow over into the next column, column A can be made narrower.

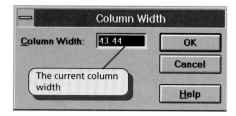

4. Select any cell in column A, pull down the **Format** menu, click the **Column** command to cascade the menu, and then click the **Width** command to display the Column Width dialog box. (The displayed width of the current column depends on your system.)

5. Type **25** in the **Column Width** text box, and then click the **OK** command button.

Changing Column Widths By Dragging

6. Select columns B through E by using the headings to select the entire columns.

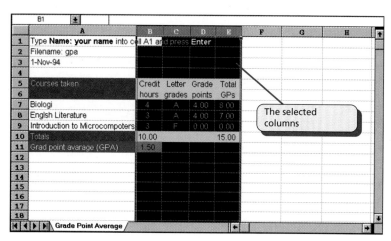

7. Point to the border between the column B and column C heading, and the mouse pointer turns into a split double arrow.

8. Hold down the left mouse button and drag the dotted line until it's in the middle of column C, then release the mouse button to change the widths of selected columns.

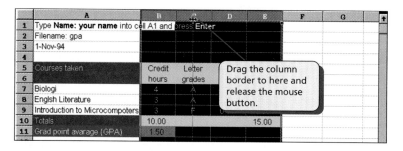

Hiding and Unhiding Rows

9. Select any cell on row 11, pull down the **Format** menu, click the **Row** command to cascade the menu, and then click the **Hide** command. Row 11 is now hidden from view. (It also wouldn't print if you printed at this point.)

10. Select any cells on rows 10 and 12, pull down the **Format** menu, click the **Row** command to cascade the menu, and then click the **Unhide** command.

Finishing Up

11. Enter your name in cell A1 and then click the **Save** button on the toolbar to save your changes.

12. Click the **Print** button on the toolbar to print the sheet.

13. Close the workbook.

PicTorial 2 Review Questions

True-False

T F **1.** Numbers automatically align with the left edge of the cell.

T F **2.** The **Undo** command will undo the effect of the last command executed.

T F **3.** Mathematical operators with a higher priority are performed first.

T F **4.** You can press [Enter ←] to remove data from the formula bar and insert it into the selected cell.

T F **5.** Clicking a row heading selects the entire row.

T F **6.** Copying leaves the source cells intact.

T F **7.** Mathematical operators with the same level of priority are calculated in the order they appear in the formula from left to right.

T F **8.** Up to 265 characters can be typed in a cell.

T F **9.** Quotation marks are used to enclose formulas within formulas.

T F **10.** When creating a formula, pressing [F9] will display the result of the formula on the formula bar.

Multiple Choice

1. All Excel formulas begin with _____.

a. Hyphens

b. Dashes

c. Equal signs

d. Apostrophes

2. You specify absolute references by adding _____ signs in front of the column or row references.

a. #

b. @

c. $

d. *

3. When the cell reference is the last one on the formula bar, press _____ to cycle through the four possible combinations of cell referencing.

a. [F5]

b. [Ctrl]+[F8]

c. [F8]

d. [F4]

4. To display the formulas used in cells instead of their calculated values, press _____.

    a. Ctrl + "

    b. Ctrl + '

    c. Ctrl + `

    d. Ctrl + ^

5. If you do not wish a cell reference to change when copied or moved to another location, use a(n) _____ cell reference.

    a. Relative

    b. Absolute

    c. Mixed

    d. Partial

6. The results of the formula =4*(2+3) would be _____.

    a. 10

    b. 9

    c. 20

    d. 11

7. To control the order of mathematical operations, use _____.

    a. Parentheses

    b. Colons

    c. Asterisks

    d. Commas

8. To enter numbers as text, type a(n) _____ as the first character.

    a. Apostrophe

    b. Quotation mark

    c. Period

    d. Exclamation point

9. The function key to use to activate the Extend feature is _____.

    a. F2

    b. F11

    c. F8

    d. F5

10. Which of the following is an example of an absolute cell reference:

    a. A1

    b. $$A$1

    c. $A1

    d. A1

Fill In the blank

1. In order to select nonadjacent areas, you must use the _____ key.

2. When you _____ a range of cells, a duplicate set of the cells' contents and formats is reproduced elsewhere on the worksheet.

3. When copying data, any data in the location where you paste it is _____.

4. To enter fractions, precede them with a _____ so Excel does not consider them to be dates.

5. When copying data, the new location to where the data is copied is call the _____ range.

6. To insert a data entry in the active cell, you can press _____, an _____, or click the _____.

7. The result of the formula =3+4*2 would be _____.

8. As you enter data into a cell, the data is displayed in the cell and on the _____ bar.

9. If, when copying, you wish the column reference to change, but not the row reference, use a(n) _____ cell reference.

10. The small square in the lower-right corner of the active cell is called a(n) _____.

PicTorial 2 Lab Activities

▶▶ COMPUTER-BASED TUTORIALS

2-1. Examples and Demos
We suggest you complete the following computer-based lessons to learn more about the features discussed in this PicTorial. To do so, pull down the **Help** menu and click the **Examples and Demos** command, click the *Topic* listed in the table "Suggested Examples and Demos to Complete," and then click the *Subtopic* listed in that same table.

Suggested Examples and Demos to Complete	
Topic	Subtopic
❏ Selecting Cells, Choosing Commands	Selecting Cells on a Worksheet
❏ Selecting Cells, Choosing Commands	Choosing Shortcut Menu Commands
❏ Entering Data	Entering Data
❏ Entering Data	Filling a Range of Adjacent Cells
❏ Creating Formulas and Links	Entering Formulas
❏ Creating Formulas and Links	Using References
❏ Editing a Worksheet	Editing Cells
❏ Editing a Worksheet	Moving and Copying Data by Dragging
❏ Formatting a Worksheet	Changing Column Width and Row Height
❏ Formatting a Worksheet	Hiding and Unhiding Columns and Rows

2-2. Quick Preview—Getting Started with Excel
Excel has a built-in Quick Preview feature that introduces you to many of the program's features. Here you use this feature to take a guided tour of getting started with Excel.

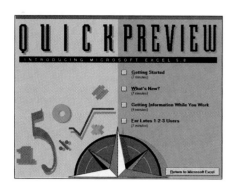

1. Pull down the **Help** menu and click the **Quick Preview** command to display its opening screen.

2. Click the **Getting Started** button to begin that lesson. Then follow the instructions that appear on the screen. The buttons you click to navigate the preview are described in the table "Quick Preview Command Buttons."

Quick Preview Command Buttons
Close returns you to the Quick Preview opening screen.
Hint displays a hint on how to complete a step.
Next takes you to the next step.
Return to Microsoft Excel closes Quick Preview and returns you to Excel.
Show Me demonstrates a procedure.

3. When finished, click the **Return to Microsoft Excel** command button.

 ▶▶ **QUICKSTEP DRILLS**

2-1A. Entering Text and Numbers into Cells

As you've seen, templates are frequently used in business. These templates have been designed so anyone can enter data into them and the formulas will calculate the correct answers. (You can specify that a workbook be saved as a template with the extension .xlt by choosing Template in the Save As dialog box's **Save File as Type** box. Then, when you use it, you save your version so the template isn't overwritten.) Here you use a checkbook-balancing template to practice entering text and numbers. When finished, your model should look like the one in the figure "The Checkbook Model."

	A	B	C	D	E	F
1	Type **Name: your name** into cell A1 and press **Enter**					
2	Filename: chkbook.xls					
3	2-Nov-94					
4						
5			Balancing a Check Book			
6						Balance
7	Check #	Date	Description	Amount	Deposit	$1,250.00
8	1	30-Jan-96	Textbook	45.62		1,204.38
9	2	2-Feb-96	Airline ticket	156.50		1,047.88
10	3	3-Feb-96	Dinner	28.70		1,019.18
11		4-Feb-96	Pay check		350.00	1,369.18
12	4	5-Feb-96	Jacket	52.80		1,316.38
13		6-Feb-96	Bank charge		(5.00)	1,311.38
14	5	7-Feb-96	Auto loan	235.75		1,075.63
15	6	9-Feb-96	Rent	525.50		550.13
16		11-Feb-96	Birthday present		25.00	575.13
17						N/A

Note You can enter data in cells with this background color. All other cells are protected.

The Checkbook Model

1. Open the *chkbook.xls* workbook stored in the *drill* directory on the *Excel Student Resource Disk (Part 1)* and enter your name into cell A1.

2. Enter the text and numbers shown in the lighter colored cells area of the template. All other cells are protected so you cannot enter data into them. As you enter numbers in columns D and E, notice how the balance automatically changes in column F.

   ▶ To enter the numbers in column A as text, type an apostrophe first.

   ▶ Enter the bank charge as -5 0r (5).

3. Save your changes, make a printout, and then close the workbook.

2-1B. Entering Text and Numbers into Cells

In this drill you practice entering numbers in different formats to see how they appear on the worksheet. When finished, your model should look like the one in the figure "The Entering Model."

The Entering Model

	A	B	C
1	Type **Name: your name** into cell A1 and press **Enter**		
2	Filename: entering		
3	2-Nov-94		
4			
5	Type each of these entries into the cell to its right	Type In this Column	Description of what's displayed
6	1.0	1	Trailing zero is dropped
7	-1.1230	-1.123	Trailing zero is dropped
8	1,581	1,581	Comma is displayed between thousands as entered
9	1.1%	1.10%	Number accepted as a decimal and decimal place is added
10	1.112%	1.11%	Number is rounded off to two decimal places
11	10e2	1.00E+03	Number displayed in scientific notation (for 1,000)
12	1 1/2	1 1/2	Number is displayed as a fraction
13	3 3/5	3 3/5	Number is displayed as a fraction
14	3/4	4-Mar	Number is assumed to be a date
15	$4.50	$4.50	Number is displayed with dollar sign
16	$1,250.00	$1,250.00	Number is displayed with dollar sign and comma
17	-78.91	-78.91	Number accepted and displayed as entered

1. Open the *entering.xls* workbook stored in the *drill* directory on the *Excel Student Resource Disk (Part 1)* and enter your name.

2. Enter data shown in column A on the same row in column B just as shown, and read the description of the results you get in column C.

3. Save your changes, make a printout, and then close the workbook.

2-2. Editing Cell Contents

In this drill you edit text in one column of a worksheet so it matches text in another column. When finished, your model should look like the one in the figure "The Whoops Model."

1. Open the *whoops.xls* workbook stored in the *drill* directory on the *Excel Student Resource Disk (Part 1)* and enter your name into cell A1.

2. Correct the words in column A on rows 7 through 11 so they match the spelling on the same rows in column C.

3. Save your changes, make a printout, and then close the workbook.

2-3. Undoing Mistakes

In this drill you delete the contents of cells and then undo the deletion to restore the cells to their original state. When finished, your model should look like the one in the figure "The Whoops Model."

Delete or format any of these cells' contents and then click the Undo button on the toolbar.

Correct the spelling of the words to the left so they match those to the right.

	A	B	C	D	E
1	Type **Name**: your name into cell A1 and press **Enter**				
2	Filename: whoops				
3	1-Nov-94				
4					
5		Undoing			
6	1	2	3		
7	4	5	6		
8	7	8	9		
9	10	11	12		
10	13	14	15		
11					
12					
13		Editing			
14	Wrong		Right		
15	Salees		Sales		
16	Expensos		Expenses		
17	Profats		Profits		
18	Boneus		Bonus		
19	Deposats		Deposits		

The Whoops Model

1. Open the *whoops.xls* workbook stored in the *drill* directory on the *Excel Student Resource Disk (Part 1)*.

2. Select any cell in the "Undoing" section that contains a number and press ⌈Delete⌉ to delete it. Then immediately click the **Undo** button on the toolbar to undo the deletion. Repeat with other cells until you are comfortable with the procedure.

3. Close the workbook without saving your changes.

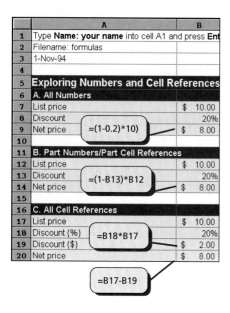

The Understanding Formulas Model

2-4. Understanding Formulas

To calculate the net price of a product when you know the list price and discount, you use the formula (100% – discount × list price). In this drill you retrieve a workbook designed to demonstrate the principles of numbers and cell references in formulas and order of operations.

1. Open the *formulas.xls* workbook stored in the *drill* directory on the *Excel Student Resource Disk (Part 1)*.

2. In the three-part section on numbers and cell references, select each of the following cells to display its formula on the formula bar:

a. **All Numbers**. In cell B9, the formula =(1-.2)*10 contains only numbers. Because the numbers are part of the formula, you cannot easily change the discount or price to calculate a new result.

b. **Part Numbers/Part Cell References**. In cell B14, the formula =(1-B13)*B12 contains both numbers and cell references. The formula subtracts the value in cell B13 from 1 (100%) and multiplies the result times the price in cell B12. The numbers in cells B12 and B13 are both variables that you can change to explore outcomes.

c. **All Cell References**. In cell B19, the formula =B18*B17 contains only references to cells and calculates the discount in dollars. In cell B20, enter the formula =B17-B19 which uses cell references to subtract the discount from the list price to calculate the net price.

3. Close the workbook without saving any changes you may have made.

2-5A. Entering Formulas

In this drill you enter formulas using various operators described in the worksheet itself. As you do so, you immediately see the results of the calculations. When finished, your model should look like the one in the figure "The Operator Model" on the following page.

1. Open the *operator.xls* workbook stored in the *drill* directory on the *Excel Student Resource Disk (Part 1)* and enter your name into cell A1.

2. Enter each formula described in column A on the same row in column B and read the description of the formula in column C. For example, type **=10+10** in cell B9.

3. Save the workbook, click the **Print** button on the toolbar to print it, and close the workbook.

	A	B	C
1	Type **Name: your name** into cell A1 and press **Enter**		
2	Filename: operator		
3	2-Nov-94		
4			
5	Price	5	
6	Number	4	
7			
8	Type each of these entries into the cell to its right	Type in this column	Description of what's calculated
9	=10+10	20	10 plus 10
10	=10*4	40	10 times 4
11	=30-5	25	30 minus 5
12	=200/5	40	200 divided by 5
13	=10^10	10000000000	10 raised to the 10th power
14	=B5+B6	9	Number in cell B5 plus number in cell B6
15	=B5*B6	20	Number in cell B5 times number in cell B6
16	=B5-B6	1	Number in cell B5 minus number in cell B6
17	=B5/B6	1.25	Number in cell B5 divided by number in cell B6
18	=B5^B6	625	Number in cell B5 raised to the power of number in cell B6
19	=10+B5	15	10 plus the number in cell B5
20	=2*B5	10	2 times the number in cell B5
21	=B5-4	1	Number in cell B5 minus 4
22	=1000/B6	250	1000 divided by the number in cell B6
23	=B6^2	16	Number in B6 raised to the second power

The Operator Model

2-5B. Entering Formulas

In this drill you enter formulas using numbers, references to other cells containing numbers, and a combination of numbers and cell references. As you do so, you immediately see the results of the calculations.

1. Open the *entrform.xls* workbook stored in the *drill* directory on the *Excel Student Resource Disk (Part 1)* and enter your name into cell A1.

2. Enter each of the formulas shown on the worksheet. When finished, your results should match those shown in the illustration in Drill 2-4.

3. Save the workbook, click the **Print** button on the toolbar to print it, and close the workbook.

2-6. Selecting Ranges of Cells

In this drill you practice selecting columns and rows and rectangular ranges. As you do so, you practice dragging with the mouse to extend the selection.

1. Open the *select.xls* workbook stored in the *drill* directory on the *Excel Student Resource Disk (Part 1)* and enter your name into cell A1.

2. Follow each of the instructions on the screen to select various parts of the worksheet. To cancel the selection, click any cell.

3. Repeat all of the steps in this drill until you have mastered selecting ranges, then close the workbook without saving any changes you may have made.

2-7. Filling Adjacent Cells

The easiest way to copy text, numbers, or formulas is to select the cell or cells you want to copy and then drag the highlight to the cells where you want them copied. In this drill, you practice this important procedure.

1. Open the *fill.xls* workbook stored in the *drill* directory on the *Excel Student Resource Disk (Part 1)* and enter your name into cell A1.

2. Select cells A8 through G8, then drag the fill handle down to row 16 and release it. Notice how the entries are each incremented by one month, number, or day.

3. Select cells A23 through G24, then drag the fill handle down to row 34 and release it. Notice how the entries are each incremented by the same amount as the first two entries were. For example, January and April in column A is incremented so there is a three-month interval between all of the copied months.

4. Save the workbook, click the **Print** button on the toolbar to print it, and close the workbook.

2-8. Copying Data

In this drill you practice copying data, first by dragging and dropping and then using the menu commands.

1. Open the *copydata.xls* workbook stored in the *drill* directory on the *Excel Student Resource Disk (Part 1)* and enter your name into cell A1.

2. Click the sheet tab at the bottom of the sheet labeled *Dragging & Dropping* to make it the active sheet if it isn't already. There are four ranges of cells you will copy: a cell, column, row, and block. These ranges are yellow with red borders and you will copy them to the ranges shown in red with yellow borders. To do so:

   ▸ Select the range to be copied (yellow cells with red borders).

   ▸ Hold down Ctrl and point to the range border so the mouse pointer is an arrow with a plus sign over it.

   ▸ Hold down the left mouse button and drag the range to the range you are copying it to. When the range's outline is superimposed over the range you are copying to (red cells with yellow borders), release the mouse button.

3. Compare the cell references in the original cells with those in the copied cells to see how they have automatically adjusted the cells they refer to.

4. Click the **Print** button on the toolbar to print the worksheet.

5. Click the tab at the bottom of the sheet labeled *Copying & Pasting* to make it the active sheet (see the illustration on the next page).

6. Use the **Edit** menu's **Copy** and **Paste** commands to copy data from the "Copy From" section to the "Copy To" section. Compare the cell references in the original cells with those in the copied cells to see how they have automatically adjusted the cells they refer to.

   ▸ In the "Copy To" section, the cells you select before pasting are highlighted with hatch marks.

   ▸ Remember that when you use the menu commands, you can copy once and paste as many times as you like until you copy another cell or cells.

7. Click the **Print** button on the toolbar to print the worksheet and then close it without saving your changes.

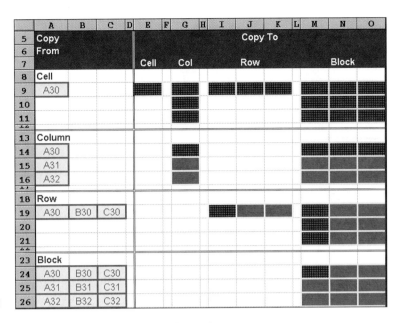

The Copying & Pasting Worksheet

2-9A. Specifying Absolute Cell References

In this drill you use a specially formatted model to see how cell references change when you copy them to a new location on the worksheet.

1. Open the *absrel.xls* workbook stored in the *drill* directory on the *Excel Student Resource Disk (Part 1)* and enter your name into cell A1.

2. Use the **Copy** and **Paste** buttons on the toolbar to copy each of the red cells with the yellow border to the yellow cell with the red border in the same section. As you do so, select first the cell you copy from and then the cell you copy to and notice how the cell references change or doesn't change when copied, depending on which part of the reference is relative and which is absolute. To help you see the results better, the cell referred to by the original formula is shown in dark blue and the one it refers to after being copied is shown in light blue. (Note that when you copy a cell, the moving border around the source cell remains flashing until you copy the next cell.)

3. Click the **Print** button on the toolbar to print the worksheet and then close it without saving your changes.

2-9B. Specifying Absolute Cell References

One common use of mixed cell references is in the preparation of tables that show a range of possible outcomes. Here you create a table that compares two subscription plans from a major telecommunication provider. One plan has a lower monthly fee but a higher hourly rate than the other. The model will tell you how many hours you must use the service to benefit from paying the higher monthly fee to get the lower hourly rate. (The fees listed are not the actual fees charged by CompuServe.) When finished, the first few rows of your model should look like the figure "The CompuServe Model."

1. Open the *compsrv.xls* workbook stored in the *drill* directory on the *Excel Student Resource Disk (Part 1)* and enter your name into cell A1.

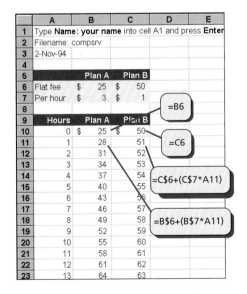

The CompuServe Model

2. Enter the formulas shown in the figure "The Compsrv Model" in cells B10, C10, B11, and C11.

3. Select cells B11 and C11 and use the fill handle to copy them to all adjacent rows down to row 37.

4. Press [Ctrl]+[`] to display formulas in their cells and notice the results of copying the formula. The only references that change are those that refer to the hours in column A where the row is relative. The references to rows 6 and 7, where the reference to the row was absolute, haven't changed when copied down the columns.

5. Press [Ctrl]+[`] to display values in their cells.

6. Save, print, and close the workbook.

2-9C. Specifying Absolute Cell References

There is a concept referred to as the time value of money which describes how money increases when invested at compound interest (future value) and decreases due to inflation (present value). To calculate compound interest, you use the formula $(1+r)^N$. To calculate the present value of an amount, the formula is $(1+r)^{-N}$. In both formulas, r is the rate of interest (or inflation) and N is the number of periods. Here you enter these formulas in a single cell and then use the fill command to copy them to other cells. The result is a table of values similar to those you find in the appendix of many accounting or finance books.

	A	B	C	D	E	F	G	H	I	J	K
1	Type **Name**: **your name** into cell A1 and press **Enter**										
2	Filename: value				=(1+B$5)^$A6						
3	2-Nov-94										
4											
5	Period	1%	2%	3%	4%	5%	6%	7%	8%	9%	10%
6	1	1.010	1.020	1.030	1.040	1.050	1.060	1.070	1.080	1.090	1.100
7	2	1.020	1.040	1.061	1.082	1.103	1.124	1.145	1.166	1.188	1.210
8	3	1.030	1.061	1.093	1.125	1.158	1.191	1.225	1.260	1.295	1.331
9	4	1.041	1.082	1.126	1.170	1.216	1.262	1.311	1.360	1.412	1.464
10	5	1.051	1.104	1.159	1.217	1.276	1.338	1.403	1.469	1.539	1.611
11	6	1.062	1.126	1.194	1.265	1.340	1.419	1.501	1.587	1.677	1.772
12	7	1.072	1.149	1.230	1.316	1.407	1.504	1.606	1.714	1.828	1.949
13	8	1.083	1.172	1.267	1.369	1.477	1.594	1.718	1.851	1.993	2.144
14	9	1.094	1.195	1.305	1.423	1.551	1.689	1.838	1.999	2.172	2.358
15	10	1.105	1.219	1.344	1.480	1.629	1.791	1.967	2.159	2.367	2.594
16	11	1.116	1.243	1.384	1.539	1.710	1.898	2.105	2.332	2.580	2.853
17	12	1.127	1.268	1.426	1.601	1.796	2.012	2.252	2.518	2.813	3.138
18	13	1.138	1.294	1.469	1.665	1.886	2.133	2.410	2.720	3.066	3.452
19	14	1.149	1.319	1.513	1.732	1.980	2.261	2.579	2.937	3.342	3.797
20	15	1.161	1.346	1.558	1.801	2.079	2.397	2.759	3.172	3.642	4.177
21	16	1.173	1.373	1.605	1.873	2.183	2.540	2.952	3.426	3.970	4.595
22	17	1.184	1.400	1.653	1.948	2.292	2.693	3.159	3.700	4.328	5.054
23	18	1.196	1.428	1.702	2.026	2.407	2.854	3.380	3.996	4.717	5.560

The Compound Sum of $1 Worksheet

1. Open the *value.xls* workbook stored in the *drill* directory on the *Excel Student Resource Disk (Part 1)* and enter your name into cell A1.

2. On the *Compound Sum of $1* sheet, enter the formula =(1+B$5)^$A6 into cell B6.

3. Select the cell with the formula and use the fill handle to fill the formula to all cells on the row out to cell K6.

4. Select cells B6 through K6 and use the fill handle to fill the formula to all rows down to row 30.

5. Print the worksheet.

6. Press [Ctrl]+[`] to display formulas in their cells and notice the results of copying the formula. The row or column references with dollar signs in front of them didn't change and those without them did. Check a few of the formulas to see exactly which rows and columns they refer to.

7. Press [Ctrl]+[`] to display values in their cells.

8. Click the tab at the bottom of the sheet labeled *Present Value of $1* to make it the active sheet.

9. Enter the formula =1/(1+B$5)^$A6 into cell B6. Repeat Steps 3 and 4 to use the fill handle to fill the formula into the cells to the right and down.

10. Repeat Steps 6 through 7 for this table to see how the formula changes when copied.

11. Save the workbook and then close it.

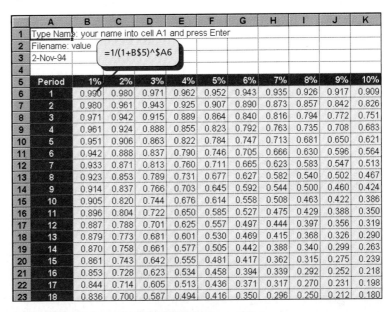

The Present Value of $1 Worksheet

2-10. Adjusting and Hiding Columns and Rows

Widening columns is often necessary to display labels and numbers correctly. However, changing the size of rows and columns allows you to control the layout on the page. In this drill you practice changing column widths and row heights by dragging with the mouse.

1. Open the *row&col.xls* workbook stored in the *drill* directory on the *Excel Student Resource Disk (Part 1)* and enter your name into cell A1.

2. Select the colored column and drag it to about half its original width.

3. Select the colored rows and drag them to about twice their original height.

4. Select the entire worksheet and use the **Row** and **Column** commands on the **Format** menu to AutoFit the text.

5. Save, print, and then close the workbook.

▶▶ SKILL-BUILDING EXERCISES

2-1. Creating a Pricing Model

Retail businesses purchase their inventory from manufacturers at a discount. They then mark up the goods so that they can sell them at a profit. In this exercise, you create a model that allows you to explore the relationship among prices, discounts, markups, and profits. When finished your model should look like the figure "The Pricing Model."[1]

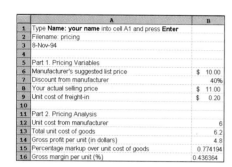

The Pricing Model

1. Open the *pricing.xls* workbook stored in the *exercise* directory on the *Excel Student Resource Disk (Part 2)* and enter your name into cell A1.

2. Use the **Format**, **Column**, **Width** command to set column A to 32.

3. In each of the four cells B12 through B16, enter the formulas described in the table "The Pricing Model's Formulas." The formulas in this table are described in English, much as they would be explained to you in class or on a job. Using these descriptions, you must figure out what cells references and operators to use to create the actual formulas you enter in the worksheet. When finished, your model should look like the figure "The Pricing Model."

4. Save the finished model and make a printout.

5. Explore the following what-ifs, and make printouts of one or more as you do so:

   ▶ What if the discount from the manufacturer is raised to 50%? What happens to the gross profit and gross margin per unit?

   ▶ What if the discount from the manufacturer is lowered to 35%? What happens to the gross profit and gross margin per unit?

   ▶ If the discount from the manufacturer is 35%, what actual selling price must you have to obtain a 44% gross margin per unit?

6. Close the workbook without saving your what-if changes.

The Pricing Model's Formulas	
Cell	Formula
B12	The *Unit cost from manufacturer* is calculated by subtracting the *Discount from manufacturer* from 100% and multiplying the result times the *Manufacturer's suggested list price*. The formula would read in English **(1- Discount from manufacturer)*Manufacturer's suggested list price**.
B13	The *Total unit cost of goods* is the *Unit Cost from manufacturer* plus the *Unit cost of freight in*.
B14	The *Gross profit per unit (in dollars)* is *Your actual selling price* minus the *Total unit cost of goods*.
B15	The *Percentage markup over unit cost of goods* is the *Gross profit per unit (in dollars)* divided by the *Total unit cost of goods*.
B16	The *Gross margin per unit (%)* is the *Gross profit per unit (in dollars)* divided by *Your actual selling price*.

2-2. Doubling a Penny Every Day

You may remember the childhood puzzle where kids would ask, "What if you put one penny in a bank on the first day and then doubled the amount every day? For example, on day two, you put two pennies in the bank; on day three, you put in four pennies; and so on. How many pennies would you have to put in at the end of the month?" The answer was always surprising. In this exercise, you create a model that answers

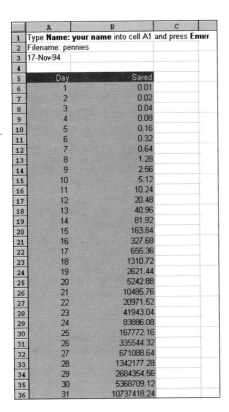

	A	B	C
1	Type **Name: your name** into cell A1 and press **Enter**		
2	Filename: pennies		
3	17-Nov-94		
4			
5	Day	Saved	
6	1	0.01	
7	2	0.02	
8	3	0.04	
9	4	0.08	
10	5	0.16	
11	6	0.32	
12	7	0.64	
13	8	1.28	
14	9	2.56	
15	10	5.12	
16	11	10.24	
17	12	20.48	
18	13	40.96	
19	14	81.92	
20	15	163.84	
21	16	327.68	
22	17	655.36	
23	18	1310.72	
24	19	2621.44	
25	20	5242.88	
26	21	10485.76	
27	22	20971.52	
28	23	41943.04	
29	24	83886.08	
30	25	167772.16	
31	26	335544.32	
32	27	671088.64	
33	28	1342177.28	
34	29	2684354.56	
35	30	5368709.12	
36	31	10737418.24	

The Pennies Model

	A	B	C
1	Type **Name: your name** into cell A1 and press **Enter**		
2	Filename: series		
3	2-Nov-94		
4			
5	Arithmetic	Geometric	Exponential
6	2	2	2
7	3	4	4
8	4	8	16
9	5	16	256
10	6	32	65,536
11	7	64	4,294,967,296

The Series Model

this question. When finished, your model should look like the figure "The Pennies Model."

1. Open the *pennies.xls* workbook stored in the *exercise* directory on the *Excel Student Resource Disk (Part 2)* and enter your name into cell A1.

2. Use the **Format**, **Column**, **Width** command to set column B to 17.

3. Enter the numbers 1 and 2 in cells A6 and A7, select both cells and use the fill handle to copy them down to row 36. This enters a linear series of numbers in the *Day* column.

4. Enter the number .01 into cell B6.

5. In cell B7, enter a formula that multiplies the amount saved on day 1 (cell B6) times 2.

6. Use the fill handle to copy the formula in cell B7 to cells B8 through B36.

7. Save the finished model and make a printout.

8. How much would you have to put in on the 31st day if you started with $1?

9. Close the workbook without saving your last what-if change.

2-3. Exploring Series of Numbers

In math, there are three common types of number series: arithmetic, geometric, and exponential. In this exercise, you enter a model that allows you to see the relationships among these three series. When finished, your model should look like the figure "The Series Model."

1. Open the *series.xls* workbook stored in the *exercise* directory on the *Excel Student Resource Disk (Part 2)* and enter your name into cell A1.

2. Use the **Format**, **Column**, **Width** command to set columns A, B, and C, to 15.

3. Enter the number 2 in cells A6, B6, and C6.

4. Enter and copy the formulas as described in the table "The Number Series Model's Formulas."

5. Save. print, and close the workbook.

The Number Series Model's Formulas	
Cell	**Formula**
A7	*Arithmetic* is a reference to the number above it plus 1. Use the cell's fill handle to copy the formula down to cell A11.
B7	*Geometric* is a reference to the number above it times 2. Use the cell's fill handle to copy the formula down to cell B11.
C7	*Exponential* is a reference to the number above raised to the power of 2. Use the cell's fill handle to copy the formula down to cell C11.

2-4. Exploring Birthday Probabilities

Whenever there is a group of people together, the possibility that any two of them share the same birthday is surprisingly high. For example, if there is one other person in the room, the probability that they do not have the same birthday as you is 364/365, or 99.18%. The probability that the two of you do have the same birthday is therefore 100% − 99.18%, or .82%. If there are two other people in the room, you can calculate the probability

	A	B	C	D
1	Type **Name: your name** into cell A1 and press **Enter**			
2	Filename: birthday			
3	2-Nov-94			
4				
5	Number of people	Individual probability	Probability not	Probability so
6	1	99.7%		
7	2	99.5%	99.2%	0.8%
8	3	99.2%	98.4%	1.6%
9	4	98.9%	97.3%	2.7%
10	5	98.6%	96.0%	4.0%
11	6	98.4%	94.4%	5.6%
12	7	98.1%	92.6%	7.4%
13	8	97.8%	90.5%	9.5%
14	9	97.5%	88.3%	11.7%
15	10	97.3%	85.9%	14.1%
16	11	97.0%	83.3%	16.7%
17	12	96.7%	80.6%	19.4%
18	13	96.4%	77.7%	22.3%
19	14	96.2%	74.7%	25.3%
20	15	95.9%	71.6%	28.4%
21	16	95.6%	68.5%	31.5%
22	17	95.3%	65.3%	34.7%
23	18	95.1%	62.1%	37.9%
24	19	94.8%	58.9%	41.1%
25	20	94.5%	55.6%	44.4%
26	21	94.2%	52.4%	47.6%
27	22	94.0%	49.3%	50.7%
28	23	93.7%	46.2%	53.8%
29	24	93.4%	43.1%	56.9%
30	25	93.2%	40.2%	59.8%

The Birthday Model

that they don't have the same birthday with the formula (364/365)*(363/365). If there were five people, you would use the formula (364/365)*(363/365)*(362/365)*(361/365)*(360/365). If there were 25 people, the formula would be five times as long. Let's see how easy it is to make this calculation by entering and copying a few simple formulas. When finished, your model should look like the figure "The Birthday Model."

1. Open the *birthday.xls* workbook stored in the *exercise* directory on the *Excel Student Resource Disk (Part 2)* and enter your name into cell A1.

2. Enter and copy the formulas described in the table "The Birthday Model's Formulas." You can see from the table that if there are 25 people in a room, the probability that two of them share a birthday is almost 60%.

3. Save, print, and close the workbook.

The Number Series Model's Formulas

Cell	Formula
B6	Enter the formula =**(365-A6)/365** and use the cell's fill handle to copy the formula down to cell B30.
C7	Enter the formula =**B7*B6**.
C8	Enter the formula =**C7*B8** and use the cell's fill handle to copy the formula down to cell C30.
D7	Enter the formula =**1-C7** and use the cell's fill handle to copy the formula down to cell D30.

2-5. Creating a Multiplication Table

Every math book you used in grade school probably had a multiplication table in the appendix. In this exercise, you create a multiplication table that allows you to display any range of numbers. When finished, your model should look like the figure "The Multiplication Table Model."

	A	B	C	D	E	F	G	H	I	J
1	Type **Name: your name** into cell A1 and press **Enter**									
2	Filename: multtabs									
3	2-Nov-94									
4										
5	Start		1							
6	Increment		1							
7										
8			1	2	3	4	5	6	7	8	9
9		1	1	2	3	4	5	6	7	8	9
10		2	2	4	6	8	10	12	14	16	18
11		3	3	6	9	12	15	18	21	24	27
12		4	4	8	12	16	20	24	28	32	36
13		5	5	10	15	20	25	30	35	40	45
14		6	6	12	18	24	30	36	42	48	54
15		7	7	14	21	28	35	42	49	56	63
16		8	8	16	24	32	40	48	56	64	72
17		9	9	18	27	36	45	54	63	72	81

The Multiplication Table Model

1. Open the *multtab.xls* workbook stored in the *exercise* directory on the *Excel Student Resource Disk (Part 2)* and enter your name into cell A1.

2. Enter the formulas described in the table "The Multiplication Table Model's Formulas," and copy the formulas to the indicated cells.

3. Save and print the worksheet.

4. Press (Ctrl)+(`) to display formulas in their cells and notice the results of copying the formula. Then press (Ctrl)+(`) to display values in their cells.

5. Change the start and increment numbers in cells B5 and B6, and watch the table change.

6. Close the workbook without saving your changes.

Cell	Formula
The Multiplication Table Model's Formulas	
A9	Enter the formula **=B5**.
A10	Enter the formula **=A9+B$6** (so that the reference to cell B6 has the row reference absolute), and use the cell's fill handle to copy the formula down to A17.
B8	Enter the formula **=B5**.
C8	Enter the formula **=B8+$B6** (so that the reference to cell B6 has the column reference absolute), and use the cell's fill handle to copy the formula out to cell J8.
B9	Enter the formula **=$A9*B$8** (so that the reference to cell A9 has the column reference absolute and B8 has the row reference absolute), and use the cell's fill handle to copy the formula first to J9, then select B9:J9 and fill down to row 17.

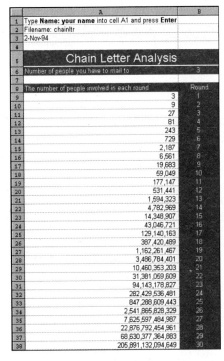

The Chain Letter Model

2-6. Exploring Chain Letters

Have you ever received a chain letter asking you to send money to the sender? These letters always promise great rewards if you do so, and if you send copies of the letter to a number of other people who will then send you money. Because these letters are illegal, they are usually couched in some other terms; for example, you send $5 to the sender to buy mailing labels, which you in turn sell to others. Generally, these chain letters are a great investment—if you are the originator. The problem with them is that the number of people involved grows so fast that before too many mailings, the entire world population has to be involved. When finished, your model should look like the figure "The Chain Letter Model."

1. Open the *chainltr.xls* workbook stored in the *exercise* directory on the *Excel Student Resource Disk (Part 2)* and enter your name into cell A1.

2. Use the **Format, Column, Width** command to set column A to 39.

3. Enter the formulas described in the table "The Chain Letter Model's Formulas," and copy the formulas to the indicated cells.

4. Save and print the worksheet.

5. Press (Ctrl)+(`) to display formulas in their cells, and notice the results of copying the formula. Then press (Ctrl)+(`) to display values in their cells.

6. The variable is the number of people that you have to mail to in cell B3. Change this to 4 and then to 5. How many people are involved on the tenth round? The thirtieth?

7. Close the workbook without saving your changes.

Cell	Formula
The Chain Letter Model's Formulas	
A9	The number of people involved at each round is a reference to the number of people you have to mail to in cell B6.
A10	The number of people involved at each round is the value in cell A9 multiplied by the number of people you have to mail to in cell B6 (an absolute reference). Use the fill handle on cell A9 to copy the formula down to cell A38.

	A	B	C	D
1	Type **Name:** your name into cell A1 and press **Enter**			
2	Filename: exchange			
3	2-Nov-94			
4				
5	Enter amount to be converted			1,000.00
6				
7		Exchange rate	Amount (in $)	Amount (in local)
8	Australia (Dollar)	0.8245	$824.50	1,212.86
9	Brazil (Cruzado)	0.00229	$2.29	436,681.22
10	Britain (Pound)	1.768	$1,768.00	565.61
11	Canada (Dollar)	0.8308	$830.80	1,203.66
12	Chile (Peso)	0.004	$4.00	250,000.00
13	Colombia (Peso)	0.0031	$3.10	322,580.65
14	Ecuador (Sucre)	0.00198	$1.98	505,050.51
15	France (Franc)	0.165	$165.00	6,060.61
16	Germany (Mark)	0.5627	$562.70	1,777.15
17	Greece (Drachma)	0.0069	$6.90	144,927.54
18	Hong Kong (Dollar)	0.1281	$128.10	7,806.40
19	Indonesia (Rupiah)	0.000586	$0.59	1,706,484.64
20	Ireland (Punt)	1.492	$1,492.00	670.24
21	Israel (Shekel)	0.6226	$622.60	1,606.17
22	Italy (Lira)	0.000758	$0.76	1,319,261.21
23	Japan (Yen)	0.0079368	$7.94	125,995.36
24	Mexico (Peso)	0.000439	$0.44	2,277,904.33
25	Philippines (Peso)	0.0483	$48.30	20,703.93
26	Singapore (Dollar)	0.5005	$500.50	1,998.00
27	United States (Dollar)	1.0000	$1,000.00	1,000.00
28				

The Currency Exchange Model

2-7. Calculating Currency Exchange Rates

With many transactions being international in nature, financial complications arise as currency exchange rates rise and fall. Profits made in one country have to be converted to the currency of the country in which a business is based. Prices and costs are frequently quoted in one currency but paid in another. To help people keep track, the daily exchange rates are always listed in the *Wall Street Journal*. In this exercise, you create a model that allows you to quickly convert from one currency to another based on that daily rate. When finished, your model should look like the figure "The Currency Exchange Model."

1. Open the *exchange.xls* workbook stored in the *exercise* directory on the *Excel Student Resource Disk (Part 2)* and enter your name into cell A1.

2. Enter and copy the formulas described in the table "The Exchange Rate Model's Formulas."

3. Save and print the workbook.

4. Explore what-ifs by changing the amount in cell D5.

5. Close the workbook without saving your what-if changes.

The Exchange Rate Model's Functions

Cell	Formula
C8	*Amount (in $)* is calculated by the formula **=B8*D$5**. Use the cell's fill handle to copy the formula down to cell C27.
D8	*Amount (in local)* is calculated by the formula **=D$5/B8**. Use the cell's fill handle to copy the formula down to cell D27.

▶▶ REAL-WORLD PROJECTS

2-1. A Balance Sheet

The accounting balance sheet is appropriately named, for it must always balance. There are two sections of the balance sheet. The left side shows the firm's assets (what the firm owns). The right side shows the liabilities (what the firm owes) and the owner equity, which together represent the claims against the assets or how the firm paid for its assets. The balance sheet is a snapshot of a firm's condition at a given point in time, such as the end of the month, quarter, or year. In simple terms, a balance sheet is a record of what the company has done with its income and the money provided by creditors, lenders, and stockholders. Managers and owners use the balance sheet not only for evaluating financial conditions but also for setting management and company goals. The balance sheet is also a window through which others, such as bankers, creditors, and stockholders, can look at a company.

In this project, you create a balance sheet for a company that compares this year's results with last year's results. After completing this project, you will be able to enter and describe the elements that make up a balance sheet and explain how they relate to one another.

A typical balance sheet is shown in the figure "The Balance Sheet." Instead of being organized into left and right sides, liabilities are entered below assets to simplify its layout on the worksheet. This balance sheet, like most others that you will encounter, contains the formulas indicat-

NOTE ON PROJECTS

Each PicTorial in this text ends with a series of real-world projects that test and build on the skills you have developed as you learn how to use Excel. The projects are typical of the applications spreadsheets are used to analyze. To complete them, you must use the procedures already discussed in the text. However, they are designed to make you think about what you're doing as you use procedures to solve real-world problems. Don't be discouraged if they take some thought and effort to work through.

	A	B	C
1	Type **Name: your name** into cell A1 and press **Enter**		
2	Filename: balance		
3	2-Nov-94		
4			
5	BALANCE SHEET		
6	PACRIM Enterprises		
7	December 31, 199X		
8		This Year	Last Year
9	CURRENT ASSETS		
10	Cash	11,200	6,400
11	Accounts receivable	20,000	20,000
12	Inventory	70,000	70,000
13	Prepaid expense	3,400	3,400
14	Total current assets	104,600	99,800
15	FIXED ASSETS		
16	Buildings & equipment	30,000	30,000
17	Less accumulated depreciation	-10,000	-5,000
18	Land	20,000	5,000
19	Total fixed assets	40,000	30,000
20	OTHER ASSETS		
21	Patents	10,000	10,000
22	Total assets	154,600	139,800
23	CURRENT LIABILITIES		
24	Accounts payable	20,000	20,000
25	Accrued wages and taxes	10,000	10,000
26	Current portion of long term debt	5,000	5,000
27	Other current liabilities	5,000	5,000
28	Total current liabilities	40,000	40,000
29	LONG-TERM DEBT		
30	Bank loans	40,000	30,000
31	Other	10,000	20,000
32	Total liabilities	90,000	90,000
33	OWNER EQUITY		
34	Common stock	37,000	37,000
35	Retained earnings	27,600	12,800
36	Total owner equity	64,600	49,800
37	Total equity and liabilities	154,600	139,800

The Balance Sheet

ed on the illustration and described below. Using these descriptions, create a balance sheet just like the one illustrated. When finished, save it as *balance.xls* in the *project* directory on the *Excel Student Resource Disk (Part 2)* and make a printout.

1. **Total current assets** is the sum of the firm's assets that are expected to be converted into cash in the course of the firm's operating year. Typical current assets include cash, marketable securities with maturities of less than a year (such as Treasury bills or money market securities), accounts receivable, notes receivable, inventory, and prepaid expenses such as insurance payments.

2. **Total fixed assets** is the sum of the assets acquired for the long-term use of the business. These assets are typically not for resale, and they are recorded on the balance sheet at their cost to the business less accumulated depreciation. Fixed assets include land, buildings, leasehold improvements, fixtures, furniture, machinery, tools, and equipment.

3. **Total assets** is the sum of total current assets, total fixed assets, and all other assets such as goodwill, patents, trademarks, and organizational costs.

	A	B	C	D
1	Type Name: your name into cell A1 and press Enter			
2	Filename: income			
3	2-Nov-94			
4				
5	PRO FORMA INCOME STATEMENT - FIRST THREE YEARS			
6	PACRIM Enterprises			
7	January 1, 199x -- December 31, 199x			
8		Year 1	Year 2	Year 3
9	SALES			
10	Gross sales	40,000	44,000	48,400
11	Discounts, returns, & allow.	2,000	2,200	2,420
12	Net sales	38,000		45,980
13				
14	COST OF GOODS SOLD			
15	Purchase price	22,800		27,588
16	Freight in	912		1,104
17	Total cost of goods sold	23,712		28,692
18	Gross profit	14,288		17,288
19				
20	OPERATING EXPENSES			
21	General and administrative	7,500		7,500
22	Selling expenses	3,750	3,750	3,750
23	Interest expenses	931		931
24	Depreciation	1,250		1,250
25	Total operating expenses	13,431		13,431
26				
27	Operating income/loss	857		3,857
28	Other income	10		15
29	Other expenses			
30	Income before taxes	867		3,872
31	Taxes	214		964
32	Net income/loss	653		2,908

The Income Statement

4. Total current liabilities is the sum of all claims of creditors against the assets of the business—in other words, debt owed by the business. Current liabilities are short-term obligations due on demand or within a year. Typical current liabilities include accounts payable for merchandise and services, loans payable within the year, taxes, and other accruals.

5. Total liabilities is the sum of the current liabilities and the itemized long-term debt items such as bank loans or bonds entered on the rows above.

6. Total owner equity (also called *net worth*) is the sum of the owners' investment and retained earnings entered on the rows above.

7. Total equity and liabilities is the sum of all liabilities and owner equity. This sum always equals total assets, and therefore, the balance sheet balances.

2-2. An Income Statement

Business owners and managers must have a way to measure the degree of success or failure of their business or department and to show the net results of subtracting expenses from sales or revenues. The income, or profit-and-loss, statement is the gauge most frequently used to determine profitability. The income statement shows the profit or loss over a period, usually a month, quarter, or year.

In this project, you create an income statement that shows the sales, expenses, and profits for a three-year period. After completing this project, you will be able to enter and describe the line items that make up an income statement and explain how they are related.

The income statement shown in the figure "The Income Statement" is typical of those used to show the performance of a business over a period of time. This income statement, like most others that you will encounter, contains the formulas indicated on the illustration and described below. Using these descriptions, create an income statement just like the one illustrated. When finished, save it as *income.xls* in the *projects* directory on the *Excel Student Resource Disk (Part 2)* and make a printout. Then display formulas in their cells instead of the calculated values, narrow columns as much as possible, and make a printout so you have a record of the formulas in the model.

1. **Net sales** is gross sales minus discounts, returns, and allowances.

2. **Total cost of goods sold** is the sum of all costs of inventory or raw materials purchased by the firm, including the freight charges of having them delivered.

3. **Gross profit** is the money available to the firm after cost of goods sold is deducted from net sales.

4. **Total operating expenses** is the sum of all costs used to operate the business. Typical operating expenses include general and administrative costs, selling expenses, interest expenses, and depreciation.

5. **Operating income or loss** is calculated by subtracting total operating expenses from gross profit.

6. **Income before taxes** is calculated by adding other income to operating income or loss and then subtracting other expenses.

7. **Net income or loss**, frequently referred to as the bottom line, is income before taxes minus taxes.

What-Ifs

Using the finished *income.xls* model, explore the following what-ifs, and list the amounts for each item in the table "Exploring Sales What-Ifs." Compare the results of the changes with the original numbers. Which changes are for the better? For the worse?

A. What if sales in Year 1 are reduced to $37,000?

B. What if sales in Year 1 are increased to $43,000?

C. What if sales in Year 1 are $38,000 and the purchase price increases to $24,700?

Exploring Sales What-Ifs				
What If	Original	A	B	C
Gross sales	_____	_____	_____	_____
Gross profit	_____	_____	_____	_____
Income before taxes	_____	_____	_____	_____

Assume that you are the manager of a small store and want to increase your profits. Using the income statement, make the following changes, and list the results from the "Year 3" column in the table "Exploring Other What-Ifs." Compare the results of the changes with the original numbers. Which changes are for the better? For the worse?

A. Assume that with better training, and no additional expenses, your sales help can increase starting sales to $50,000.

B. Return starting sales to the original $40,000, and then assume that you can strike a better deal with your supplier that will decrease purchase price to $20,900.

C. Return purchase price to the original $22,800, and then assume that by hiring a part-time salesperson sales can be increased. To do so, you must increase general and administrative expenses to $9,000 to increase starting sales to $45,000.

Exploring Other What-Ifs				
What If	Original	A	B	C
Gross sales	_____	_____	_____	_____
Gross profit	_____	_____	_____	_____
Income before taxes	_____	_____	_____	_____
Net income/loss	_____	_____	_____	_____

2-3. Scaling Times

Have you ever wondered how people figure out those wonderful analogies about sizes and times—ones where the history of the earth is condensed into 24 hours? Well, here's an excerpt from a textbook on astronomy that does something similar.

"*Some people have trouble comprehending millions and billions of years. These are big numbers, and after a while they lose their meaning. To better understand Earth's history, consider an analogy. Imagine the entire lifetime of Earth to be 50 years rather than 5 billion years. This time scale is then comparable to the human life span, making various highlights of Earth's history more understandable.*

With this analogy in mind, we can say that there is no record whatever for the first 10 years of Earth's existence. Rocks hardened and life arose quickly thereafter. In particular, life originated about at least 35 years ago, when Earth was only 15 years old in our analogy. Our planet's middle age is largely a mystery, although we can be sure that life continued to evolve, and that mountain chains and oceanic trenches steadily built up and eroded down. Not until 5 years ago, in our 50-year analogy, did abundant life flourish throughout Earth's oceans. Life came ashore about 4 years ago, plants and animals mastered the land about 2 years ago, and dinosaurs reached their peak about 1 year ago, only to die suddenly about 8 months ago. Human-like apes changed into humans only last week, and the last major ice ages occurred only a few days ago. Homo Sapiens—our species—did not emerge in this 50-year analogy of Earth's history until about 4 hours ago. In fact, the invention of agriculture is only 1 hour old, and the Renaissance only 3 minutes old!"[1]

The model shown in the figure "The Scale Model" is one the author could have used to calculate these numbers. The formulas in it are numbered and described below. Using these descriptions, create a model just like the one illustrated. When finished, save it as *scale.xls* in the *projects* directory on the *Excel Student Resource Disk (Part 2)* and make a printout.

The Scale Model

	A	B	C	D	E	F
1	Type **Name: your name** into cell A1 and press **Enter**					
2	Filename: scale					
3	2-Nov-94					
4						
5	Scaling Times					
6						
7	Age of Earth	5,000,000,000				
8	Scale to (in years)	50				
9	Scaling factor	0.00000001				
10						
11		Actual Age	Scaled Time	Scaled Time	Scaled Time	Scaled Time
12			(in years)	(In days)	(In hours)	(In minutes)
13	Earth	5,000,000,000	50	18250	438000	26280000
14	First life	3,500,000,000	35	12775	306600	18396000
15	Dinosaurs	500,000,000	5	1825	43800	2628000
16	Man	1,500,000	0.015	5.475	131.4	7884
17	First use of fire	500,000	0.005	1.825	43.8	2628
18	Agriculture	10,000	0.0001	0.0365	0.876	52.56
19	Renaisance	500	0.000005	0.001825	0.0438	2.628

(Markers 1–5 point to cells B9, C11, D11, E11, F11 respectively.)

1. **Scaling factor** is calculated by dividing the *Scale to (in years)* value by the age of the earth.
2. **Scaled time (in years)** is the actual age times the scaling factor.
3. **Scaled time (in days)** is the scaled time in years times 365.
4. **Scaled time (in hours)** is the scaled time in days times 24.
5. **Scaled time (in minutes)** is the scaled time in hours times 60.

[1] Eric Chaisson, *Universe: An Evolutionary Approach to Astronomy* (Englewood Cliffs, N.J.: Prentice-Hall, 1988), p. 7.

PicTorial 3

Formatting and Revising Models

drill

3-1 → 3-5 .

Exercise

3-1 → 3-5 .

P81 - 91 .

After completing this PicTorial, you will be able to:

▶ Format text and numbers automatically and by using the toolbar and menus

▶ Copy formats to other cells

▶ Delete and clear the contents and formats from cells

▶ Change the page setup for printing

▶ Insert and delete rows and columns

▶ Move data from one location to another

One of the best features of a spreadsheet is its revisability. You can start with small, simple models, and then add to their power and readability. For example, to change existing data or formulas in a model, you can edit them or erase them. To expand or condense your model, you can insert or delete rows. When you want your models, whether on the screen or in printouts, to be attractive and easy to read, you use formats to align labels and format numbers or use patterns, borders, and fonts to highlight items.

3-1. AUTOFORMATTING

Excel's AutoFormat feature makes formatting fast and easy. All you have to do is select the area you want formatted and choose a professionally designed format from a list. The formats not only add borders and patterns; they also change column width and format numbers.

QUICKSTEPS: AUTOFORMATTING

1. Select a single cell in the model you want formatted or select all of the cells you want formatted. (When you select more than one cell, only those cells are formatted. If you select just one cell, Excel analyzes the sheet and guesses at which cells should be formatted. Occasionally it will guess wrong.)

2. Pull down the **Format** menu and click the **AutoFormat** command to display the AutoFormat dialog box.

3. Select a format from the **Table Format** list, and it is illustrated in the *Sample* window.

4. Click the **Options** command button to display a list of formats you can turn on or off. Turn off any that you want to preserve in the table. For example, if you have formatted numbers in the Currency format and don't want that format to change, click the **Number** check box to turn it off (☐).

5. Click the **OK** command button to apply the selected format to the table.

TUTORIAL

In this tutorial you are introduced to the command that automatically formats your model. The model you use is the one that calculates your budget.

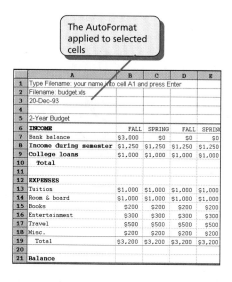

The AutoFormat command is such a useful feature that you should take the time to explore it. Pause here to repeat Steps 2 through 4 to select one or more additional formats.

Getting Started

1. Open the *budget.xls* workbook stored in the *tutorial* directory on the *Excel Student Resource Disk (Part 1)*.

Formatting a Table

2. Select cells A6 through E21, pull down the **Format** menu, and click the **AutoFormat** command to display the AutoFormat dialog box.

3. Select the *Accounting 2* format from the **Table Format** list, and it is illustrated in the *Sample* window.

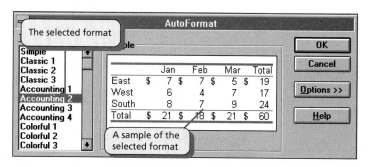

4. Click the **OK** command button to apply the selected format to the table. Click anywhere outside of the table so you can see the formats without their being highlighted.

5. Click the **Save** button on the toolbar to save your changes.

6. Click the **Print** button on the toolbar to print the sheet.

Finishing Up

7. Close the workbook without saving your changes.

3-2. FORMATTING TEXT AND NUMBERS USING THE TOOLBAR

If you want to format cells individually instead of using AutoFormat, you can apply the most commonly used formats by clicking buttons on the toolbar.

FONTS AND SIZES

With Excel, you can select cells and then change the fonts used to format the cell contents. When you do so, you can select a new font design or a new size. The font design, called its *typeface*, determines the overall look of the type. Some fonts of a kind known as TrueType fonts are supplied with Windows. They include Arial, Courier New, and Times New Roman.

Many other fonts may be added to a system. The fonts available to you depend on what printer has been selected. If you change the printer selection, you may see a different list of fonts when you format characters.

The font size determines the height and width of the characters and is specified in a unit of measurement called *points*. (Available font sizes vary depending on the capabilities of your printer.) A point is about 1/72 of an inch, so 72-point type is 1 inch high, 36-point type is fi inch high,

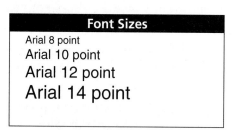

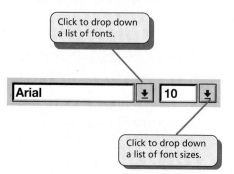

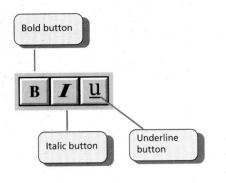

Bold button

Italic button

Underline button

and 18-point type is / inch high. Normally, body text in books, magazines, and newspapers will be 10 to 12 points in size.

FONT STYLE BUTTONS

The **Bold**, **Italic**, and **Underline** buttons on the toolbar will **boldface**, *italicize*, or underline the contents of selected cells.

ALIGNMENT BUTTONS

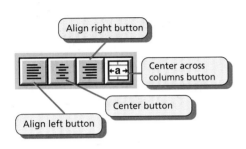

Align right button

Center across columns button

Center button

Align left button

The **Align Left**, **Center**, and **Align Right** buttons on the toolbar align data in selected cells with the left or right edge of the cells or center it between the edges.

The **Center Across Columns** button is a little different. If you enter a heading or other text in the leftmost cell, and then select that cell and any number of cells to the right, clicking this button will center the text in the selected range. The text itself, however, remains in the leftmost cell in case you need to delete or edit it.

	A	B	C	D	E
1	2-Year Budget				
2	INCOME	FALL	SPRING	FALL	SPRING
3	Bank balance	$3,000	$0	$0	$0

Text centered across columns A through E

NUMBER FORMAT BUTTONS

The **Currency Style** ($100.00), **Percent Style** (10%), and **Comma Style** (1,000) buttons on the toolbar apply those styles to numbers in selected cells. You can also click the **Increase Decimal** or **Decrease Decimal** buttons to increase or decrease decimal places in selected numbers.

BORDER AND PATTERN BUTTONS

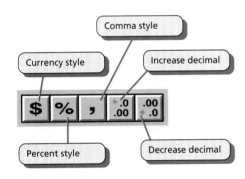

Comma style

Currency style

Increase decimal

Percent style

Decrease decimal

Many worksheets look much more attractive when borders are used to set off headings and sections. You can also apply colors to the borders, as background in cells, and to text and numbers. Although these colors will not print in color on most printers, they can still improve the worksheet's appearance on the screen. (Colors may print as various shades of gray on many printers, so you may have to run some tests to see if you like the results.)

▸ Clicking the **Borders** drop-down arrow (⬇) on the toolbar displays a palette of borders. Click the one you want to apply to the selected cells.

▸ Clicking the **Color** drop-down arrow (⬇) on the toolbar displays a palette of colors. Click the one you want as a background in selected cells. The left part of the **Color** button shows the currently selected color. If you click that part of the button it assigns the color to selected cells.

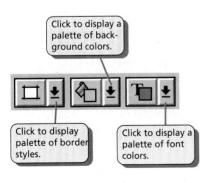

Click to display a palette of background colors.

Click to display palette of border styles.

Click to display a palette of font colors.

▸ Clicking the **Font Color** drop-down arrow (⬇) on the toolbar displays a palette of colors. Click the one you want to apply to text and numbers in the selected cells. The left part of the **Font Color** button shows the currently selected color. If you click that part of the button it assigns the color to selected text.

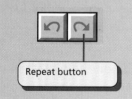
TUTORIAL

In this tutorial you format a table using the buttons on the toolbar. The model you format is the one that calculates a five-year plan.

Getting Started

1. Open the *5yrplan.xls* workbook stored in the *tutorial* directory on the *Excel Student Resource Disk (Part 1)*.

Centering Text across Columns

2. Select cells A5 through F5 and click the **Center Across Columns** button on the toolbar to center the heading across the selected columns.

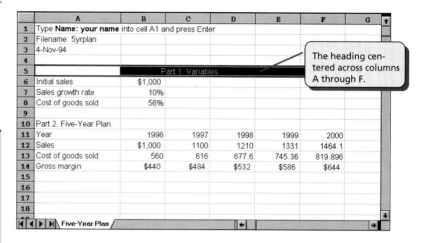

The heading centered across columns A through F.

3. Select cells A10 through F10 and click the **Center Across Columns** button on the toolbar to center the heading across the selected columns.

Formatting Numbers as Currency

4. Select cells B12 through F14 and click the **Currency Style** button on the toolbar to add dollar signs to the numbers.

5. With cells B12 through F14 still selected, click the **Decrease Decimal** button on the toolbar twice to remove decimal places from the numbers.

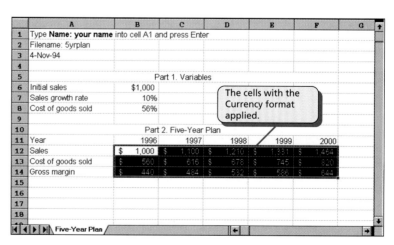

The cells with the Currency format applied.

Formatting Numbers with Commas

6. Select cells B13 through F13 and click the **Comma Style** button on the toolbar to remove dollar signs from the numbers.

7. With cells B13 through F13 still selected, click the **Decrease Decimal** button on the toolbar twice to remove decimal places from the numbers but retain the commas that separate thousands.

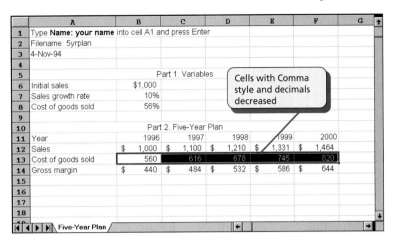

Using Colored Patterns

8. Select cells A5 through F5 and click the **Color** drop-down arrow (⬇) on the toolbar to display a palette of colors.

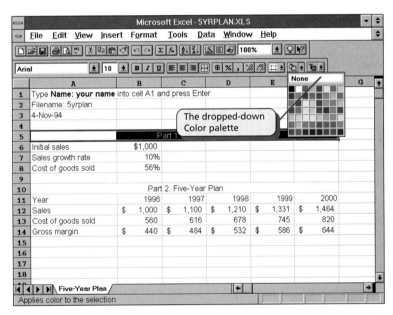

9. Click the first color on the second row (a deep red or brick color) to format the selected cells. (In this and the following steps, you might want to click outside of the formatted area to see your results when they are not selected.)

10. Select cells A10 through F10 and press F4 to repeat the format command.

Using Colored Text

11. Select cells A5 through F5 and click the **Font Color** drop-down arrow (⬇) on the toolbar to display a palette of colors.

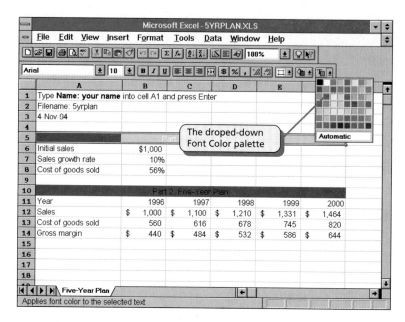

The dropped-down Font Color palette

12. Click the second color from the left on the first row (white) to format the selected cells so they display white text against a deep red background.

13. Select cells A10 through F10 and click the **Repeat** button on the toolbar to repeat the format command.

14. Select cells A6 through F8 and click the **Color** drop-down arrow () on the toolbar to display a palette of colors.

15. Click the third color from the left on the third row (light yellow) to format the selected cells.

16. Select cells A11 through F14 and click the **Repeat** button on the toolbar to repeat the format command.

Finishing Up

17. Save, print, and close the workbook. Compare the printout to the screen display to see how various colors have printed.

3-3. FORMATTING TEXT AND NUMBERS USING THE MENU

When you want complete control over cell formats, you use the Format Cells dialog box.

> **QUICKSTEPS: FORMATTING TEXT AND NUMBERS USING THE MENU**
>
> 1. Select the cells you want to format.
>
> 2. Pull down the **Format** menu and click the **Cells** command to display the Format Cells dialog box.
>
> 3. Choose any of the setting described in the box "Understanding the Format Cells Dialog Box."
>
> 4. Click the **OK** command button to apply the selected formats to the cells.

UNDERSTANDING THE FORMAT CELLS DIALOG BOX

When you pull down the **Format** menu and click the **Cells** command, the Format Cells dialog box appears. This dialog box contains six tabs with formats you can apply to the selected cells. To select a tab, click it, and it moves to the front of the pack. Change any settings you want to change, and then click the **OK** command button to apply them to the selected cells.

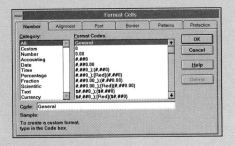

The *Number* tab lists formats you can apply to numbers. Click the desired category of formats in the **Category** list to display that category's formats in the **Format Codes** list. Click the desired format code to select it.

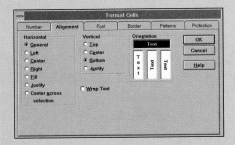

The *Alignment* tab lists horizontal and vertical alignments you can apply to text. Most of these are self-evident, but here are a few you may not already know:

Fill repeats the cell's entry so it fills the entire width of the cell. For example, if you enter / into a cell and apply this format, the cell will display //////.

Justify wraps text wider than the cell to more than one line and expands it so it has even left and right margins.

Wrap Text wraps the text to more than one line in the cell if it is too long to fit in the cell. The row height adjusts automatically to make room for the extra line(s).

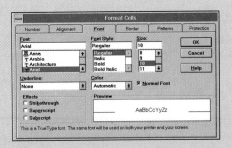

The *Font* tab lists fonts, styles, sizes, and colors that you can apply to text and numbers.

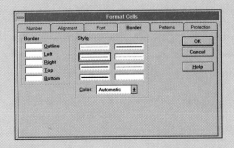

The *Border* tab lists border styles and border colors that you can apply.

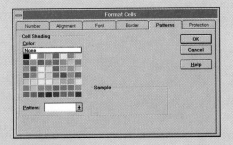

The *Patterns* tab lists background colors and patterns that you can apply.

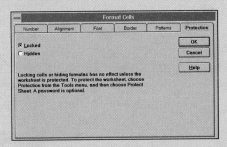

The *Protection* tab locks or unlocks selected cells. When locked, you cannot enter data into them when Protection is turned on. (To turn it on, pull down the **Tools** menu, click the **Protection** command to cascade the menu, and click **Protect Sheet** or **Protect Workbook**.)

TUTORIAL

In this tutorial you format a table using menu commands. The model you format is the one that calculates your budget.

Getting Started

1. Open the *budget.xls* workbook stored in the *tutorial* directory on the *Excel Student Resource Disk (Part 1)*.

Formatting Numbers as Currency

2. Select cells B7 through E21, pull down the **Format** menu, and click the **Cells** command to display the Format Cells dialog box.

3. Click the *Number* tab to make it active.

4. Click *Accounting* under the **Category** list to select it and display available accounting formats in the **Format Codes** list.

5. Click the format that begins (*$*#,##0_)* on the **Format Codes** list, and then click the **OK** command button. Some of the numbers are now too large to be displayed in their cells so the cells display pound signs (######) instead.

	A	B	C	D	E	F	G	H
1	Type Filename: your name into cell A1 and press Enter							
2	Filename: budget.xls							
3	20-Dec-93							
4								
5	2-Year Budget							
6	INCOME	FALL	SPRING	FALL	SPRING			
7	Bank balance	######	$ -	$ -	$ -			
8	Income during semester	######	######	######	######			
9	College loans	######	######	######	######			
10	Total							
11								
12	EXPENSES							
13		######	######	######	######			
14		######	######	######	######			
15		$ 200	$ 200	$ 200	$ 200			
16		$ 300	$ 300	$ 300	$ 300			
17	Travel	$ 500	$ 500	$ 500	$ 500			
18	Misc.	$ 200	$ 200	$ 200	$ 200			
19	Total	######	######	######	######			
20								
21	Balance							
22								

Columns too narrow for their contents

6. Pull down the **Format** menu, click the **Column** command to cascade the menu, then click the **AutoFit Selection** command to automatically adjust column widths.

	A	B	C	D	E	F	G
1	Type Filename: your name into cell A1 and press Enter						
2	Filename: budget.xls						
3	20-Dec-93						
4							
5	2-Year Budget						
6	INCOME	FALL	SPRING	FALL	SPRING		
7	Bank balance	$3,000	$ -	$ -	$ -		
8	Income during semester	$1,250	$1,250	$1,250	$1,250		
9	College loans	$1,000	$1,000	$1,000	$1,000		
10	Total						
11							
12	EXPENSES						
13		$1,000	$1,000	$1,000	$1,000		
14		$1,000	$1,000	$1,000	$1,000		
15		$ 200	$ 200	$ 200	$ 200		
16		$ 300	$ 300	$ 300	$ 300		
17	Travel	$ 500	$ 500	$ 500	$ 500		
18	Misc.	$ 200	$ 200	$ 200	$ 200		
19	Total	$3,200	$3,200	$3,200	$3,200		
20							
21	Balance						
22							

Numbers are fully displayed.

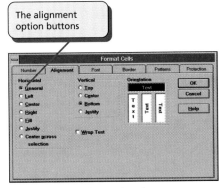

The alignment option buttons

The Format Cells Dialog Box

Formatting Numbers with Commas

7. Select cells B8 through E9, pull down the **Format** menu, and click the **Cells** command to display the Format Cells dialog box. The *Number* page should still be displayed and the *Accounting* category still selected.

8. Click the format that begins *(*#,##0_)* on the **Format Codes** list, and then click the **OK** command button.

9. Select cells B14 through E18 and press F4 to repeat the command.

Aligning Text

10. Select cells B6 through E6, pull down the **Format** menu, and click the **Cells** command to display the Format Cells dialog box (see top margin illustration).

11. Click the *Alignment* tab to make it active.

12. Click the **Center** option button under the *Horizontal* heading to turn it on (◉), then click the **OK** command button.

Finishing Up

13. Save, print, and close the workbook.

QUICKSTEPS: COPYING FORMATS
Copying Formats to a Single Range

1. Select the cell that has the format you want to copy.

2. Click the **Format Painter** button on the toolbar, and a paintbrush appears on the mouse pointer.

3. Select the range you want to apply the copied format to. When you release the mouse button, the paintbrush disappears from the mouse pointer.

Copying Formats to Multiple Ranges

1. Select the cell that has the format you want to copy.

2. Double-click the **Format Painter** button on the toolbar, and a paintbrush appears on the mouse pointer.

3. Select the ranges you want to apply the copied format to. When you release the mouse button after painting each range, the paintbrush remains on the mouse pointer.

4. Click the **Format Painter** button on the toolbar to turn it off.

3-4. COPYING FORMATS

Excel's Format Painter allows you to quickly copy the format from one cell to any other cells.

TUTORIAL

In this tutorial you copy formats from one range to another. The model you format is one designed to demonstrate the effects of these commands and others.

Getting Started

1. Open the *clear.xls* workbook stored in the *tutorial* directory on the *Excel Student Resource Disk (Part 1)* and enter your name into cell A1.

Copying Formats

2. Click cell A5 to select it, then click the **Format Painter** button on the toolbar. The mouse pointer now has a paintbrush attached to it.

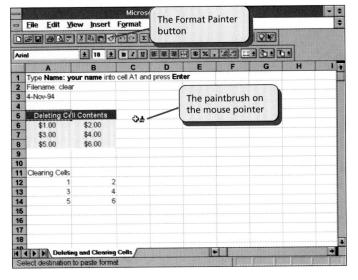

The Format Painter button

The paintbrush on the mouse pointer

3. Select cells A11 through B11 to copy the format to those cells.

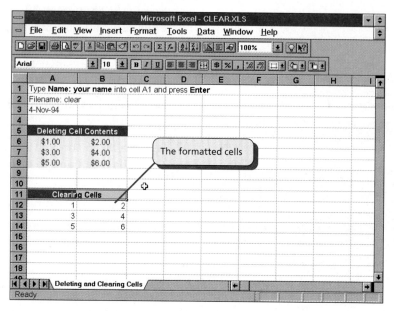

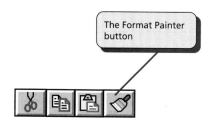

4. Click cell A6 to select it, then click the Format Painter button on the toolbar. The mouse pointer again has a paintbrush attached to it.

5. Select cells A12 through B14 to copy the format to those cells.

Finishing Up

6. Save, print, and close the workbook.

3-5. DELETING AND CLEARING CELL CONTENTS

When revising a model, you can delete the contents of cells without deleting formats, or you can clear formats, contents, or both. (To delete the cells themselves, see Section 3-9, "Deleting Rows, Columns, and Cells").

> **QUICKSTEPS: DELETING AND CLEARING CELL CONTENTS**
> ▶ To delete the contents of cells (text, numbers, or formulas), select the cells and press Delete. This does not delete any formats applied to the cell.
>
> ▶ To clear the contents of cells (text, numbers, or formulas), select the cells, click the right mouse button in the highlighted area to display the shortcut menu, and then click the **Clear Contents** command. This does not delete any formats applied to the cell.
>
> ▶ To clear contents, formats, or notes from cells, select the cells, pull down the **Edit** menu and click the **Clear** command to cascade the menu. Click one of the following:
> > ▶ **All** to clear all (formats, contents, and notes)
> > ▶ **Formats** to clear just formats
> > ▶ **Contents** to clear just contents
> > ▶ **Notes** to clear notes. (Notes are beyond the scope of this text.)

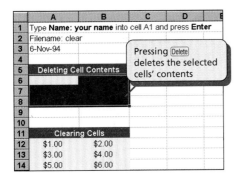

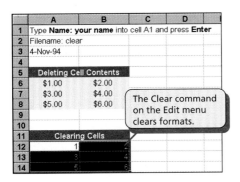

TUTORIAL

In this tutorial you explore the differences between deleting and clearing cells. The model you work on is one designed to demonstrate the effects of these commands and others.

Getting Started

1. Open the *clear.xls* workbook stored in the *tutorial* directory on the *Excel Student Resource Disk (Part 1)*.

Deleting the Contents of Cells

2. Select cells A6 through B8 and then press Delete to delete their contents.

3. Type the numbers **1** through **6** back into the cells in any order and you'll see that the formats for the cell were not deleted along with their contents. All of the numbers are displayed as currency with two decimal places.

Clearing Cell Formats

4. Select cells A12 through B14, pull down the **Edit** menu and click the **Clear** command to cascade the menu.

5. Click **Formats** to clear just the formats.

Finishing Up

6. Click the **Print** button on the toolbar to print the sheet.

7. Close the workbook without saving your changes.

QUICKSTEPS: PREVIEWING PRINTOUTS

1. Click the **Print Preview** button on the toolbar, or pull down the **File** menu and click the **Print Preview** command.

2. Click any of the buttons described in the box "Understanding the Print Preview Toolbar."

3. Click the **Close** command to return to your previous view of the worksheet.

3-6. PRINTING AND PAGE SETUP

Up till now you have printed sheets by clicking the **Print** button on the toolbar. Although fast and easy, this procedure doesn't give you much control over the results. To control your printouts, you need to be familiar with the Print dialog box and page setup commands. However, you can also save a lot of paper if you use the Print Preview command before you print the worksheet to see how the printout will look.

USING PRINT PREVIEW

You can preview what a worksheet will look like when printed. The advantage of Print Preview is that it lets you catch layout mistakes before wasting time and paper printing the document. In this view, you can also adjust margins and column widths.

UNDERSTANDING THE PRINT PREVIEW TOOLBAR

When you display the Print Preview toolbar, you have access to the following command buttons.

Next and **Previous** scroll you though the workbooks pages as they will appear when printed. If the worksheet will print on a single sheet, these buttons are dimmed.

Zoom zooms and unzooms the display. You can also do this by clicking the screen with the magnifying-glass-shaped mouse pointer.

Print prints the document.

Setup displays the Page Setup dialog box described below in "Changing Page Setup."

Margins displays handles on the page that you can drag to change margins and column widths.

Close returns you to your previous view of the worksheet.

USING THE PRINT DIALOG BOX

To print an entire workbook, specific sheets, or a selected block of cells, you use the **Print** command on the **File** menu to display the Print dialog box.

UNDERSTANDING THE PRINT DIALOG BOX

When you pull down the **File** menu and click the **Print** command, the Print dialog box appears. This box allows you to control all aspects of the printout.

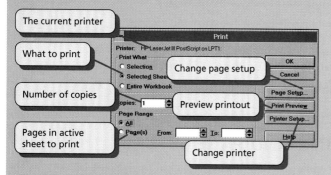

Print What Section

Normally, the active sheet is printed, but you can print just selected cells or all sheets in the workbook

Selection prints selected cells in selected sheets.

Selected Sheet(s) prints the entire print area in selected sheets.

Entire Workbook prints all sheets in the workbook.

Copies Section

Copies specifies the number of copies to be printed.

Page Range Section

All prints all pages of the selected sheets.

Pages prints only the specified pages of the selected sheets. You enter the first page to print in the **From** text box and the last page in the **To** text box. To see what prints on what pages, click the **Print Preview** command button and then click the **Next** or **Previous** command buttons to page through the document. After you've done this, page breaks (the places where new pages begin) are shown on the sheet with dotted gridlines. These same gridlines appear after you have printed a document once.

Command Buttons

OK begins printing the workbook with the current settings in effect.

Cancel closes the dialog box without printing the document.

Page Setup (see the box "Understanding Page Setup").

Print Preview displays the document on the screen just the way it will look when printed.

Printer Setup displays the Printer Setup dialog box so you can specify a different printer for the document. The printer that the workbook is going to be printed on is listed at the top of the dialog box following the *Printer* heading.

CHANGING PAGE SETUP

To change the orientation of the printed page, change margins, add headers and footers, or turn gridlines and row and column headings on or off, you have to change the page setup.

QUICKSTEPS: CHANGING PAGE SETUP

1. Pull down the **File** menu and click the **Print** command to display the Print dialog box, and then click the **Page Setup** command button; or pull down the **File** menu and click the **Page Setup** command.

2. Change any of the settings described in the box "Understanding Page Setup."

3. Click the **OK** command button to return to the Print dialog box or to the workbook. If you return to the Print dialog box, click the **OK** command button to begin printing.

UNDERSTANDING PAGE SETUP

When you choose **Page Setup** from the **File** menu or click the Print dialog box's **Page Setup** command button, the Page Setup tabbed dialog box appears. To change aspects of page setup, click the appropriate tab.

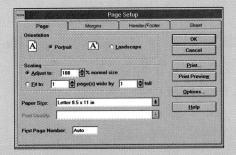

The *Page* tab lists options for paper orientation, scaling, and size. It also allows you to change the page number printed on the first and subsequent pages. One of the unique features on this tab is the **Fit to** spin buttons (⬍) that allow you to specify how many pages the document will be shrunk to. This is most useful when your model is just a little too wide or too long to print on a single sheet.

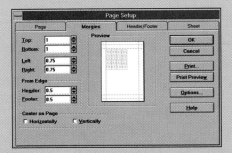

The *Margins* tab lists options for page margins and header and footer spacing. It also contains check boxes you can click to horizontally or vertically center the printout on the page. (You can also change margins by using the **Print Preview** command and then dragging handles on the margins.)

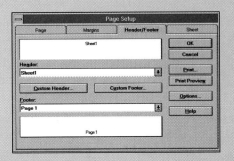

The *Header/Footer* tab has two drop-down arrows (⬍) that display lists from which you can select headers and footers for the printout or create your own. Samples of each are shown above and below the drop-down lists.

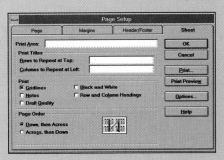

The *Sheet* tab allows you to print the same rows and columns on each page. It also allows you to choose whether gridlines and row and column headings are printed along with the model.

Print Titles are used when a model is too wide or long to print on a single sheet of paper. For example, if you use column A for row titles and print a wide model, column A appears only on the first page of the printout. This makes it hard to identify the contents of the rows on the second and subsequent pages. The same is true if you use row 1 for column titles and print a long model. The titles appear only at the top of the first page. In either case, if you specify that these columns or rows be treated as titles, they are printed on each page of the printout. To set print titles, click in the **Rows to Repeat at Top** or **Columns to Repeat at Left** text boxes and then select the rows or columns that you want to repeat.

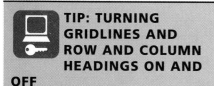

TIP: LANDSCAPE ORIENTATION

With Excel it's easy to print a document on most laser printers across either the width or length of the page. The direction is called the orientation, and it can be either portrait or landscape. *Portrait orientation* is that of a normal printout—that is, text is printed across the width of the page. *Landscape orientation* rotates the printout 90 degrees so that it is printed along the length of the page. This orientation is useful when you are printing wide models.

TIP: TURNING GRIDLINES AND ROW AND COLUMN HEADINGS ON AND OFF

When you are working on a model, it helps to print gridlines and row and column headings because they guide you in checking your results and troubleshooting any mistakes. However, you may not want to print them on the final printout. The best way to turn them off is to use the Page Setup dialog box's Sheet tab. However, you can also turn them off both on the screen and printout. To do so, pull down the **Tools** menu and click the **Options** command to display the Options dialog box. Click the *View* tab to select it, and then click the **Gridlines** or **Row and Column Headers** check boxes to turn them on (⊠) or off (☐).

TUTORIAL

In this tutorial you use page setup commands to change a printout's orientation and gridlines. The model you print is the one you use to forecast a five-year business plan.

Getting Started

1. Open the *5yrplan.xls* workbook stored in the *tutorial* directory on the *Excel Student Resource Disk (Part 1)*.

2. Pull down the **File** menu and click the **Print** command to display the Print dialog box.

Changing Page Setup

3. Click the **Page Setup** command button to display the Page Setup dialog box.

4. Click the *Margins* tab to select it, and then click the **Horizontally** and **Vertically** check boxes under the *Center on Page* heading to turn them on (⊠).

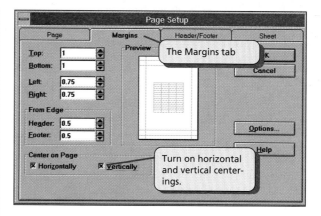

5. Click the *Sheet* tab to select it, and then turn off the **Gridlines** and **Row and Column Headings** check boxes under the *Print* heading by clicking either of them that has an X in it (⊠) to turn them off.

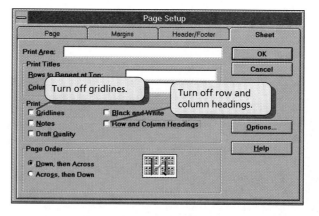

6. Click the *Header/Footer* tab to select it, and then click the **Header** box's drop-down arrow (⬇) to display a list of possible headers.

7. Click the header that reads *Page 1 of ?* to select it, and a sample is displayed in the box above.

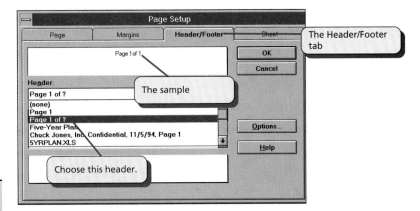

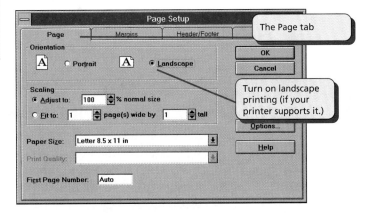

STOP: DOES YOUR PRINTER SUPPORT LANDSCAPE PRINTING?

Step 8 should be completed only if your printer supports landscape printing. If you are not sure, ask. If it doesn't, skip this step and proceed directly to Step 9.

8. If your printer supports landscape printing, click the *Page* tab to select it, and then click the **Landscape** option button to turn it on (◉). If your printer does not support landscape printing, skip to Step 9.

9. Click the **OK** command button to return to the Print dialog box.

10. Click the **Print Preview** command button to preview the way the sheet will look when you print it.

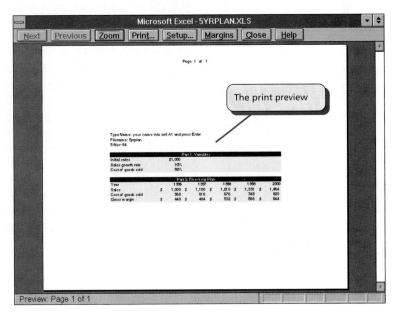

11. Click the **Print** command button on the Preview screen's button bar to print the worksheet.

Printing Row and Column Headers and Gridlines

12. Pull down the **File** menu and click the **Page Setup** command to display the Page Setup dialog box.

13. Click the *Sheet* tab to select it, then click both the **Gridlines** and **Row and Column Headings** check boxes under the *Print* heading so they have Xs in them(⊠) to turn them on.

14. If you changed to landscape orientation in Step 8, click the *Page* tab to select it, then click the **Portrait** option button to turn it on (◉).

15. Click the **Print** command button to display the Print dialog box.

16. Click the **OK** command button to print the worksheet again. Compare this printout with the first one you made to see the effects of the changes you made.

Finishing Up

17. Click the **Save** button on the toolbar to save your changes. Changes to Page Setup are saved along with the workbook.

18. Close the workbook.

3-7. SPELL-CHECKING A WORKSHEET

Excel contains a built-in spelling checker that compares words in your spreadsheet with those in its dictionary. When it finds a word in your spreadsheet that it can't find in its dictionary (the word isn't necessarily misspelled), it highlights the word and displays a list of words you can use to replace it.

Click to ignore one or all.

Click to change one or all.

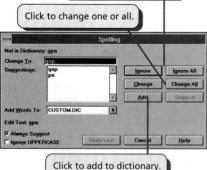

Click to add to dictionary.

QUICKSTEPS: SPELL-CHECKING A SHEET

1. Select the cells to be spell-checked, or select one cell to spell-check the entire sheet. If you select one cell, the sheet is checked from that cell down, and then a dialog box asks *Continue checking at beginning of sheet?* Click **Yes** to continue or **No** to close the Spelling dialog box.

2. Click the **Spelling** button on the toolbar, or click pull down the **Tools** menu and click the **Spelling** command to display the Spelling dialog box. (See the margin illustration.)

3. When a word is found that isn't in the dictionary, it is listed following the *Not in Dictionary* heading. A list of possible replacement words is displayed in the **Suggestions** list, and the word Excel believes to be the most likely replacement is shown in the **Change To** box.

   ▸ To replace the word in the workbook with the word in the **Change To** box, click the **Change** command button.

   ▸ To select another word in the **Suggestions** list, click it and then click the **Change** command button.

   ▸ To replace the word throughout the workbook, click the **Change All** button.

   ▸ To ignore this occurrence of the word, click the **Ignore** button.

   ▸ To ignore this occurrence of the word and all subsequent occurrences, click **Ignore All**.

QUICKSTEPS: SPELL-CHECKING A SHEET (CONTINUED)

> ▶ To add the word to the dictionary so it won't be highlighted again in this or any other workbook, click the **Add** button. (You should not do this on a lab computer, or the next student won't get the same results you do.)

> ▶ To edit the entry displayed in the **Change To** box, click the box to move the insertion point there, or press ← or → to remove the highlight from the current entry. Then edit the entry and click the **Change** command button to replace the word in the document with the edited word. If the edited word isn't in the dictionary, a dialog box tells you it isn't in the dictionary and asks *Change anyway?* Click **Yes** to change it.

The Spelling button

The "mispelled" word

List of suggested replacements

Correcting Spelling

Highlighted Word	Action
your name	Ignore
gpa	Ignore
Biologi	Change to *Biology*
Englsh	Change to *English*
microcompoters	Change to *microcomputers*
avarage	Change to *average*
GPA	Ignore

TUTORIAL

In this tutorial you check and correct the spelling in a model. The model you spell-check is the one that calculates a grade point average.

Getting Started

1. Open the *gpa.xls* workbook stored in the *tutorial* directory on the *Excel Student Resource Disk (Part 1)*.

Spelling Checking the Worksheet

2. Select cell A1, then click the **Spelling** button on the toolbar to begin spell-checking the document.

3. When Excel finds a word that is not in its dictionary (such as your name), it displays the Spelling dialog box. The "misspelled" word is displayed following the *Not in Dictionary* heading. A list of possible replacement words is displayed in the **Suggestions** window. The word that Excel thinks is the most likely choice is displayed in the **Change To** text box. (Remember you can grab the dialog box by the title bar and drag it out of the way if it hides the word it has highlighted.)

4. Click the **Change** command button to accept one of Excel's suggestions or click the **Ignore** command button to leave the word unchanged and continue spell-checking. (For help, see the table "Correcting Spelling.") A dialog box tells you spell-checking is finished.

5. Click the **OK** command button to end spell-checking. (Notice how the spelling checker did not find the word *Grad* in cell A11 that should read *Grade*. The word is spelled correctly; it's just the wrong word.)

Finishing Up

6. Save, print, and close the workbook.

3-8. INSERTING ROWS, COLUMNS, AND CELLS

Often you may find it necessary to insert rows or columns into the middle of an existing model. You can do this easily, and all formulas automatically adjust so that they continue to refer to the correct cells. If rows, columns, or cells are inserted within a range referred to by a formula, the range expands to include the new rows or columns. If rows or columns are inserted on the edge of the range, they are not included.

To insert rows, columns, or cells, you must select the adjoining area to tell Excel where the insertion should be made. The contents of the selected cells are not affected, but the cells move down or to the right to make room for the inserted cells.

TIP: USING THE SHORTCUT MENU

After selecting rows, columns, or cells, you can click with the right mouse button in the selected area to display a shortcut menu. You then click the menu's **Insert** command to insert rows, columns, or cells.

QUICKSTEPS: INSERTING ROWS, COLUMNS, AND CELLS

▶ To insert a single row or column, select the row above or the column to the right of where you want the insertion. Then pull down the **Insert** menu and click the **Rows** or **Columns** command.

▶ To insert multiple rows or columns, select the row above or the column to the right of where you want the insertion. Then extend the selection so you have selected as many rows or columns as you want inserted. Pull down the **Insert** menu and click **Rows** or **Columns** command.

▶ To insert cells, select a range the same size and in the same position as the one you want inserted. Then pull down the **Insert** menu and click the **Cells** command to display the Insert dialog box. Click one of the following option buttons to turn it on, (◉) and then click the **OK** command button to insert the cells:

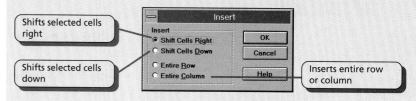

▶ **Shift Cells Right** to insert the cells and have the currently selected cells move to the right to make room for the new cells.

▶ **Shift Cells Down** to insert the cells and have the currently selected cells move down to make room for the new cells.

▶ **Entire Row** to insert entire rows.

▶ **Entire Column** to insert entire columns.

UNDERSTANDING INSERTING CELLS

When you insert cells into a worksheet, Excel guesses whether you want the selected cells shifted down or to the right to make room for the inserted cells. You can accept the program's guess or click another choice.

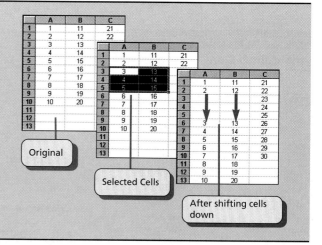

TUTORIAL

In this tutorial you insert rows to expand the model that calculates grade point averages. This allows you to add additional courses as you progress closer to a degree.

Getting Started

1. Open the *gpa.xls* workbook stored in the *tutorial* directory on the *Excel Student Resource Disk (Part 1)*.

Inserting Rows

2. Using the row heading, select the entire row 10, pull down the **Insert** menu, and click the **Rows** command to insert one row.

3. Press Ctrl + ` to display formulas in the cells instead of calculated results. Notice how the functions in cells B11 and E11 have not adjusted their ranges to include the new row. This is because the row you selected was at the bottom of the previous range.

4. Edit the function in cell B11 so it reads =SUM(B7:B10). Then edit the function in cell E11 to read =SUM(E7:E10).

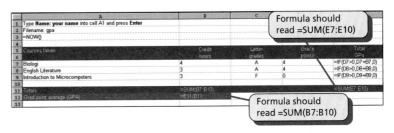

5. Using the row headings, select the entire rows 10 through 15.

6. Click with the RIGHT mouse button in the highlighted area to display the shortcut menu and click the **Insert** command to insert six rows. Notice how the functions have correctly adjusted their ranges to include the new rows. This is because the first row you selected was included in the previous range.

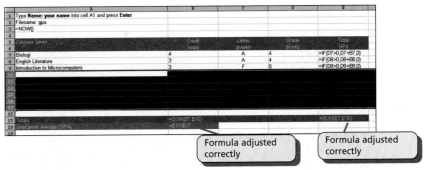

7. Press Ctrl + ` to display calculated results in the cells instead of formulas.

Finishing Up

8. Save, print, and close the workbook.

3-9. DELETING ROWS, COLUMNS, AND CELLS

Deleting rows, columns, or cells has almost the same effect as inserting them. The worksheet closes up, and all formulas automatically adjust to refer to the correct cells.

There is one exception to the way formulas automatically adjust. If you delete any cells that remaining formulas refer to, those formulas display error values. For this reason, it is wise to save a workbook before

QUICKSTEPS: DELETING ROWS, COLUMNS, AND CELLS

▸ To delete rows or columns, first select the rows or columns to be deleted. Then pull down the **Edit** menu and click the **Delete** command. (Immediately click the **Undo** button on the button bar if you think you may have made a mistake.)

▸ To delete cells, first select the range to be deleted. Then pull down the **Edit** menu and click the **Delete** command. If you have selected a range of cells rather than a range of rows or columns, the Delete dialog box appears. Click one of the following option buttons and then click the **OK** command button:

  ▸ **Shift Cells Left** to delete the cells and have those to the right move left to fill the deleted area.

  ▸ **Shift Cells Up** to delete the cells and have those below move up to fill the deleted area.

  ▸ **Entire Row** to delete the entire row.

  ▸ **Entire Column** to delete the entire column.

making deletions. After making deletions, check to see if any error values (especially #REF!) appear in the cells. If you have any doubts, click the **Undo** button on the toolbar or save the worksheet under a new filename so that you do not store it on top of, and erase, the original version.

If you do not delete the upper-left or lower-right corner of a range referred to by a formula, the range contracts or expands to accommodate the change. If these corners are deleted, the range is erased. If any formulas or functions refer to the range, they display a #REF! error value.

COMMON WRONG TURNS: WHOOPS, WHERE DID MY BUDGET GO?

When you delete a row or column, you delete it entirely, including any data that it contains. If some data aren't currently displayed on the screen, you may not even know you deleted them by mistake until later when you need them. A good way to check for unseen data in a row or column is to select a cell in the row of column to be deleted and press [End] and then one of the arrow keys. This shoots the selected cell along the row or column out to the boundary of the sheet unless it encounters data along the way.

Experienced model builders take this problem into consideration when they lay out a model. Sections are added stepwise rather than side by side or one above another. This way rows or columns can be deleted in one section without deleting them in another.

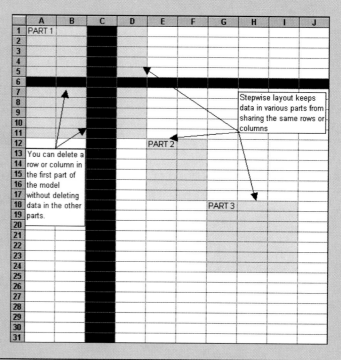

TUTORIAL

In this tutorial you delete rows in the model that calculates grade point averages. The purpose here is to just see how it's done. You then undo the changes and close the model without saving it.

Getting Started

1. Open the *gpa.xls* workbook stored in the *tutorial* directory on the *Excel Student Resource Disk (Part 1)*.

Deleting and Undeleting Rows

2. Press Ctrl+` to display formulas in the cells instead of calculated results.

3. Using the row headings, select the entire rows 10 through 16, pull down the **Edit** menu, and click the **Delete** command to delete the selected rows. Notice how the functions in cells B10 and E10 have adjusted their ranges.

4. Click the **Undo** button on the toolbar to undo the deletion.

5. Click the **Undo** button on the toolbar again to redo the deletion.

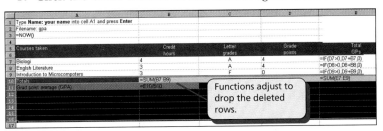

Functions adjust to drop the deleted rows.

7. Press Ctrl+` to display calculated results in the cells instead of formulas.

Finishing Up

8. Close the workbook without saving your changes.

TIP: VIEWING & ZOOMING WORKSHEETS

You have a great deal of control over the way a worksheet is displayed on your screen.

▶ To display the worksheet full screen so the toolbar and formula bars are hidden, pull down the **View** menu and click the **Full Screen** command. Click the **Full Screen** button that appears when you want to return to the normal view.)

▶ To zoom the worksheet on the screen from its normal view to other settings between 25% and 200%, click the **Zoom Control** drop-down arrow (⬇) on the toolbar and click the percentage you want to use. Or pull down the **View** menu and click the **Zoom** command to display a dialog box. Click one of the zoom option buttons to turn it on (◉), and then click the **OK** command button.

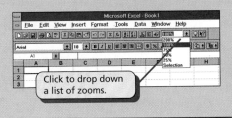

Click to drop down a list of zooms.

3-10. MOVING DATA

You can move the contents of cells to other locations on the worksheet. Moving allows you to reorganize models as you create or revise them. To begin, you first select the cells you want to move. You then drag the selected cells' contents to a new location or cut them to Windows' Clipboard so you can paste them elsewhere in the workbook. Because they remain on the Clipboard until you cut (or copy) other cells or exit Windows, you can paste them in more than one place.

When you move a range of cells, a duplicate of the cells' contents and formats is moved to the new position, and then the contents of the cells in the original location are automatically deleted.

▶ If the cells in the new position contain any data, a dialog box asks you if you want to replace the contents of the destination cells. If you choose to do so, the contents of the destination cells are overwritten, and the old data is lost.

▶ All formulas pasted into a new position will continue to refer to the same cells they referred to before they were cut.

▶ If any formulas refer to cells in the destination area, they display the error value *#REF!*.

TIP: INSERTING DRAGGED CELLS

To insert the moved cells into existing cells so the existing cells move aside to make room for them, hold down ⇧Shift while you drag and release them. When you point to the area where you want to insert the dragged cells, the mouse pointer turns into a horizontal or vertical I-beam shape (⌶). When vertical, the cells to the right move to the right to make room for the dragged cells. When horizontal, the cells below move down to make room.

QUICKSTEPS: MOVING BY DRAGGING AND DROPPING

1. Select the cells to be moved.
2. Point to the border around them, and the mouse pointer will turn into an arrow.
3. Hold down the left mouse button, drag the outline of the cells to where you want it, and release the mouse button.

QUICKSTEPS: MOVING BY CUTTING AND PASTING

1. Select the cells to be moved.
2. Click the **Cut** button on the toolbar, or pull down the **Edit** menu and click the **Cut** command. The selected cells are highlighted by a moving border.
3. Select the cell that will be in the upper-left corner of the range of cells to be pasted in.
4. Click the **Paste** button on the toolbar, or pull down the **Edit** menu and click the **Paste** command. The cells highlighted by the moving border are moved to the new location.

TIP: MOVING SHORTCUTS

Many Excel commands have shortcut key combinations you can use instead of menu commands. Some that you may find most useful are those that move cell contents.

▶ Select the cells to be moved, and then press ⇧Shift+Delete to cut them from the sheet to the Windows Clipboard. Then select the cell in the upper-left corner of where you want them moved and press ⇧Shift+Insert.

▶ Select the cells to be moved, click the right mouse button in the selection to display the shortcut menu, and choose **Cut**. Click the upper-left corner of where you want the cells moved, click the right mouse button to display the shortcut menu, and choose **Paste**.

TUTORIAL

In this tutorial you move data from one part of a model to another. The model you use is the one that calculates a five-year plan.

Getting Started

1. Open the *5yrplan.xls* workbook stored in the *tutorial* directory on the *Excel Student Resource Disk (Part 1)*.

Moving a Range with Menu Commands

2. Select the range of cells from A5 to F14, pull down the **E̲dit** menu and click the **Cu̲t** command. The selection is outlined with a moving border.

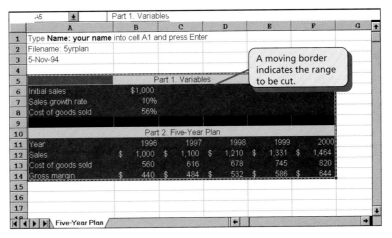

3. Select cell A6, pull down the **E̲dit** menu and click the **P̲aste** command. The entire selected area is moved down one row. Check the formulas in the moved cells, and you'll find that they have all automatically adjusted and still refer to the correct cells.

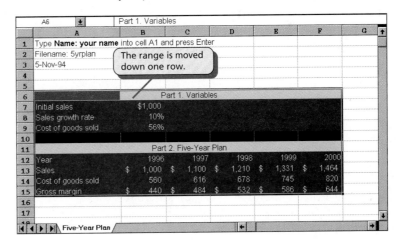

Moving a Range with Toolbar Buttons

4. Select the range of cells from A6 to F15 and click the **Cut** button on the toolbar. The selection is outlined with a moving border.

5. Select cell A5 and click the **Paste** button on the toolbar. The selection is moved back up one row.

Finishing Up

6. Close the workbook without saving your changes.

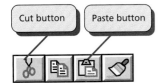

True-False

T F 1. You can delete the contents of cells without deleting cell formats.

T F 2. You do not have the option to print selected cells in a worksheet, just entire worksheets.

T F 3. The portrait mode is useful when you are printing wide models.

T F 4. The Print Titles range should not be included in the Print Area range.

T F 5. You cannot enter data into a cell when Protection is turned on.

T F 6. Before using the AutoFormat feature, select the area you want formatted.

T F 7. You can clear formats of cells without deleting the contents.

T F 8. The font size determines the height and width of characters.

T F 9. When formatting text using the **Center Across Columns** command, the text remains in the rightmost column.

T F 10. When a cell is locked, you can enter data into that cell.

Multiple Choice

1. _____ mode is the orientation of a normal printout.
   a. Landscape
   b. Portrait
   c. Snapshot
   d. Picture

2. _____ are used when a model is too wide or long to print on a single sheet of paper.
   a. Print Outlines
   b. Print Profiles
   c. Print Titles
   d. Gridlines

3. If a column is not wide enough to display a value, _____ may appear in the column.
   a. ####
   b. ****
   c. !!!!
   d. """"

4. A font design is called its _____.
   a. Font face
   b. Font style
   c. Type style
   d. Typeface

5. A good way to check for unseen data in a row or column is to select a cell in the row or column to be deleted and press _____.

   a. End and one of the arrow keys

   b. Ctrl+End

   c. Home and one of the arrow keys

   d. Alt+End

6. Italic is an example of a _____.

   a. Font style

   b. Font face

   c. Typeface

   d. Type style

7. To insert a single column, select the column _____ where you want the insertion.

   a. To the right of

   b. To the left of

   c. Above

   d. Below

8. To repeat a cell's entry so it fills the entire width of a cell, use the **Format, Cells, _____** command.

   a. **Fill**

   b. **Full**

   c. **Fulfill**

   d. **Repeat**

9. _____ mode rotates the printout 90 degrees so that it is printed along the length of the page.

   a. Landscape

   b. Portrait

   c. Snapshot

   d. Picture

10. To change the orientation of the printed page, you have to change the page's _____.

   a. Size

   b. Typeface

   c. Column widths

   d. Setup

Fill In the Blank

1. The _____ determines the height and width of characters.

2. The _____ command is used to change printing modes, change margins, and add headers to a worksheet.

3. Font size is specified in a unit of measurement called _____.

4. To insert a single row, select the row _____ where you want the insertion.

5. To copy the same format to another range, use the _____.

6. To horizontally and vertically center a printout on the page, select the _____ tab in the **File**, **Page Setup** dialog box.

7. Instead of using AutoFormat to format cells individually, you can apply the most commonly used formats by clicking buttons on the _____.

8. The _____ button is used to repeat the previous command.

9. When you want complete control over cell formats, use the _____ Cells dialog box.

10. To have Excel's spelling checker skip over a word and all subsequent occurrences of the word, select the _____ command button.

Pictorial 3 Lab Activities

▶▶ COMPUTER-BASED TUTORIALS

We suggest you complete the following computer-based lessons to learn more about the features discussed in this PicTorial. To do so, pull down the **Help** menu and click the **Examples and Demos** command, click the *Topic* listed in the table "Suggested Examples and Demos to Complete" and then click the *Subtopic* listed in that same table. (If you need more help on using the system, see the "Computer-Based Tutorials" section at the end of PicTorial 1.)

Suggested Examples and Demos to Complete	
Topic	Subtopic
☐ Editing a Worksheet	Inserting and Deleting Rows and Columns
☐ Editing a Worksheet	Deleting or Clearing Cells
☐ Formatting a Worksheet	Aligning Worksheet Data
☐ Formatting a Worksheet	Assigning a Number, Date, or Time Format
☐ Formatting a Worksheet	Formatting with Borders, Patterns, and Color
☐ Formatting a Worksheet	Formatting Characters in Cells
☐ Formatting a Worksheet	Formatting a Range Using AutoFormat
☐ Formatting a Worksheet	Copying Formats Using the Format Painter Button
☐ Printing	Setting Up a Sheet for Printing

▶▶ QUICKSTEP DRILLS

3-1. AutoFormatting

When you use the **AutoFormat** command, you can choose from a list of predefined formats. In this drill you apply some of those to a model so you can see what they look like on the screen and printouts. When finished, your model should look like the figure "The Autoform Model."

1. Open the *autoform.xls* workbook stored in the *drill* directory on the *Excel Student Resource Disk (Part 1)* and enter your name into cell A1.

	A	B	C	D	E
1	Type **Name: your name** into cell A1 and press **Enter**				
2	Filename: autoform				
3	5-Nov-94				
4					
5	**Profit & Loss**				
6	**Year**	1997	1998	1999	***Total***
7	Sales	$1,000.00	$1,200.00	$1,500.00	$3,700.00
8	Expenses	1,100.00	1,000.00	1,200.00	3,300.00
9	*Profits*	$ (100.00)	$ 200.00	$ 300.00	$ 400.00
10					
11					
12	**Profit & Loss**				
13	**Year**	1997	1998	1999	Total
14	Sales	$1,000.00	$1,200.00	$1,500.00	$3,700.00
15	Expenses	1,100.00	1,000.00	1,200.00	3,300.00
16	Profits	$ (100.00)	$ 200.00	$ 300.00	$ 400.00
17					
18					
19	Profit & Loss				
20	Year	*1997*	*1998*	*1999*	***Total***
21	*Sales*	$1,000.00	$1,200.00	$1,500.00	$3,700.00
22	*Expenses*	1,100.00	1,000.00	1,200.00	3,300.00
23	**Profits**	$ (100.00)	$ 200.00	$ 300.00	$ 400.00
24					
25					
26	**Profit & Loss**				
27	**Year**	1,997	1,998	1,999	Total
28	Sales	$1,000.00	$1,200.00	$1,500.00	$3,700.00
29	Expenses	1,100.00	1,000.00	1,200.00	3,300.00
30	Profits	$ (100.00)	$ 200.00	$ 300.00	$ 400.00

The Autoform Model

2. Use the **AutoFormat** command on the **Format** menu to format each of the four models (including the *Profit & Loss* heading). Use a different Accounting format for each. As you do so, type the name of the format you used in column G so you can use the printout as a guide in your other work.
3. Save, print, and then close the workbook.

	A	B	C
1	Type **Name: your name** into cel		
2	Filename: toolform		
3	5-Nov-94		
4			
5	**P&L Summary-Before**		
6	Sales	$11,000	100%
7	Expenses	7,000	64%
8	Profits	$ 4,000	36%

The Toolform Model

3-2. Formatting Text and Numbers Using the Toolbar

Formatting isn't always necessary when the model is for your personal use but it's important when you are sharing a model or printout with others. Good formatting makes a worksheet easier to read. Here you format an existing model and when finished, your results should match those shown in the figure " The Toolform Model."

1. Open the *toolform.xls* workbook stored in the *drill* directory on the *Excel Student Resource Disk (Part 1)* and enter your name into cell A1.
2. Select cells A5:C5 and use the **Center Across Columns**, **Color**, and **Font Color** buttons to format the range.
3. Select cell A5 and use the **Font Size** button to change the heading's font size to 12.
4. Select cells B6 and then B8 one at a time and use the **Currency** and **Decrease Decimal** buttons to format them with dollar signs and no decimal places.
5. Select cell B7 and use the **Comma** and **Decrease Decimal** buttons to format it with a comma and no decimal places.
6. Select cells C6:C8 and use the **Percent Style** button to format the range as percentages.
7. Save, print, and then close the workbook.

	A	B	C	D
1	Type **Name: your name** into cell A1 and press **Enter**			
2	Filename: menuform			
3	5-Nov-94			
4				
5	**Number Formats**	**General Format**	**Positive Values**	**Negative Values**
6	0	10000	10000	-10000
7	0.00	10000	10000.00	-10000.00
8	#,##0	10000	10,000	-10,000
9	#,##0.00	10000	10,000.00	-10,000.00
10	#,##0_);(#,##0)	10000	10,000	(10,000)
11	#,##0_);[Red](#,##0)	10000	(10,000)	(10,000)
12	#,##0.00_);(#,##0.00)	10000	$10,000	($10,000)
13	#,##0.00_);[Red](#,##0.00)	10000	10,000.00	(10,000.00)
14				
15	**Accounting Formats**	**General Format**	**Positive Values**	**Negative Values**
16	_($*#,##0_);_($*#,##0);_($*"-"_);	10000	$ 10,000	$ (10,000)
17	_(*#,##0_);_(*#,##0);_($*"-"_);_@	10000	10,000	(10,000)
18	_($*#,##0.00_);_($*#,##0.00);_($*"-"_);	10000	$ 10,000.00	$ (10,000.00)
19	_(*#,##0.00_);_(*#,##0.00);_($*"-"_);_@	10000	10,000.00	(10,000.00)
20				
21	**Percentage Formats**	**General Format**	**Positive Values**	**Negative Values**
22	0%	0.55555	56%	-56%
23	0.00%	0.55555	55.56%	-55.56%
24				
25	**Fraction Formats**	**General Format**	**Positive Values**	**Negative Values**
26	# ?/?	0.5	1/2	- 1/2
27	# ??/??	0.5	1/2	- 1/2
28				
29	**Scientific Formats**	**General Format**	**Positive Values**	**Negative Values**
30	0.00E+00	10000	1.00E+04	-1.00E+04
31	##0.0E+0	10000	10.0E+3	-10.0E+3
32				
33	**Text Formats**	**General Format**	**Positive Values**	**Negative Values**
34	@	10000	10000	10000
35				
36	**Currency Formats**	**General Format**	**Positive Values**	**Negative Values**
37	$#,##0_);($#,##0)	10000	$10,000	($10,000)
38	$#,##0_);[Red]($#,##0)	10000	$10,000	($10,000)
39	$#,##0.00_);($#,##0.00)	10000	$10,000.00	($10,000.00)
40	$#,##0.00_);[Red]($#,##0.00)	10000	$10,000.00	($10,000.00)

The Menuform Model

3-3A. Formatting Text and Numbers Using the Menu

When you pull down the **Format** menu and click the **Cells** command, the Format Cells dialog box is displayed. You can then click the *Number* tab to display a list of formats you can apply to values in selected cells. In this drill, you use many of these formats in a document that you can then use as a reference since it illustrates the results of each format. When finished, your results should match those shown in the figure "The Menuform Model."

1. Open the *menuform.xls* workbook stored in the *drill* directory on the *Excel Student Resource Disk (Part 1)* and enter your name into cell A1.
2. Select each pair of numbers in columns C and D of the *Number Formats* section—for example, cells C6:D6. Then use the **Format**, **Cells** command to apply the format to them described in column A on the same row. The formats needed for each section of the model are those listed when you display the Format Cells dialog box and then select **Number**, **Accounting**, **Percentage**, **Fraction**, **Scientific**, **Text**, and **Currency** from the **Category** list.
3. Save, print, and close the workbook.

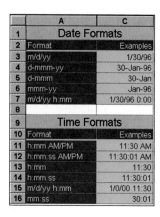

	A	C
1	**Date Formats**	
2	Format	Examples
3	m/d/yy	1/30/96
4	d-mmm-yy	30-Jan-96
5	d-mmm	30-Jan
6	mmm-yy	Jan-96
7	m/d/yy h:mm	1/30/96 0:00
8		
9	**Time Formats**	
10	Format	Examples
11	h:mm AM/PM	11:30 AM
12	h:mm:ss AM/PM	11:30:01 AM
13	h:mm	11:30
14	h:mm:ss	11:30:01
15	m/d/yy h:mm	1/0/00 11:30
16	mm:ss	30:01

The Date and Time Formats Model

3-3B. Formatting Text and Numbers Using the Menu

Not all formatting commands are listed on the toolbar. In this drill you practice formatting using dialog boxes that are displayed when you choose menu commands. When finished, your results should match those shown in the figure "The Date and Time Formats Model."

1. Open the *d&tfrmts.xls* workbook stored in the *drill* directory on the *Excel Student Resource Disk (Part 1)* and enter your name into cell A1.

2. Use the **Format**, **Cells**, **Number**, **Date** (or **Time**) commands to format each of the dates and times in column B with the format described on the same row in column A. The numbers currently displayed in the cells have two parts. The first part, before the decimal, is the number of days between January 1, 1900 and today. The part after the decimal is a fraction representing the time from 0 (12:00:00 A.M.) to .99999999 (11:59:59 P.M.).

5. Save, print, and close the workbook.

3-4. Copying Formats

Once you have formatted one range, there is no need to repeat the same commands again elsewhere on the worksheet. Instead you can use Format Painter as you do in this drill.

1. Open the *copyform.xls* workbook stored in the *drill* directory on the *Excel Student Resource Disk (Part 1)* and enter your name into cell A1.

2. Use the **Format Painter** button on the toolbar to copy formats from the formatted model to the other three unformatted models. If you make any mistakes, click the **Undo** button on the toolbar to undo them or just copy the formats again. When finished your three formatted models should look just like the top one.

3. Close the workbook without saving your changes.

3-5. Deleting and Clearing Cell Contents

Deleting removes cell contents; clearing removes that and more. In this drill you practice deleting and clearing to explore the differences between these two procedures. In the process, you also practice using the **Undo** command.

1. Open the *whoops.xls* workbook stored in the *drill* directory on the *Excel Student Resource Disk (Part 1)*.

2. Select any cells on rows 6 through 10 in the *Undoing* section that contain numbers and press Delete to delete them. Then immediately click the **Undo** button on the toolbar to undo the deletions. Repeat with other cells until you are comfortable with the procedure.

3. Select any cell on rows 6 through 10 that contain numbers, then pull down the **Edit** menu and click first **Clear** then **All** to clear both the contents and formats from the cells. Immediately click the **Undo** button on the toolbar to undo the changes. Repeat with other cells until you are comfortable with the procedure.

4. Close the workbook without saving your changes.

3-6. Printing and Page Setup

When working with application programs it's easy to go through lots of expensive paper as you make revisions. For this reason many programs have a print preview command that shows the worksheet on the screen just as it will look when printed. In this drill you use this feature to explore some of the setup options you can use on your printouts.

1. Open the *formulas.xls* workbook stored in the *drill* directory on the *Excel Student Resource Disk (Part 1)* and enter your name into cell A1.

2. Using the **Page Setup** command on the **File** menu, make the following changes to the document.
   ▶ On the **Page** tab change the orientation to **Landscape**.
   ▶ On the **Margins** tab, change the left margin to 2, and center the page horizontally and vertically.
   ▶ On the **Header/Footer** tab use the drop-down arrows (⬇) to select the header *Understanding Formulas* and the footer *Page 1 of ?*.
   ▶ On the **Sheet** tab, turn off both gridlines and row and column headings.

3. Use the **Print Preview** command button to see the results.

4. Close the document without saving any changes.

3-7. Spell-Checking a Worksheet

As you have seen, checking the spelling in a document is very easy. In this drill you use Excel's spelling checker to check a document with built-in mistakes. You then use it to check the spelling in any workbooks you have entered text into.

1. Open the *spelling.xls* workbook stored in the *drill* directory on the *Excel Student Resource Disk (Part 1)* and enter your name into cell A1.

2. Click cell A1 to select it, then click the **Spelling** button on the toolbar to correct any spelling mistakes in the worksheet.

3. Save and close the workbook.

4. For additional practice, repeat Steps 1 through 4 with any of your own workbooks.

3-8. Inserting Rows, Columns, and Cells

One of the best things about spreadsheets is how you can revise models on the fly. One of the main procedures you use to do so is inserting rows, columns, and cells. In this drill you practice those procedures. When finished your model should look like the figure on the following page, "The Insert Model."

1. Open the *insert.xls* workbook stored in the *drill* directory on the *Excel Student Resource Disk (Part 1)* and enter your name into cell A1.

2. Select all cells in column B between rows 5 and 14 inclusive and use the **Insert, Cells** command to insert cells. When prompted, have them shift to the right. Enter data in the inserted cells in the upper model so it matches the lower model.

	A	B	C	D	E
1	Type **Name: your name** into cell A1 and press **Enter**				
2	Filename: insert				
3	5-Nov-94				
4					
5			Inventory		
6	**Item**	*Stock #*	*Quantity*	*Price*	*Total value*
7	Computer, desktop	1001	100	$ 1,300.00	$ 130,000
8	Computer, laptop	1002	20	1,500.00	30,000
9	Computer, notebook	1003	150	2,500.00	375,000
10	Printer, dot-matrix	1004	25	300.00	7,500
11	Printer, laser	1005	75	1,200.00	90,000
12	Printer, ink-jet	1006	25	500.00	12,500
13	Monitor, 17"	1007	125	350.00	43,750
14	Monitor, 21"	1008	25	1,800.00	45,000
15	Modem, 1200 baud	1009	10	50.00	500
16	Modem, 9600 baud	1010	100	175.00	17,500
17	CD-ROM drive	1011	200	300.00	60,000
18	*Total*		855		811,750

The Insert Model

3. Select row 9 and use the **Insert**, **Rows** command to insert a row.

4. Select row 12 and use the **Insert**, **Rows** command to insert a row.

5. Select rows 15 and 16 and use the **Insert**, **Rows** command to insert two rows.

6. Select cell E8 and use the cell's fill handle to copy the formula down the column to the last blank cell.

7. Enter data in the inserted rows to match the illustration.

8. Check all of the formulas in the model, and you'll see that they have adjusted to refer to the correct cells.

9. Save and then close the workbook.

	A	B	C	D
1	Type **Name: your name** into cell A1 and press **Enter**			
2	Filename: delete			
3	5-Nov-94			
4				
5				
6	**Item**	*Quantity*	*Price*	*Total value*
7	Computer, desktop	100	$1,300.00	$ 130,000
8	Computer, laptop	20	1,500.00	30,000
9	Printer, dot-matrix	25	300.00	7,500
10	Printer, laser	75	1,200.00	90,000
11	Monitor, 17"	125	350.00	43,750
12	Monitor, 21"	25	1,800.00	45,000
13	CD-ROM drive	200	300.00	60,000
14	*Total*	570		406,250

The Delete Model

3-9. Deleting Rows, Columns, and Cells

Models, unlike our waistlines, don't always expand. Sometimes they shrink. The procedure you use to reduce them in size is the deletion or rows and columns. In this drill you practice those procedures. When finished your model should look like the figure "The Delete Model."

1. Open the *delete.xls* workbook stored in the *drill* directory on the *Excel Student Resource Disk (Part 1)* and enter your name into cell A1.

2. Select each of the rows and columns with the deep red (brick) background color one at a time and use the **Edit**, **Delete** command to delete them..

3. Check all of the formulas in the model, and you'll see that they have adjusted to refer to the correct cells.

4. Save and then close the workbook.

3-10. Moving Data

In addition to inserting and deleting rows and columns, one of the other major revision tools at your disposal is moving data. In this drill you practice moving data from one place to another on the worksheet.

1. Open the *movedata.xls* workbook stored in the *drill* directory on the *Excel Student Resource Disk (Part 1)* and enter your name into cell A1.

	A	B	C	D	E	F	G	H
1	Type **Name: your name** into cell A1 and press **Ente**[r]							
2	Filename: movedata							
3	5-Nov							
4								
5	Cut From				Paste To			
6								
7	Cell							
8					A25			
9								
10	Column							
11					A25			
12					A26			
13					A27			
14								
15	Row							
16					A25	B25	C25	
17								
18	Block							
19					A25	B25	C25	
20					A26	B26	C26	
21					A27	AB7	C27	
22								

The Cutting & Pasting Sheet

2. On the *Cutting & Pasting* sheet, use the **Cut** and **Paste** buttons on the toolbar to cut each of the cell ranges with a yellow background and red border and paste them into the ranges with a red background and yellow border. When you do so, notice how none of the cell references change. They refer to the same cells in their new position as they did in their old. When finished, your model should look like the figure "The Cutting & Pasting Sheet."

3. On the *Dragging & Dropping* sheet, drag each of the four ranges of cells with a yellow background and red border from the Drag From section and drop them in the indicated spaces in the Drag To section. When finished your model should look like the figure "The Dragging & Dropping Sheet."

4. Close the workbook without saving your changes.

	A	B	C	D	E	F	G	H
1	Type Name: your name into cell A1 and press Enter							
2	Filename: movedata							
3	5-Nov							
4								
5	Drag From				Drag To			
6								
7	Cell							
8					A25			
9								
10	Column							
11					A25			
12					A26			
13					A27			
14								
15	Row							
16					A25	B25	C25	
17								
18	Block							
19					A25	B25	C25	
20					A26	B26	C26	
21					A27	AB7	C27	
22								

The Dragging & Dropping Sheet

▶▶ SKILL-BUILDING EXERCISES

3-1. Formatting and Revising the Pricing Model

In this drill you revise and format the *pricing.xls* model that you created in the exercises at the end of PicTorial 2. When finished, you model should look like the one shown in the figure "The Formatted Pricing Model."

1. Open the *pricing.xls* workbook stored in the *exercise* directory on the *Excel Student Resource Disk (Part 2)*.

2. Change the width of column A to 45.

3. Select the cell range A5:B5 and center the heading using the **Center Across Columns** button on the toolbar. Do the same for the cell range A11:B11.

4. Format cells B12:B14 as currency with two decimal places using the **Format**, **Cells**, **Number** command. Note the format is different than it is in cells B6, B8, and B9. What caused the difference? Which format do you prefer? (The **Currency** button was used for the first entries; the **Format** menu for the later entries.)

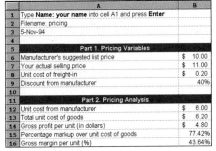

	A	B
1	Type **Name: your name** into cell A1 and press **Enter**	
2	Filename: pricing	
3	5-Nov-94	
4		
5	Part 1. Pricing Variables	
6	Manufacturer's suggested list price	$ 10.00
7	Your actual selling price	$ 11.00
8	Unit cost of freight-in	$ 0.20
9	Discount from manufacturer	40%
10		
11	Part 2. Pricing Analysis	
12	Unit cost from manufacturer	$ 6.00
13	Total unit cost of goods	$ 6.20
14	Gross profit per unit (in dollars)	$ 4.80
15	Percentage markup over unit cost of goods	77.42%
16	Gross margin per unit (%)	43.64%

The Formatted Pricing Model

5. Copy the format from cell B6 to the cell range B12:B14 using the **Format Painter** button on the toolbar.

6. Select the cell range A5:B5, click the **Color** button on the toolbar, and choose red on the first row of the palette. Do the same for the cell range A11:B11.

7. Select the cell range A5:B5, click the **Font Color** button on the toolbar, and choose white on the first row of the palette. Do the same for the cell range A11:B11.

8. Select the cell range A5:B5 and click the **Bold** button on the toolbar. Do the same for the cell range A11:B11.

9. Select the cell range A5:B5, click the **Font Size** button on the toolbar, and choose *12*. Do the same for the cell range A11:B11.

10. Select row 10 and use the **Insert**, **Rows** command to insert a blank row.

11. Use the **Cut** and **Paste** buttons on the toolbar to move the cell range A7:B7 to the range A10:B10.

12. Delete the now blank row 7 using the **Edit**, **Delete** command.

13. Format the cell range B15:B16 as percentages with two decimal places using the **Format**, **Cells**, **Number** command.

14. Turn off gridlines and row and column headings using the **File**, **Page Setup** command.

15. Print the workbook, save it, and then close it.

3-2. **Formatting and Revising the Model That Doubles a Penny Every Day**

In this drill you revise and format the *pennies.xls* model that you created in the exercises at the end of PicTorial 2. When finished, your model should look like the one shown in part in the figure "The Formatted Pennies Model."

1. Open the *pennies.xls* workbook stored in the *exercise* directory on the *Excel Student Resource Disk (Part 2)*.

2. Format cells B12:B14 as currency with two decimal places using the **Format**, **Cells**, **Number** command.

3. Using the **Color** button on the toolbar, change the background colors of the following ranges:

   ▶ Cells A5 and B5 to dark blue (on the fourth row of the palette). Then use the **Bold** button on the toolbar to boldface the text in those cells.

   ▶ Cells A6:A36 to lime green (fourth from the left on the top row of the palette)

   ▶ Cells B6:B36 to bright blue (far right on the first row of the palette)

4. Using the **Font Color** button on the toolbar, change the colors of the contents in cells A6:B36 to dark blue (on the first row of the palette).

5. Use the **Copy** and **Paste** buttons on the toolbar to copy the entries in A5:B36 to cells D5:E36. This gives you a second copy of the

	A	B
1	Type **Name: your name** into cel
2	Filename: pennies	
3	5-Nov-94	
4		
5	Day	Saved
6	1	$0.01
7	2	$0.02
8	3	$0.04
9	4	$0.08
10	5	$0.16
11	6	$0.32
12	7	$0.64
13	8	$1.28
14	9	$2.56
15	10	$5.12

The Formatted Pennies Model

model which you can use to practice clearing formats and data.

6. Select the new entries in columns D and E and use the **Edit**, **Clear** command to clear first the formats and then the contents.

7. Use the **File**, **Page Setup** command turn off the gridlines and row and column headings.

8. Save, print, and then close the workbook.

3-3. Formatting and Revising the Model That Explores Series of Numbers

In this drill you revise and format the *series.xls* model that you created in the exercises at the end of PicTorial 2. When finished, your model should look like the one shown in the figure "The Formatted Series Model."

1. Open the *series.xls* workbook stored in the *exercise* directory on the *Excel Student Resource Disk (Part 2)*.

2. Change the entries in cells A5:C5 to 14 point bold using the **Font Size** and **Bold** buttons on the toolbar.

3. Use the **Cut** and **Paste** commands to rearrange the order of the data in columns A, B, and C. The column C data should be inserted in Column A and the Column A data should be inserted in column C. Tip: You will have to move column A data to column D, then once column C is empty, move the column D data to column C or delete column C.

4. Use the **Bold** button on the toolbar to boldface all of the numbers in the cell range A6:C11.

5. Use the **Copy** and **Paste** buttons on the toolbar to copy the cell range A11:C11 to rows 12 through 19. Notice how some of the numbers in column A are too large to be displayed.

6. Double-click the heading border between columns A and B to widen the column to fit the largest entry. The numbers in column A on rows 16 through 19 are too large to be calculated.

7. Select rows 16 through 19 and use the **Edit**, **Delete** command to delete them.

8. Use the **File**, **Page Setup** command turn off the gridlines and change to landscape orientation, then click the **Print Preview** button to preview your results.

9. Close Print Preview, and use the **Edit**, **Delete** command to delete rows 13 through 15.

10. Select column A and use the **Format**, **Column**, **AutoFit Selection** command to narrow the column.

11. Print the workbook.

12. Use the **File**, **Page Setup** command to return to portrait orientation.

13. Save and then close the workbook.

3-4. Formatting and Revising the Birthday Model

In this exercise you revise and format the *birthday.xls* model that you created in the exercises at the end of PicTorial 2. When finished, your model should look like the one shown in the figure "The Formatted Birthday Model."

The Formatted Series Model

	A	B	C
1	Name: Your Name		
2	Filename: series		
3	18-Nov-94		
4			
5	Exponential	Geometric	Arithmetic
6	2	2	2
7	4	4	3
8	16	8	4
9	256	16	5
10	65,536	32	6
11	4,294,967,296	64	7
12	18,446,744,073,709,600,000	128	8

The Formatted Birthday Model

	A	B	C	D	E
1	Type **Name: your name** into cell A1 and press **Enter**				
2	Filename: birthday				
3	5-Nov-94				
4					
5	Number of people		Individual probability	Probability not	Probability so
6	1		99.7%		
7	2		99.5%	99.2%	0.8%
8	3		99.2%	98.4%	1.6%
9	4		98.9%	97.3%	2.7%
10	5		98.6%	96.0%	4.0%
11	6		98.4%	94.4%	5.6%
12	7		98.1%	92.6%	7.4%
13	8		97.8%	90.5%	9.5%
14	9		97.5%	88.3%	11.7%
15	10		97.3%	85.9%	14.1%
16	11		97.0%	83.3%	16.7%
17	12		96.7%	80.6%	19.4%
18	13		96.4%	77.7%	22.3%
19	14		96.2%	74.7%	25.3%
20	15		95.9%	71.6%	28.4%
21	16		95.6%	68.5%	31.5%
22	17		95.3%	65.3%	34.7%
23	18		95.1%	62.1%	37.9%
24	19		94.8%	58.9%	41.1%
25	20		94.5%	55.6%	44.4%
26	21		94.2%	52.4%	47.6%
27	22		94.0%	49.3%	50.7%
28	23		93.7%	46.2%	53.8%
29	24		93.4%	43.1%	56.9%
30	25		93.2%	40.2%	59.8%

1. Open the *birthday.xls* workbook stored in the *exercise* directory on the *Excel Student Resource Disk (Part 2)*.

2. Select cells A5:D5 and use the **Font Size** button on the toolbar to change the font to 12 point.

3. Select the cells on row 10 and use the **Format, Cells, Border** command to insert a bottom line border for the row of entries.

4. Use the **Edit, Repeat Format Cells** command to insert the bottom line border for entries in Row 15, 20, 25, and 30.

5. Use the **Center** button on the toolbar to center the entries in the range A5:A30.

6. Use the **Insert, Columns** command to insert a new column between columns A and B and change the width of the new column B to 2.

7. Use the **Color** button on the toolbar to change the background color to the same blue used for the headings for the entries in B6:B30. (It's the blue on the second row of the palette.)

8. Use the **File, Page Setup, Margins** command to vertically and horizontally center the page.

9. Save, print, and then close the workbook.

3-5. Formatting and Revising the Multiplication Table

In this exercise you revise and format the *multtab.xls* model that you created in the exercises at the end of PicTorial 2. When finished, your model should look like the one shown in the figure "The Formatted Multiplication Table Model."

	A	B	C	D	E	F	G	H	I	J
1	Type **Name: your name** into cell A1 and press **Enter**									
2	Filename: multtabs									
3	5-Nov-94									
4										
5	**Start**	1								
6	**Increment**	1								
7										
8		1	2	3	4	5	6	7	8	9
9	1	1	2	3	4	5	6	7	8	9
10	2	2	4	6	8	10	12	14	16	18
11	3	3	6	9	12	15	18	21	24	27
12	4	4	8	12	16	20	24	28	32	36
13	5	5	10	15	20	25	30	35	40	45
14	6	6	12	18	24	30	36	42	48	54
15	7	7	14	21	28	35	42	49	56	63
16	8	8	16	24	32	40	48	56	64	72
17	9	9	18	27	36	45	54	63	72	81

The Formatted Multiplication Table Model

1. Open the *multtab.xls* workbook stored in the *exercise* directory on the *Excel Student Resource Disk (Part 2)*.

2. Select cells A5 and A6 and use the **Bold** button on the toolbar to boldface them.

3. Select all of the cells with numbers and use the **Center** button on the toolbar to center them.

4. Use the **File, Page Setup**, command to center the page horizontally and vertically on the page and to have row and column headings displayed but not gridlines.

5. Save, print, and then close the workbook.

3-6. Formatting On Your Own

In this exercise you put to work all that you have learned so far by formatting one or more models of your choice as you think best.

1. Open one of the files *chainltr.xls*, *exchange.xls*, or *metric.xls*.
2. Format the model as you think best.
3. Save, print, and close the workbook.
4. Repeat Steps 1 through 3 for another model if you have time.

▶▶ REAL-WORLD PROJECTS

3-1A. Balance Sheet

There are standard ways to format a balance sheet including the type of underlines used, number formats, spacing, and such. Here you use those rules to revise and format the *balance.xls* workbook stored in the *projects* directory on the *Excel Student Resource Disk (Part 2)* so it matches the one shown in the figure "The Formatted Balance Sheet." As you complete each sequence of corrections or formats, check them off on the "Balance Sheet Revision Checklist." When finished, save, print and close the workbook.

A	B	C
1	Type **Name: your name** into cell A1 and press **Enter**		
2	Filename: balance		
3	5-Nov-94		
4			
5	BALANCE SHEET		
6	PACRIM Enterprises		
7	December 31, 199X		
8		This Year	Last Year
9	**CURRENT ASSETS**		
10	Cash	$ 11,200	$ 6,400
11	Accounts receivable	20,000	20,000
12	Inventory	70,000	70,000
13	Prepaid expense	3,400	3,400
14	Total current assets	$ 104,600	$ 99,800
15			
16	**FIXED ASSETS**		
17	Buildings & equipment	$ 30,000	$ 30,000
18	Less accumulated depreciation	(10,000)	(5,000)
19	Land	20,000	5,000
20	Total fixed assets	$ 40,000	$ 30,000
21			
22	**OTHER ASSETS**		
23	Patents	$ 10,000	$ 10,000
24	Total assets	$ 154,600	$ 139,800
25			
26	**CURRENT LIABILITIES**		
27	Accounts payable	$ 20,000	$ 20,000
28	Accrued wages and taxes	10,000	10,000
29	Current portion of long term debt	5,000	5,000
30	Other current liabilities	5,000	5,000
31	Total current liabilities	$ 40,000	$ 40,000
32			
33	**LONG-TERM DEBT**		
34	Bank loans	$ 40,000	$ 30,000
35	Other	$ 10,000	$ 20,000
36	Total liabilities	$ 90,000	$ 90,000
37			
38	**OWNER EQUITY**		
39	Common stock	$ 37,000	$ 37,000
40	Retained earnings	27,600	12,800
41	Total owner equity	$ 64,600	$ 49,800
42	Total equity and liabilities	$ 154,600	$ 139,800

The Formatted Balance Sheet

Balance Sheet Revision Checklist
☐ Center the heading across columns and format its color, size, and style
☐ Boldface subheadings in the balance sheet
☐ Format the indicated values as currency
☐ Add single or double borders below number sections

3-2. An Income Statement

There are also standard ways to format a income statements including the type of underlines used, formats, spacing, and such. Here you use those rules to revise and format the *income.xls* workbook stored in the *projects* directory on the *Excel Student Resource Disk (Part 2)* so it matches the one shown in the figure "The Formatted Income Statement" on page 116. As you complete each sequence of corrections or formats, check them off on the "Income Statement Revision Checklist." When finished, save, print and close the workbook.

Income Statement Revision Checklist
☐ Center the heading across columns and format its size and style
☐ Insert new row below heading
☐ Center the three annual column headings and change their color and style
☐ Correct and revise all text
☐ Boldface subheadings in the balance sheet
☐ Format the indicated values as currency
☐ Move the three annual columns to reverse their order
☐ Add single or double borders below number sections

	A	B	C	D
1	Type Name: your name into cell A1 and press Enter			
2	Filename: income			
3	18-Nov-94			
4				
5	PRO FORMA INCOME STATEMENT - FIRST THREE YEARS			
6	PACRIM Enterprises			
7	January 1, 199x -- December 31, 199x			
8				
9		Year 3	Year 2	Year 1
10	SALES			
11	Gross sales	$ 48,400	$ 44,000	$ 40,000
12	Discounts, returns, & allowances	2,420	2,200	2,000
13	Net sales	$ 45,980	$ 41,800	$ 38,000
14				
15	COST OF GOODS SOLD			
16	Purchase price	$ 27,588	$ 25,080	$ 22,800
17	Freight in	1,104	1,003	912
18	Total cost of goods sold	28,692	26,083	23,712
19	Gross profit	$ 17,288	$ 15,717	$ 14,288
20				
21	OPERATING EXPENSES			
22	General and administrative	$ 7,500	$ 7,500	$ 7,500
23	Selling expenses	3,750	3,750	3,750
24	Interest expenses	931	931	931
25	Depreciation	1,250	1,250	1,250
26	Total operating expenses	13,431	13,431	13,431
27				
28	Operating income/loss	$ 3,857	$ 2,286	$ 857
29	Other income	15		10
30	Other expenses		12	
31	Income before taxes	3,872	2,274	867
32	Taxes	964	571	214
33	Net income/loss	$ 2,908	$ 1,703	$ 653

The Formatted Income Statement

WORKING WITH FUNCTIONS

Drill 4-1
↓
4-4

Exercise 4-2
↓
4-4.

After completing this PicTorial, you will be able to:

▶ Understand how functions work
▶ Use AutoSum and Function Wizard to enter functions
▶ Use names in functions and formulas
▶ Enter and calculate dates and times
▶ Use comparison operators and logical functions
▶ Use text in formulas and functions

You have already been introduced to formulas. In this PicTorial you are introduced to a special type a formula called a function. A function will either perform a complex calculation or make a long formula simple to enter.

4-1. UNDERSTANDING FUNCTIONS

Excel contains many functions that have been built in to perform commonly used calculations. You enter them just like formulas, by typing them into cells.

SPECIFYING RANGES

Functions frequently refer to a group, or *range* of cells. For example, a function can add all of the values entered into cells A1 through A5. This range of cells is specified in the function as A1:A5, where the colon means "through," as in *cells A1 through A5*.

To specify a range of cells falling on a row, you specify the leftmost and rightmost cells in the range, separated by a colon.

To specify a range of cells falling in a column, you specify the top and bottom cells in the range, separated by a colon.

To specify a range of cells falling in a rectangle, you specify the upper-left and lower-right cells in the range, separated by a colon.

THE PURPOSE OF FUNCTIONS

As mentioned earlier, functions will either make a complex formulas simple to enter, or perform complex calculations. Let's look at some examples.

Functions often simplify the entry of long formulas. For example, to calculate the average of a list of 6 numbers in cells A1 through A6, you would have to enter the formula =(A1+A2+A3+A4+A5+A6)/6. The same calculation can be made with the function =AVERAGE(A1:A6). If the list of numbers were expanded to a hundred numbers, imagine how long the formula would be. The function, on the other hand, would be simply =AVERAGE(A1:A100)

In addition to simplifying formulas, functions can also perform complex calculations. We will see a few such functions in this PicTorial, but the most complex functions are beyond the scope of this text.

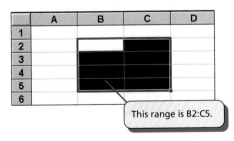

This range is A2:D2.

A row range

This range is B1:B6.

A column range

This range is B2:C5.

A rectangular range

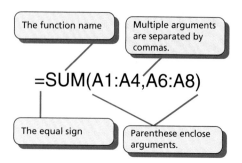

The function name

Multiple arguments are separated by commas.

=SUM(A1:A4,A6:A8)

The equal sign

Parenthese enclose arguments.

THE STRUCTURE OF FUNCTIONS

Functions have a structure, or syntax, that you must follow when you enter them. The syntax includes an equal sign, a function name, and usually one or more values, called arguments, on which the function performs its calculations.

For example, the name of the function that sums the values in a range of cells is SUM, and the name of the function that averages the values in a range of cells is AVERAGE.

Arguments follow the function's name. The most common kind of argument is the numbers that are to be calculated, or references to other cells containing the numbers.

▸ The arguments must be enclosed in parentheses that tell Excel where they begin and end.

▸ The arguments can be numbers, cell references, ranges, formulas, or other functions. For example, the function =SUM(10,20,30) sums the three numbers, and the function =SUM(A1:A5) sums the values in the range A1 through A5.

▸ If there is more than one argument, the arguments must be separated from each other by commas. (Do not use commas to separate thousands when you enter numbers into a function.) For example, the function =SUM(A1:A5,A7:A9) sums the values in the ranges A1:A5 and A7:A9.

▸ A few functions, such as PI or RAND, do not require arguments, but they must still have the parentheses for Excel to recognize them. For example, the function =PI() will calculate the value of pi for you, and =RAND() will generate a random number between 0 and 1.

▸ Some functions have optional arguments that you can enter but that are not required for the function to make a calculation.

Let's look at an example of function used to calculate monthly payments on a loan. The function's syntax is =PMT(*rate,nper,–pv*). The function's name is PMT (for **PayMenT**). The arguments are *rate* (the interest rate), *nper* (number of payment periods), and *–pv* (present value of the loan—that is, the amount of the loan—expressed as a negative). The three arguments are separated from one another by commas and are enclosed in parentheses. You can substitute numbers in the function (see the middle margin illustration). The function =PMT(.14/12,48,–10000) calculates and displays monthly payments of $273.26 on a $10,000 loan at 14% for 48 months (the 14% loan is divided by 12 in the function to convert it to a monthly rate that matches the term, which is expressed in months. You could also leave the .14 undivided by 12 and express the term in years (4) to calculate an annual payment.)

Instead of entering numbers as arguments in a function, you can enter them into other cells and then enter references to those cells as arguments in the function. The values in the referred-to cells are calculated just as if they were a part of the function (see the bottom margin illustration). Entering the values into their own cells makes it easy to change them when updating a model or exploring what-ifs.

Functions can also be used in combinations. For example, the functions =ROUND(SUM(A1:A7),2) round the sum of the values in cells

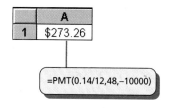

	A
1	$273.26

=PMT(0.14/12,48,–10000)

	A	B
1	rate	14%
2	nper	48
3	pv	$10,000
4	Payment	$273.26

=PMT(B1/12,B2,–B3)

	A	B
1	**Function with Multiple Arguments**	
2	Interest rate (rate)	1%
3	Number of periods (nper)	48
4	Present value (pv)	$ 10,000.00
5	Payment	$263.34

A function's arguments

With descriptions
=PMT(rate,nper,–pv)

With cell references
=PMT(B2,B3,-B4)

With numbers
=PMT(.01,48,–10000)

A1:A7 to two decimal places. When you include one function in another like this, the functions are *nested*.

TUTORIAL

In this tutorial you look at a number of functions to see how they are structured. The functions you look at include those with no arguments, those with a range of cells as an argument, and those with multiple arguments.

1. Open the *funcform.xls* workbook stored in the *tutorial* directory on the *Excel Student Resource Disk (Part 1)* and enter your name into cell A1.

Exploring Functions

2. Press **Ctrl**+**`** to display functions in the cells instead of their calculated values. Scroll the screen to see how the functions all work.

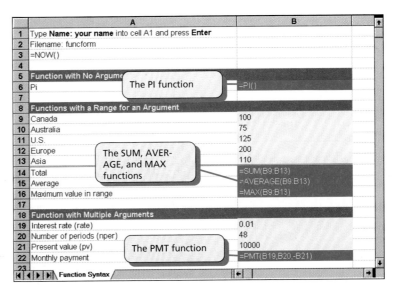

3. Notice how the function in cell B6 (which calculates the mathematical constant pi (π) to 15 digits) has no argument within its parentheses. A few functions don't require arguments—but they still require the parentheses.

4. Cells B14, B15, and B16 each contain a function that refers to the same range of cells, B9:B13. The function in cell B14 sums the range, the one in cell B15 calculates the average value of the range, and the one in cell B16 calculates the maximum value in the range.

5. The function in cell B22 calculates the monthly payment on a loan. It has three arguments separated by commas. Its syntax is =PMT(*rate,nper,–pv*). Since it is referring to cells, it's calculating the numbers in those cells as =PMT(.01,48,–10000). Three ways to think of these arguments are shown in the figure "A Function's Arguments."

6. Press **Ctrl**+**`** again to return to displaying calculated values.

Finishing Up

7. Close the workbook without saving it.

QUICKSTEPS:
USING AUTOSUM

1. Select the cells to be summed as described in the box "Selecting Cells to Be Summed" on the next page.

2. Click the **AutoSum** button on the toolbar to enter the SUM function(s). If you selected a single cell, Excel enters the function for you and highlights the range of cells with a moving border.

   ▶ If the range is correct, press Enter↵, click the Enter box (☑), or click the **AutoSum** button on the formula bar again.

   ▶ If the range isn't correct, edit the range highlighted in the active cell, and then press Enter↵ or click the Enter box (☑). (You can also click the Cancel box (☒), select the range manually, and then repeat this step.)

4-2. USING AUTOSUM

The function that people use most frequently is the one that totals, or sums, columns or rows of numbers. This SUM function can be typed directly into a cell in the format =SUM(*range*). For example, to total all of the numbers in column B from rows 3 to 8 you would enter the function as =SUM(B3:B8).

	A	B	C	D	E
1	Sales: First Quarter				
2	Item	*Jan*	*Feb*	*Mar*	*Total*
3	Computer	$10,000	$11,000	$12,100	$33,100
4	Printer	300	330	363	$ 993
5	CD-ROM	400	440	484	$ 1,324
6	Monitor	250	275	303	$ 828
7	Mouse	50	55	61	$ 166
8	Software	350	385	424	$ 1,159
9	Total	$11,350	$12,485	$13,734	$37,569

=SUM(B3:B8)

However, you can also enter this function quickly and automatically using the **AutoSum** button on the toolbar. When you do so, Excel analyzes the data and automatically enters a SUM function and guesses at the range of cells to be added. If it guesses correctly, you just have to click the Enter box (☑) on the formula bar or press Enter↵ to complete the entry.

TIP: ENTERING GRAND TOTALS

If you use the SUM function to calculate subtotals, you can then select the range that includes those subtotals and click the **AutoSum** button to calculate grand totals. Excel ignores all numbers in the selected range and just sums those calculated by other SUM functions.

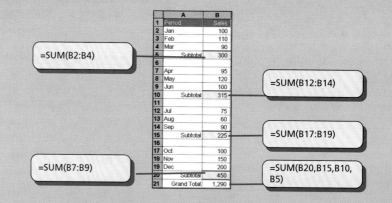

In this figure, cell B21 was selected, and then the **AutoSum** button was clicked. The function summed the number in cells B5, B10, B15, and B20—ignoring the other numbers in the column.

SELECTING CELLS TO BE SUMMED

When you click the **AutoSum** button on the toolbar, your results depend on what cells you have selected.

▶ Select one blank cell below or to the right of the cells to be summed to sum the adjacent column or row.

	A	B	C	D
1	1	2	3	
2	4	5	6	
3	7	8	9	
4	12			
5				
6				

▶ Select a range of blank cells below or to the right of the cells to be summed to sum the adjacent columns or rows.

	A	B	C	D
1	1	2	3	
2	4	5	6	
3	7	8	9	
4	12	15	18	
5				
6				

▶ Select the cells to be summed to sum them on the row below the selected range.

	A	B	C	D
1	1	2	3	
2	4	5	6	
3	7	8	9	
4	12	15	18	
5				
6				

▶ Select the cells to be summed and the row below and column to the right to sum both rows and columns.

	A	B	C	D
1	1	2	3	6
2	4	5	6	15
3	7	8	9	24
4	12	15	18	45
5				
6				

TUTORIAL

In this tutorial you are introduced to the **AutoSum** command. You use it to quickly sum columns of income and expense numbers in the budget model.

Getting Started

1. Open the *budget.xls* workbook stored in the *tutorial* directory on the *Excel Student Resource Disk (Part 1)*.

2. Select any of the cells on the *Total* lines to see their formulas on the formula bar. You may remember all of the typing or pointing you had to do to enter these formulas that sum the cells above them. You are about to see how easily the same thing can be done.

3. Select cells B10 through E10 and then press Delete to delete their contents. (Don't worry that some of the cells fill with number signs.)

4. Select cells B19 through E19 and then press Delete to delete their contents.

Using AutoSum

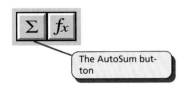

The AutoSum button

5. Select cells B10 through E10 and click the **AutoSum** button on the toolbar to sum the columns of data above. Click any cell on the row to see how SUM functions were automatically entered (see the model on the following page).

6. Select cells B19 through E19 and click the **AutoSum** button on the toolbar to sum the columns of data above. Click any cell on the row to see how SUM functions were automatically entered.

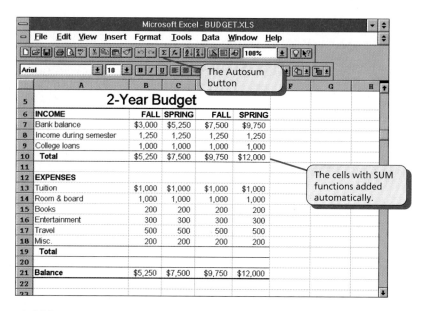

Finishing Up

7. Save, print, and close the workbook.

4-3. USING THE FUNCTION WIZARD

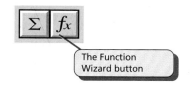

The Function Wizard button

Although you can type a function directly into a cell, Excel's Function Wizard makes the process much easier. When you use the Function Wizard, a dialog box displays functions grouped by category. When you select the function you want to enter, you can then display a second dialog box that guides you through entering the arguments. The types of functions you will encounter are summarized in the box "Understanding the Types of Excel Functions."

UNDERSTANDING THE TYPES OF EXCEL FUNCTIONS

Excel has hundreds of functions from which you can choose. To help you locate them, related functions are grouped into the following families:

Database & List functions calculate averages and medians, count cells, and find maximum and maximum values, standard deviations, sums, and variances of databases and lists.

Date & Time functions calculate the current date and time or add or subtract dates and times.

Engineering functions perform calculations used by programmers, scientists, and engineers.

Financial functions calculate depreciation, present and future values, internal rates of return, periodic payments of an annuity, interest rates, and yields.

Information functions determine what type of data is in cells.

Logical functions perform conditional calculations (if x then y), and connect arguments so one, both, or neither must be true for a conditional calculation to be performed in a given way.

Lookup & Reference functions look up values in a table and find locations of row and column references.

Math & Trig functions calculate absolute values, logarithms, pi , and random numbers.

Statistical functions calculate averages and medians, count cells, and find minimum and maximum values, standard deviations, sums, and variances.

Text functions convert text to numbers and vice versa, compare text entries, remove nonprintable text characters, join several text items into one item, compare two text values to see if they are identical, and change the case of characters.

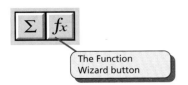

The Function Wizard button

QUICKSTEPS: USING THE FUNCTION WIZARD

1. Select the cell in which you want to enter the function, or begin entering a formula in which you want to enter a function.

2. Click the **Function Wizard** button on the toolbar, or pull down the **Insert** menu and click the **Function** command to display the Function Wizard Step 1 of 2 dialog box.

3. Click the type of function you want to use in the **Function Category** list to select it and display that kind of function in the **Function Name** list. (The box "Understanding the Types of Excel Functions" describes some of the functions available in Excel—others are described in later sections.)

4. Click the name of the desired function in the **Function Name** list to select it. A brief description of the function and its arguments is displayed below the lists.

5. Click the **Next** command button to display the Function Wizard Step 2 of 2 dialog box. (You can then click the **Back** command button at any point to return to Step 1 of 2.)

6. Enter the arguments for the function in the argument edit boxes, and then click the **Finish** command button to enter the function in the cell.

UNDERSTANDING THE FUNCTION WIZARD'S DIALOG BOXES

When you click the **Function Wizard** button on the toolbar, the Function Wizard Step 1 of 2 dialog box is displayed. After selecting a function, you normally click the **Next** command button to display the Step 2 of 2 dialog box. (If you click the **Finish** command button, the selected function is entered into the active cell with the argument names inserted as placeholders. For example, if you insert the PMT function this way, the function =PMT(*rate,nper,pv,fv,type*) is entered in the cell and displayed on the formula bar so you can substitute values for the placeholders in the arguments.)

The Function Wizard Step 2 of 2 dialog box is where you enter a function's arguments (if any are required). The names of required arguments are boldfaced and the names of optional arguments are displayed in lighter type. When you enter a formula or cell reference in one of the argument edit boxes, the arguments are shown to the right of the edit box. The current calculated value of the function is displayed in the *Value* box in the upper-right corner of the dialog box.

You can click the **Function Wizard** button to the left of any argument in an edit box to open another instance of the Function Wizard dialog box. This lets you insert another function as an argument within the first one.

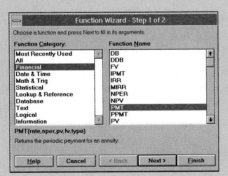

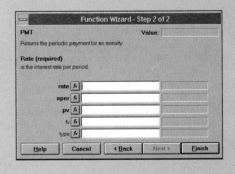

TIP: FUNCTION NAMES

When you enter a function name in lowercase letters, Excel will automatically convert it to uppercase when you press [Enter ←] or click the Enter box. If it doesn't convert it to uppercase, and #NAME? is displayed in the cell, check for typos in the name.

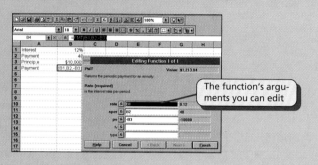
TUTORIAL

In this tutorial you use Excel's Function Wizard to enter a variety of commonly used functions. The model you use already has all of the arguments for each of the functions you enter. All you have to do is be sure you refer to the correct cells when entering the arguments asked for by the Function Wizard.

Getting Started

1. Open the *function.xls* workbook stored in the *tutorial* directory on the *Excel Student Resource Disk (Part 1)* and enter your name into cell A1.

Entering a Function with the Function Wizard

2. Select cell C11 and click the **Function Wizard** button on the toolbar to display the Function Wizard's Step 1 of 2 dialog box.

3. Click *Financial* in the **Function Category** list to select it and display financial functions in the **Function Name** list (see the upper margin illustration).

4. Click *DDB* in the **Function Name** list to select it, and notice how a description of the selected function, the double declining balance method of depreciating assets, is displayed at the bottom of the dialog box.

5. Click the **Next** command button to display the Function Wizard Step 2 of 2 dialog box (see bottom illustration in the margin).

6. Enter into the edit boxes the arguments shown in the bottom margin illustration. The easiest way to enter an argument is to click in the argument's edit box to move the insertion point there, then click the appropriate cell in the model. If necessary, you can drag the dialog box out of the way. (You must enter only those arguments that are boldfaced in the dialog box—the others are optional.)

List of financial functions

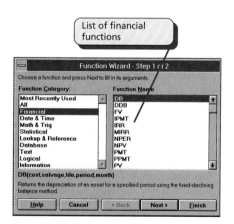

Step 3

The function's arguments

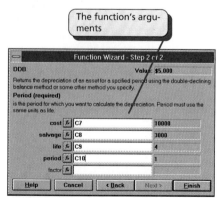

Step 5

7. Click the **Finish** command button to enter the function in its cell.

Entering Other Functions

8. Select cell C16 and use Function Wizard to select the function *FV* (the future value of an investment) and specify the arguments as cells **C13** (*rate*), **C14** (*nper*), and **C15** (*pmt*). Then click the **Finish** command button. The result should be $98,347.

9. Select cell C23 and use Function Wizard to select the function *IRR* (the internal rate of return) and specify the arguments as cells **B19:B23** (*values*) and **C19** (*guess*). Then click the **Finish** command button. The result should be 34.90%.

10. Select cell C28 and use Function Wizard to select the function *PMT* (payment) and specify the arguments as cells **C25** (*rate*), **C26** (*nper*), and **C27** (*pv*). Then click the **Finish** command button. The result should be $1,338.79.

11. Select cell C33 and use Function Wizard to select the function *PV* (the present value of an investment) and specify the arguments as cells **C30** (*rate*), **C31** (*nper*), and **C32** (*pmt*). Then click the **Finish** command button. The result should be $9,818.

12. Click the **Save** button on the toolbar to save your changes.

13. Click the **Print** button on the toolbar to print the sheet.

Exploring What-Ifs

14. Change any of the arguments for any of the functions, and watch the functions calculate new results.

Finishing Up

15. Close the workbook without saving your what-if changes.

4-4. USING NAMES

You can name ranges of cells and then refer to them by name rather than by their reference when entering formulas and functions, selecting cells, or completing dialog boxes. Names are useful because they are easy to remember. For example, a formula =A6–A7 has no meaning without referring to the referenced cell's descriptive labels. However, if you name cell A6 *Sales* and A7 *Expenses*, you could enter the formula as =*Sales–Expenses* and know immediately what it calculated. Also, you can use names instead of cell addresses or ranges in functions. For example, the function =SUM(*sales*) will total all of the numbers that fall in the range named *sales*.

When you first open a new workbook, there are no named ranges. However, you can name them using the Name box on the formula bar or by pulling down the **Insert** menu and clicking the **Name** command.

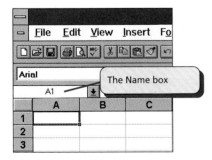

NAMES AND THE NAME BOX

You can use the Name box on the formula bar to define names and then use those names to select cells or refer to them in formulas. To name a range of cells, select the range and then type a name into the Name box.

QUICKSTEPS: NAMING RANGES USING THE NAME BOX

1. Select the range of cells to be named.

2. Click the Name box on the formula bar, type a name, and then press Enter↵. The names you can use are described in the box "Understanding Names."

UNDERSTANDING NAMES

▶ The first character in the name must be a letter or underscore character. The characters that follow the first can also include numbers and periods.

▶ Spaces are not allowed in names. To separate words, enter underscore characters. For example, to name a range *Fall Sales*, enter the name as *Fall_Sales*.

▶ You can use upper- and lowercase letters, but Excel is not case-sensitive when you refer to names. For example, if you name a range *Sales*, the functions =SUM(sales), =SUM(Sales), and =SUM(SALES) all work identically.

USING NAMES IN FORMULAS AND FUNCTIONS

Once you have named ranges, you can use the names by clicking the Name box's drop-down arrow (⬇) to display them and then click one of the names to select it. What happens then depends on where you are in a procedure:

▶ If the formula bar is active (as it is after you press =), the selected name is inserted into the formula or function. The name in the formula or function acts just as the cell reference would and would be entered at the same point. For example, if the range A1:A5 has been named *sales*, the function =SUM(sales) is the same as the function =SUM(A1:A5). To enter this function, you type **=SUM(** and then click the Name box's drop-down arrow (⬇) to select the name *sales*. At this point the function would read *=SUM(sales*. You would then type) to end the function and press Enter↵ to enter it in the cell.

▶ If the formula bar is not active, the range of cells to which the name has been assigned is selected. For example, if the range A1:A5 has been named *Sales*, that range is highlighted when you click *Sales* on the drop-down list. In other words, clicking the name is like using the **Go To** command on the **Edit** menu.

	A	B	C	D	E
1		January	February	March	April
2	Sales	1000	1500	2000	2500
3	Expenses	600	900	1200	1500
4	Profit	400	600	800	1000

Select the range that includes the names, and then pull down the **Insert** menu, click the **Name** command, and use the **Create** command to create names in the top row and left column.

NAMES AND THE INSERT MENU

	A	B	C	D	E
1		January	February	March	April
2	Sales	1000	1500	2000	2500
3	Expenses	600	900	1200	1500
4	Profit	400	600	800	1000

This row will be names *Sales*.

This column will be named *January*.

NAMES AND THE INSERT MENU

You can define names using the **Name** command on the **Insert** menu, but it isn't as fast as using the Name box on the formula bar. The reason you use the **Name** command is that it allows you to delete names and apply names to cells based on the text in adjacent cells.

QUICKSTEPS: NAMING RANGES WITH THE INSERT MENU

1. Select the range of cells that includes the cells containing the names and the cells to be named.
2. Pull down the **Insert** menu and click the **Name** command to cascade the menu.
3. Make any of the choices described in the table "Understanding the Name Menu."

UNDERSTANDING THE NAME MENU

When you pull down the **Insert** menu and click the **Name** command, the menu cascades to list the following commands.

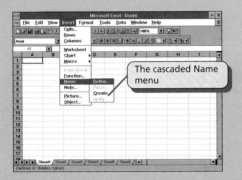

Define displays the Define Name dialog box. All defined names are displayed in the **Names in Workbook** window. You can enter a new name in the **Names in Workbook** text box and click the **Add** button to create a new name. You can also select any name on the list and click the **Delete** command button to delete it.

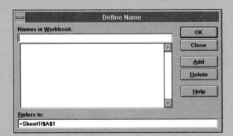

Paste inserts the selected name into the formula displayed on the formula bar.

Create displays the Create Names dialog box where you assign names to selected cells using the text in adjacent selected cells.

▶ **Top Row** uses the text in the top row to name the cells on the rows below. The name in the top cell of the selected range is applied to all of the selected cells below it in the column.

▶ **Left Column** uses the text in the left column to name the cells in the columns to the right. The name in the leftmost cell in the selected range is applied to all of the selected cells to the right of it on the row.

▶ **Bottom Row** uses the text in the bottom row to name the cells on the rows above.

▶ **Right Column** uses the text in the right column to name the cells in the columns to the left.

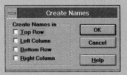

Apply replaces cell references in formulas with the selected name wherever the ranges match exactly. It does this for a selected range of cells, or for the entire worksheet when only a single cell is selected.

TUTORIAL

In this tutorial you define a name with the Name box on the formula bar. Then you use Excel's **Name** command to name cells by assigning them the row labels to their left and the column labels above them. You then enter formulas that use the assigned names rather than the cell addresses to which they refer.

Getting Started

1. Open the *names.xls* workbook stored in the *tutorial* directory on the *Excel Student Resource Disk (Part 1)* and enter your name into cell A1.

Naming a Range

2. Select cells B6 through B9.

3. Click the Name box on the formula bar to select the cell's address, then type the name **sales** and press Enter↵.

Selecting a Named Range

4. Click anywhere on the worksheet outside of the named range.

5. Click the Name box's drop-down arrow (⬇) to display a list of names on the worksheet (*sales* is now the only one), and click the name *sales*. The range of that name is immediately selected.

Referring to a Named Range in a Function

6. Select cell B10 and type the function **=SUM(sales)** and press Enter↵. The function sums the range just as if you had entered it as B6:B9.

Creating Names

7. Select the range of cells from A15 to D17.

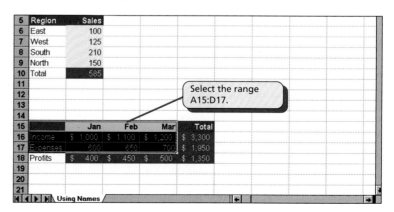

8. Pull down the **Insert** menu and click the **Name** command to cascade the menu.

9. Click the **Create** command to display the Create Names dialog box. The check boxes for **Top Row** and **Left Column** should both be on (⊠). If they are not, click them on.

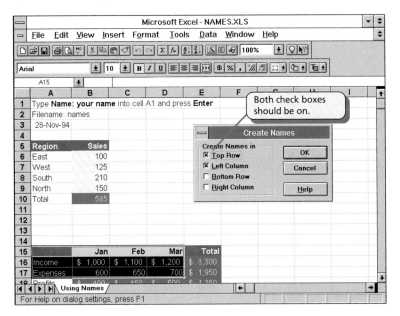

10. Click the **OK** command button to create the names.

Using Created Names in Formulas

11. Select cell B18, type the formula **=income–expenses** and press Enter ↵.

12. Select cell B18 and point to the fill handle on the cell border so the mouse pointer turns into a small plus sign (+). Hold down the left mouse button, drag the fill handle to cell D18, and release the mouse button. The formula is copied to each of the cells you dragged the outline over.

13. Select cell E16, then type **=SUM(** and click the Name box's drop-down arrow (⬇) to display a list of names on the worksheet.

14. Click *Income* to select it, then type **)** and press Enter ↵.

15. Select cell E17, then type **=SUM(expenses)** and press Enter ↵.

16. Select cell E18, then type **=SUM(income)–SUM(expenses)** and press Enter ↵.

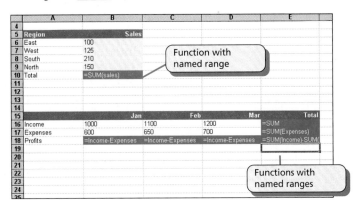

Displaying Formulas

17. Press `Ctrl`+`'` to display formulas in the cells instead of their calculated values. If necessary, scroll the screen to see how the formulas all work.

18. Press `Ctrl`+`'` again to return to displaying calculated values.

Finishing Up

19. Save, print, and close the workbook.

4-5. ENTERING DATES AND TIMES

To calculate with dates and times you must enter them in a specific way but you can then format them so they are displayed in a variety of formats.

ENTERING DATES AND TIMES

When entering dates and times, if you enter them in a way that Excel recognizes, it will allow you to calculate with them and automatically format the cell to display them correctly. When they are entered correctly, Excel stores dates and times as values called *serial numbers* that it can add and subtract. For example, you can subtract two dates to see how many days fell between them. When they are entered in such a way that Excel does not recognize the format, they are stored as text. When entering dates or times, keep the following points in mind:

▸ To enter dates and times as text, precede them with an apostrophe.

▸ To enter today's date, press `Ctrl`+`;`

▸ To enter the current time, press `Ctrl`+`:`

▸ To enter dates, separate days, months, and years with slashes (/) or hyphens (-). For example, enter January 30, 1996 as 1/30/96 or 1-30-96.

▸ To have Excel display a time in AM or PM format, type the time, then a space, then the AM or PM. If you leave out the space, Excel treats the entry as text. If you do not type AM or PM, you must use 24-hour format to type a time. Thus, for 1:00 PM you would type 13:00.

▸ To enter a date and time in the same cell, separate them with a space.

USING AUTOFILL TO ENTER A SERIES OF DATES AND TIMES

When you want to enter a series of dates quickly, you can use Excel's AutoFill feature. Select the cell containing a date and drag the fill handle to cells where you want the date added. As you do so, the date that will be entered into the current cell is displayed in the Name box on the formula bar. When you release the mouse button, the cells are filled with incremented dates. The same procedure will fill in a series of times incremented by one hour.

FORMATTING DATES AND TIMES

When you enter a date or time function, its format depends on the format you used to enter it. However, you can change the format at any time with the **Format**, **Cells**, **Number** dialog box. The formats you can use are shown in the margin.

	A	C
1	Date Formats	
2	Format	Examples
3	m/d/yy	1/30/96
4	d-mmm-yy	30-Jan-96
5	d-mmm	30-Jan
6	mmm-yy	Jan-96
7	m/d/yy h:mm	1/30/96 0:00
8		
9	Time Formats	
10	Format	Examples
11	h:mm AM/PM	11:30 AM
12	h:mm:ss AM/PM	11:30:01 AM
13	h:mm	11:30
14	h:mm:ss	11:30:01
15	m/d/yy h:mm	1/0/00 11:30
16	mm:ss	30:01

TUTORIAL

In this tutorial you see how to enter dates and times in formats that Excel recognizes. You then see how they increment if you use the Fill command to copy them to adjacent cells.

Getting Ready

1. Open the *datetime.xls* workbook stored in the *tutorial* directory on the *Excel Student Resource Disk (Part 1)* and enter your name in cell A1.

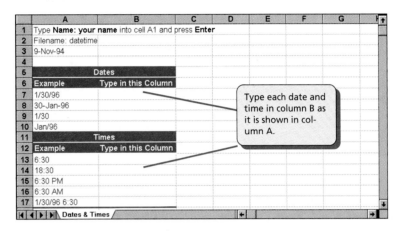

Entering Dates and Times

2. Column A shows some example forms in which you can enter dates and times so Excel recognizes them. Enter each date and time in column B as shown in the cell to its left. Not all entries will be displayed exactly as you type them. (The entries in column A are text because an apostrophe (') was typed before typing the date or time. Don't type this apostrophe in column B.)

Filling Adjacent Cells

3. Click cell B7 to select it, then point to the fill handle on the lower-right corner of the cell until the mouse pointer turns into a small plus sign.

4. Drag the fill handle two cells to the right, and then release the mouse button to fill the cells with dates that increment by one day.

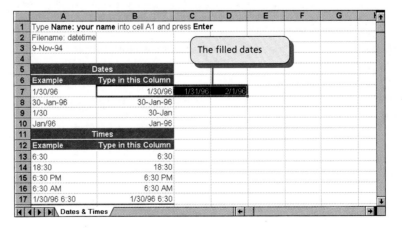

5. Click cell B16 to select it, then point to the fill handle on the lower-right corner of the cell until the mouse pointer turns into a small plus sign.

6. Drag the fill handle two cells to the right, and then release the mouse button to fill the cells with times that increment by one hour.

Finishing Up

7. Save, print, and close the workbook.

4-6. DATE AND TIME FUNCTIONS

Dates and times are important elements of many types of analysis. For example, a business's accounts payable and accounts receivable are due on certain dates. The time that a measurement is made in biology may have an influence on the results of an experiment. Since dates and times are so important, Excel provides functions that automatically calculate or operate on them for you.

GENERATING DATE AND TIME SERIAL NUMBERS

To work with dates and times, you first have to enter them as described in Section 4-5 or generate them as serial numbers using one of the functions described in the table "Functions That Generate Date and Time Serial Numbers." These functions assign a numeric serial number to days and times.

▸ Date serial numbers are the number of days since January 1, 1900 inclusive. The serial number for that date is 1.

▸ Time serial numbers are fractional equivalents of the 24-hour period. For example, midnight is 0, noon is .5, and just before midnight is .999.

Functions That Generate Date and Time Serial Numbers	
Function	Description
DATE	Calculates the serial number of the specified date
DATEVALUE	Calculates the serial number of date entered as text
NOW	Calculates the serial number of the current date and time number based on your system's internal clock. When you use the =NOW() function, it updates whenever you open or recalculate the worksheet. You can use this to display the current date and time on the screen.
TIME	Calculates the serial number of the specified time
TIMEVALUE	Calculates the serial number of a time entered as text
TODAY	Calculates the serial number of today's date

CALCULATING WITH DATES AND TIMES

Since dates and times are actually numbers, you can add and subtract them, for example, to find the number of days between two dates or the number of hours, minutes, and seconds between two times. To enter dates or times in formulas, enclose them in double quotation marks. For example, to subtract one date from another, enter the formula as ="1/30/96"–"1/30/95". You can also manipulate date and time serial numbers with the functions described in the table "Functions That Calculate with Date and Time Serial Numbers."

Functions That Calculate with Date and Time Serial Numbers	
Function	Description
DAY	Converts a serial number to a day of the month
HOUR	Converts a serial number to an hour
MINUTE	Converts a serial number to a minute
MONTH	Converts a serial number to a month
SECOND	Converts a serial number to a second
WEEKDAY	Converts a serial number to a day of the week
YEAR	Converts a serial number to a year

TUTORIAL

In this tutorial you use date functions to calculate the number of days, weeks, and years that you have been alive.

Getting Started

1. Open the *dates.xls* workbook stored in the *tutorial* directory on the *Excel Student Resource Disk (Part 1)* and enter your name into cell A1.

Entering Dates

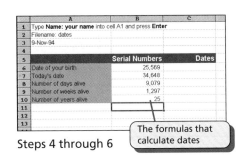

The two date functions

Steps 2 and 3

2. In cell B6, type **=DATE(70,1,1)** and press Enter↵ to display the number of days from January 1, 1900 to January 1, 1970 inclusive.

3. In cell B7, type **=NOW()** and press Enter↵ to calculate the number of days from January 1, 1900 to today. (Some numbers will be different from those in the illustration because today's date depends on which day you do this tutorial.) See the art in the margin.

Calculating Dates

4. In cell B8, enter the formula **=B7–B6** to calculate the number of days you have been alive as of today if you had been born on January 1, 1970.

5. In cell B9, enter the formula **=B8/7** to calculate the number of weeks you have been alive as of today.

6. In cell B10, enter the formula **=B8/365** to calculate the number of years you have been alive as of today (see the art in the margin.)

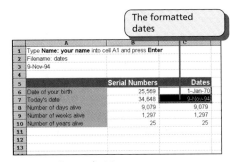

The formulas that calculate dates

Steps 4 through 6

Formatting The Dates

7. Select cells B6 through B10 and drag the fill handle one column to the right to copy the dates and formulas into column C.

8. Select cells C6 and C7, point to the selected cells and click the **RIGHT** mouse button to display a shortcut menu.

9. Click the **Format Cells** command to display the Format Cells dialog box.

10. Click the *Number* tab to display that dialog box, and click *Date* in the **Category** list to display date formats.

11. Click the *d-mmm-yy* format in the **Format Codes** list, and then click the **OK** command button to apply the selected format to the cells (see the art in the margin).

The formatted dates

Steps 7 through 11

Finishing Up

12. Save and print the workbook.

13. Edit the date function in cell C6 so that it is your birth date (or a friend's). Replace the 70 with the year you were born, the first 1 with the month (1-12), and the second 1 with the day of the month (1-31). The numbers in cells C8 through C10 now are accurate for you or your friend.

14. Close the workbook without saving your changes.

4-7. COMPARISON OPERATORS AND LOGICAL FUNCTIONS

When entering functions and formulas, some of the most powerful tools that you have are comparison operators and logical functions. These operators determine the truth or falsity of statements. For example, they can determine if Sally's sales are higher or lower than John's. When used with IF functions, these operators can cause a calculation to branch to two or more possible outcomes. For example, the function can calculate that if Sally's sales are higher, she gets a bonus; if John's are higher, he gets it.

COMPARISON OPERATORS

You use comparison operators to evaluate the relationship between two values. Excel then checks to see if the comparison is true or false. Using these operators, you can determine if one number is equal to, less than, or greater than another number. For example, the comparison operator > (greater than) in the formula =A1>1000 calculates TRUE if the value in cell A1 is larger than 1000 and FALSE if it is less than or equal to 1000. (TRUE has the numeric value of 1 and FALSE has the numeric value of 0.)

Comparison Operators	
Operator	Description
=	Equal to
>	Greater than
<	Less than
>=	Greater than or equal to
<=	Less than or equal to
<>	Not equal to

LOGICAL FUNCTIONS

The logical functions AND, OR, and NOT are used to test one or more statements. For example, the statement =OR(A1>1000,A2>1000) calculates 1 (TRUE) if the value in either cell A1 or A2 is larger than 1000 and 0 (FALSE) if both are less than or equal to 1000.

Logical Operators	
Operator	Description
AND	Both conditions must be met
OR	Either condition must be met
NOT	Following condition must not be met

IF FUNCTIONS

You use Excel's IF function to "branch" calculations. You do so by establishing a logical test that must be met. If the criterion is true, one calculation is made. If the criterion is false, another calculation is made. For example, let's say your business gave a 20% discount for all orders over $100. You could use the IF function =IF(order amount>100,order amount*discount,0) to calculate "IF the order amount is greater than $100, then multiply the order amount by 20% to calculate the discount; otherwise the discount is zero."

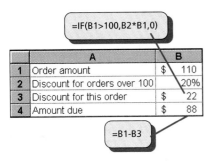

=IF(B1>100,B2*B1,0)

	A	B
1	Order amount	$ 110
2	Discount for orders over 100	20%
3	Discount for this order	$ 22
4	Amount due	$ 88

=B1-B3

The Discount Model—Original

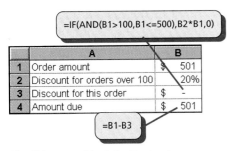

=IF(AND(B1>100,B1<=500),B2*B1,0)

	A	B
1	Order amount	$ 501
2	Discount for orders over 100	20%
3	Discount for this order	$ -
4	Amount due	$ 501

=B1-B3

The Discount Model—Revised

Since the functions normally refer to cells where the arguments are entered, the IF function we're describing might actually look like the one shown in the figure "The Discount Model—Original." It would actually read =IF(B1>100,B2*B1,0), where B1 is the order amount and B2 is the discount. Let's look closely at this function. The logical test B1>100 branches the calculation to one of two following possibilities depending on whether it is true or not. If the order is over $100, the B2*B1 part of the function calculates a discount. If the order is less than $100, the 0 part of the function is calculated.

You can expand on the model by using an AND function so the discount only applies to orders over $100 and less than or equal to $500. The function would state "IF the order is greater than $100 and less than or equal to $500, then multiply the order by 20% to calculate the discount, otherwise the discount is zero." The statement as shown in the figure "The Discount Model—Revised" would actually read =IF(AND(B1>100,B1<=500),B2*B1,0).

IF statements are also used to prevent #DIV/0! error messages from being displayed in cells. These error messages are displayed whenever you use the division operator (/) in a formula and the cell containing the denominator is blank. For example, if you enter the formula =B1/B2, it displays #DIV/0! when cell B2 is blank or contains a zero.

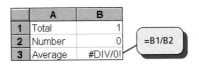

	A	B
1	Total	1
2	Number	0
3	Average	#DIV/0!

=B1/B2

To prevent this error message, you embed the formula in an IF function. For example, IF(B2>0,B1/B2,"N/A"). This formula now reads, "If the value in cell B2 is greater than 0, then divide the value in cell B1 by the value in cell B2; otherwise, display N/A."

IF
(what , True, False)

	A	B
1	Total	1
2	Number	0
3	Average	N/A

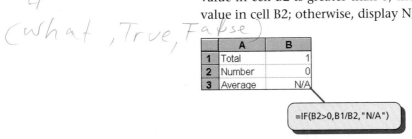

=IF(B2>0,B1/B2,"N/A")

TUTORIAL

If you are running a successful business, you might be confronted with the need to spend money to increase sales beyond present production capacity. In this tutorial you enter an IF function in a model that calculates how your breakeven point changes when you have to invest in expansion. Since the goal of most businesses is to keep breakeven as low as possible, a higher breakeven point may be a source of concern. When finished with the model, it will look like the one shown in the figure "The Breakeven Model" on the following page.

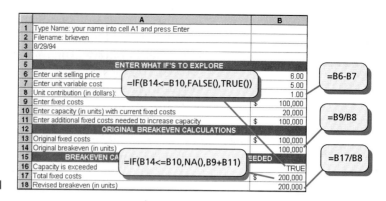

The Breakeven Model

The figure shows a spreadsheet with columns A and B:

	A	B
1	Type Name: your name into cell A1 and press Enter	
2	Filename: brkeven	
3	8/29/94	
4		
5	ENTER WHAT IF'S TO EXPLORE	
6	Enter unit selling price	6.00
7	Enter unit variable cost	5.00
8	Unit contribution (in dollars):	1.00
9	Enter fixed costs	$ 100,000
10	Enter capacity (in units) with current fixed costs	20,000
11	Enter additional fixed costs needed to increase capacity	$ 100,000
12	ORIGINAL BREAKEVEN CALCULATIONS	
13	Original fixed costs	$ 100,000
14	Original breakeven (in units)	100,000
15	BREAKEVEN CA[...]EEDED	
16	Capacity is exceeded	TRUE
17	Total fixed costs	$ 200,000
18	Revised breakeven (in units)	200,000

Callouts: `=IF(B14<=B10,FALSE(),TRUE())`, `=IF(B14<=B10,NA(),B9+B11)`, `=B6-B7`, `=B9/B8`, `=B17/B8`

Getting Started

1. Open the *brkeven.xls* workbook stored in the *tutorial* directory on the *Excel Student Resource Disk (Part 1)* and enter your name into cell A1.

Entering Formulas and Functions

2. Enter the formulas and the function shown in the figure "The Breakeven Model":

   ▸ The first function in cell B16 reads in English "If the original breakeven is less than or equal to the capacity with current fixed costs, then display FALSE in the cell; otherwise display TRUE."

   ▸ The second function in cell B17 reads in English "If the original breakeven is less than or equal to the capacity with current fixed costs, then display #NA in the cell; otherwise add additional fixed costs to increase capacity to fixed costs."

Finishing Up

3. Save, print, and close the workbook.

4-8. WORKING WITH TEXT

Excel lets you use text in IF functions to display messages that can make your models easy for others to use. When you do so, you enclose the text in quotation marks.

TUTORIAL

In this tutorial you explore using text instead of numbers in functions. The model you create displays the terms *Fire* or *Promote* depending on how a salesperson performs.

Getting Started

1. Open the *iffire.xls* workbook stored in the *tutorial* directory on the *Excel Student Resource Disk (Part 1)* and enter your name into cell A1.

Entering And Copying A Function

2. In cell C6, type **=IF(B6<10000,"Fire","Promote")** and press Enter ↵. The function displays the character string *Promote* because sales in cell B6 are not less than 10000.

	A	B	C	D
1	Type **Name: your name** into cell A1 and press Enter			
2	Filename: iffire			
3	11-Nov-94			
4				
5	Name	Sales	Action	
6	Smith	10,000	Promote	
7	Jones	9,000	Fire	
8	Lewis	12,000	Promote	
9	Washington	15,000	Promote	
10	Lee	23,000	Promote	
11	Gonzalez	11,000	Promote	

Entering and Copying a Function

	A	B	C	D
1	Type **Name: your name** into cell A1 and press Enter			
2	Filename: iffire			
3	09-Nov-94			
4				
5	Name	Sales	Action	
6	Smith	10,000	Retain	
7	Jones	9,000	Fire	
8	Lewis	12,000	Promote	
9	Washington	15,000	Promote	
10	Lee	23,000	Promote	
11	Gonzalez	11,000	Promote	

Revising the Function

3. Use the cell's fill handle to copy the function in cell C6 to cells C7 through C11. If sales in a cell in column B are less than 10000, the function in the adjoining cell displays *Fire*. If any value in a cell in column B is 10000 or more, the function displays *Promote*.

Revising The Function

4. Revise the function in cell C6 so that it reads =IF(B6=10000,"Retain",IF(B6<10000,"Fire","Promote")). To do so, add **=IF(B6=10000,"Retain"**, at the front of the function (including the ending comma) and) at the end.

5. Use the cell's fill handle to copy the function in cell C6 to cells C7 through C11. The functions now work just as they did before; however, they now display *Retain* in any cell where sales are equal to 10000.

6. Change some of the numbers in column B to numbers more than, less than, or equal to, 10,000 and watch the function change the displayed string.

Finishing Up

7. Save, print, and close the workbook.

PicTorial 4 Review Questions

 True-False

T	F	1.	Spaces are not allowed in range names.
T	F	2.	The formula **=A1>1000** calculates **TRUE** if the value in cell A1 is greater than or equal to 1000.
T	F	3.	When referred to in a function's range, cells containing text or blank cells have a numeric value of 1.
T	F	4.	There can be more than one argument in a function.
T	F	5.	When you enter a function name in lowercase letters, Excel will automatically convert it to uppercase letters when you press Enter↵.
T	F	6.	Numbers cannot be used in range names.
T	F	7.	Time serial numbers are fractional equivalents of the 24-hour period.
T	F	8.	You can add and subtract dates.
T	F	9.	The statement **=OR(A1>1000,A2>1000)** calculates **1** if the value in either cell is larger than 1000.
T	F	10.	IF functions are used to branch calculations.

1. All functions begin with a(n) _____.
   a. =
   b. +
   c. @
   d. "

2. Arguments in functions must be enclosed in _____.
   a. Quotation marks
   b. Colons
   c. Parentheses
   d. Asterisks

3. The symbol used to separate the beginning and ending of a range is a(n) _____.
   a. Quotation mark
   b. Colon
   c. Parentheses
   d. Apostrophe

4. Which of the following is not an example of a logical function:
   a. AND
   b. IF
   c. OR
   d. NOT

5. To enter dates and times as text, type a(n) _____ before typing the date or time.
   a. Quotation mark
   b. Equal symbol
   c. Plus symbol
   d. Apostrophe

6. To enter today's date, type _____ and press Enter↵.
   a. =NOW
   b. Ctrl+:
   c. Ctrl+⇧Shift+:
   d. =TODAY

7. Date serial numbers are the number of days since _____.
   a. January 1, 1900
   b. January 1, 1950
   c. January 1, 0001
   d. None of the above

8. Which of the following is not an example of a comparison operator:
   a. +
   b. =
   c. >
   d. <

9. The first character in a range name must be a(n) _____.
   a. Letter or an underscore
   b. Quotation mark
   c. Equal symbol
   d. Plus symbol

10. When entering strings directly into formulas or functions, enclose the strings in _____.
    a. Quotation marks
    b. Double quotation marks
    c. Parentheses
    d. Apostrophes

Fill In the Blank

1. You can use _____ operators to determine if one number is equal to another number.

2. In functions, _____ must be enclosed in parentheses.

3. _____ functions are used to convert text to numbers and vice versa.

4. The _____ displays functions grouped by category.

5. To enter a date and time in the same cell, separate them with a(n) _____.

6. The _____ function calculates the serial number of today's date.

7. Arguments in functions can be _____, _____, _____, _____, or _____.

8. To specify a range of cells falling in a rectangle, you specify the _____ left and _____ right cells in the range, separated by a colon.

9. AND is an example of a _____ function.

10. When using comparison operators, TRUE has a numeric value of _____ and FALSE has a numeric value of _____.

▶▶ COMPUTER-BASED TUTORIALS

We suggest you complete the following computer-based lessons to learn more about the features discussed in this PicTorial. To do so, pull down the **Help** menu and click the **Examples and Demos** command, click the *Topic* listed in the table "Suggested Examples and Demos to Complete" and then click the *Subtopic* listed in that same table. (If you need more help on using the system, see the "Computer-Based Tutorials" section at the end of PicTorial 1.)

Suggested Examples and Demos to Complete	
Topic	Subtopic
☐ Creating Formulas and Links	Using the Function Wizard
☐ Creating Formulas and Links	Working with Names

▶▶ QUICKSTEP DRILLS

4-1. Understanding Functions

In this drill you enter a PMT function in a model that calculates the monthly payment on a loan at any given interest rate, term, and loan amount. When finished, your model should look like the one in the figure "The Loan Model."

1. Open the *loan.xls* workbook stored in the *drill* directory on the *Excel Student Resource Disk (Part 1)* and enter your name into cell A1.

2. Type the function **=PMT(B6/12,B7,-B8)** into cell B9 and press Enter↵. With cell B9 selected, look at the function displayed on the formula bar and notice the order in which the cells are listed.

3. Change the interest rate to 8% and look at the new monthly payment.

4. Save, print, and close the workbook.

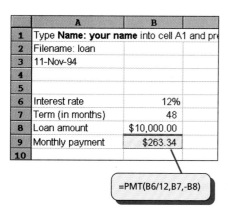

The Loan Model

4-2. Using AutoSum

The function that people use most often is SUM. Because it is used so extensively, Excel has an AutoSum feature that automatically sums numbers. In this drill you practice using that feature. When finished, your model should look like the one in the figure "The AutoSum Model."

1. Open the *autosum.xls* workbook stored in the *drill* directory on the *Excel Student Resource Disk (Part 1)* and enter your name into cell A1.

2. Select the cells with the red borders in each group but the last and then click the **AutoSum** button on the toolbar to automatically enter the function in the selected cell(s). When you select only one cell, you have to click the Enter box (☑) on the toolbar to complete the entry.

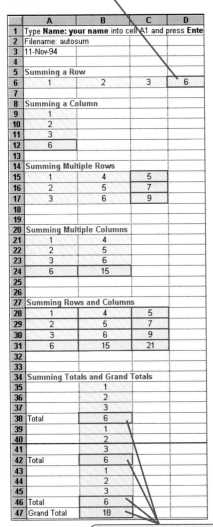

INSTRUCTIONS
Select the cells with the red borders in each group and then click the AutoSum button on the toolbar. The SUM functions will appear in the cells with the green background. Click the Enter box on the formula bar to complete the entry when necessary.

INSTRUCTIONS
Select the four cells with the red borders in order and use AutoSum individually for each of them.

The AutoSum Model

3. In the last group ("Summing Totals and Grand Totals") select each cell individually and in sequence from top to bottom. For each, click the **AutoSum** button on the toolbar, and then click the Enter box (☑) on the toolbar to complete the entry.

4. Save, print, and close the workbook.

4-3. Using the Function Wizard

Excel's Function Wizard makes it easy to enter functions step by step. In this drill you use Function Wizard to enter a series of statistical functions that all calculate the same list of numbers. When finished, your model should look like the one in the figure "The Stat Model."

	A	B
1	Type **Name: your name** into cell A1 and press **Enter**	
2	Filename: stat	
3	11-Nov-94	
4		
5	**Region**	**Sales**
6	Central	678
7	East	1,018
8	Northeast	1,515
9	Northwest	1,956
10	Southeast	965
11	Southwest	965
12	West	1,789
13		
14	Average (AVERAGE)	1269.428571
15	Count (COUNT)	7
16	Max (MAX)	1956
17	Min (MIN)	678
18	Standard deviation (STDEVP)	447.2132304
19	Sum (SUM)	8886
20	Variance (VARP)	199999.6735

The Stat Model

1. Open the *stat.xls* workbook stored in the *drill* directory on the *Excel Student Resource Disk (Part 1)* and enter your name into cell A1.

2. Use the Function Wizard to enter the functions listed on rows 14 through 20 in column B on the same row as its name.

   ▸ The name of each function is listed in column A, for example, AVERAGE, COUNT, and MAX.

   ▸ The functions are all under the *Statistical* **Function Category** in Function Wizard's first dialog box except SUM, which is *Math & Trig*.

   ▸ The functions all have the same argument, the range of cells (B6:B12). You can select the range by pointing to cell B6, holding down the mouse button, and dragging the outline down to cell B12.

3. Save the model and make a printout.

4. Change any of the sales for one or more regions and watch the statistical functions calculate new results.

5. Close the screen without saving your what-if changes.

4-4. Using Names

When you name cells or ranges of cells, you can then use those names in formulas and functions instead of cell references. In this drill you open an existing model and enter new functions that refer to a named range. When finished, your model should look like the one in the figure "The Stat Model with Names."

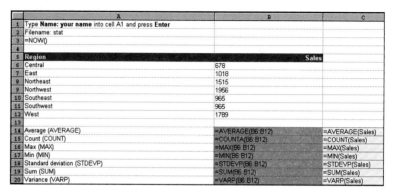

The Stat Model with Names

1. Open the *stat. xls* workbook stored in the *drill* directory on the *Excel Student Resource Disk (Part 1)*.

2. Select the range of cells B6:B12, click in the Name box on the formula bar, and enter the name *Sales*.

3. In cells C14 through C20 enter the same functions entered into column B on the same rows, but this time specify the range as *Sales*. For example, in cell C14, enter the function =AVERAGE(sales) not =AVERAGE(B6:B12).

4. Save the workbook.

5. Press Ctrl+` to display the formulas and functions in their cells, narrow column A, and make a printout.

6. Close the workbook without saving your changes.

4-5. Entering Dates and Times

The form in which you enter dates affects their format and the way they are displayed. In this drill you practice entering dates in a variety of formats. When finished, your model should look like the one in the figure "The Dates Model."

	A	B	C
1	Type **Name: your name** into cell A1 and press **Enter**		
2	Filename: dates2		
3	11-Nov-94		
4			
5	Type each of these entries into the cell to its right	Type in this column	Description of what's displayed
6	1/30/96	1/30/96	m/d/y format
7	30-Jan-96	30-Jan-96	d-mmm-yy format
8	1/30	30-Jan	d-mmm format
9	Jan-30	30-Jan	d-mmm format
10	Jan-96	Jan-96	mmm-yy format
11	1:30 PM	1:30 PM	h:mm format
12	1/30/96 1:30	1/30/96 1:30	m/d/yy h:mm format
13	Press Ctrl+;	8/29/94	Enters current date based on computer's clock
14	Press Ctrl+	3:34 PM	Enters current time based on computer's clock

The Dates Model

	A	B
1	Type **Name: your name** into cell A1 and press **Enter**	
2	Filename: mydates	
3	11/19/94	
4		
5	**Exploring Date Functions & Formats**	
6	Date function	=DATE(96,1,11)
7	Serial number	35075
8	m/d/yy	1/11/96
9	d-mmm-yy	11-Jan-96
10	d-mmm	11-Jan
11	mmm-yy	Jan-96
12	m/d/y h:mm	1/11/96 0:00
13		
14		
15	**Exploring Time Functions & Formats**	
16	Time function	=TIME(12,1,45)
17	Serial number	0.501215278
18	h:mm AM/PM	12:01 PM
19	h:mm:ss AM/PM	12:01:45 PM
20	h:mm	12:01
21	h:mm:ss	12:01:45
22	m/d/yy h:mm	1/0/00 12:01
23	mm:ss	01:45
24	mm:ss.0	01:45.0
25	[h]:mm:ss	12:01:45

The Mydates Model

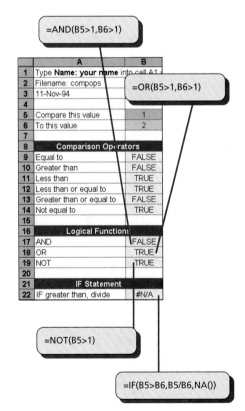

The Comparison Operators Model

1. Open the *dates2.xls* workbook stored in the *drill* directory on the *Excel Student Resource Disk (Part 1)* and enter your name into cell A1.

2. Enter dates shown in column A on the same row in column B and read the description of the results you get in column C. The last two entries enter dates and times when you press Ctrl+; and Ctrl+⇧ Shift+; (expressed on the model as Ctrl+:). After pressing the correct keys, you must press Enter↵ to complete the entry.

3. Save, print, and close the workbook.

4-6. Date and Time Functions

After you have entered dates or times, you can change their format. In this drill you enter date and time functions and format them using the available formats. When finished, your model should look like the one in the figure "The Mydates Model."

1. Open the *mydates.xls* workbook stored in the *drill* directory on the *Excel Student Resource Disk (Part 1)* and enter your name into cell A1.

2. Enter the function **=DATE(96,1,11)** in cell B6, and use the cell's fill handle to copy the function to cells B7 through B12. Use the **Format Painter** button on the toolbar to copy the red line in cell B25 back into cell B6 where it was erased by the fill command.

3. Enter the time function **=TIME(12,1,45)** in cell B16, and use the cell's fill handle to copy the function to cells B17 through B25. Use the **Format Painter** button on the toolbar to copy the line in cell B6 back into cell B25.

4. Format the cells as follows:
   ▶ Edit the contents of cells B6 and B16 to enter an apostrophe in front of the equal sign. This will display the function in the cell as text.
   ▶ Format cells B7 and B17 using the General format using the **Format**, **Cells**, **Number**, **All** commands.
   ▶ Format each of the other functions using the date or time formats listed on the same row in column A. To do so, use the **Format**, **Cells**, **Number**, **Date** or **Time** commands.

5. Save, print, and close the workbook.

4-7. Comparison Operators and Logical Functions

You can create a truth table for comparison operators. By changing the numbers in cells B5 and B6, you can establish if the relationships are true or false. When finished, your model should look like the one in the figure "The Comparison Operators Model."

1. Open the *compops.xls* workbook stored in the *drill* directory on the *Excel Student Resource Disk (Part 1)* and enter your name into cell A1.

2. In the sections "Comparison Operators" enter formulas that compare the value in cell B5 with the value in B6. For example, in cell B9 the formula is =B5=B6 and in B10 it is =B5>B6. Only the comparison operator changes in each formula.

3. In the section "Logical Functions" enter the formulas and function shown in the figure "The Comparison Operators Model."

4. In cell B22, enter the function =IF(B5>B6,B5/B6,NA()) and press [Enter ↵].

5. Save and print the workbook.

6. Change the values in cells B5 and B6 to combinations such as 1 and 1, 1 and 2, and 2 and 1 to see how the formulas and functions calculate. Try to figure out why each one calculates what it does when you change the numbers.

   ▸ What combination of the numbers 1 and 2 make cell B22 display a value? Why?

   ▸ What combination of the numbers 1 and 2 make NOT false? Why?

7. Close the workbook without saving your changes.

4-8. Working with Text

If you owned a store, you might want to separate daily cash transactions from charge account transactions. In this drill you create a model that does so with two IF functions that evaluate text entered into the model. The first function in cell D6 checks to see if you have entered Y into cell C6. If the cell does contain a Y, the function carries the amount the customer spent to the *Cash Amount* column. The other function checks to see if cell C6 contains any text other than a Y. If so, the function carries the amount the customer spent to the *Charge Amount* column. When finished, your model should look like the one in the figure "The Text Model."

The Text Model

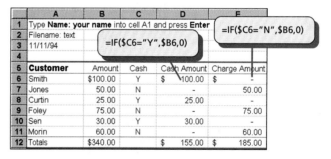

	A	B	C	D	E
1	Type **Name: your name** into cell A1 and press **Enter**				=IF($C6="N",$B6,0)
2	Filename: text			=IF($C6="Y",$B6,0)	
3	11/11/94				
4					
5	**Customer**	Amount	Cash	Cash Amount	Charge Amount
6	Smith	$100.00	Y	$ 100.00	$ -
7	Jones	50.00	N	-	50.00
8	Curtin	25.00	Y	25.00	-
9	Foley	75.00	N	-	75.00
10	Sen	30.00	Y	30.00	-
11	Morin	60.00	N	-	60.00
12	Totals	$340.00		$ 155.00	$ 185.00

1. Open the *text.xls* workbook stored in the *drill* directory on the *Excel Student Resource Disk (Part 1)* and enter your name into cell A1.

2. In cells D6 and E6, enter the two functions shown in the figure "The Text Model."

3. Select cells D6:E6 and use the fill handle to copy the formulas down to row 11.

4. Save and print the workbook.

5. Change any Y to N or N to Y in column C and watch the values move between the *Cash Amount* and *Charge Amount* columns.

6. Close the workbook without saving your changes.

▶▶ SKILL-BUILDING EXERCISES

4-1. Balancing a Checkbook

One of the chores that each of us has to perform is balancing our checkbook. If we don't do it, or don't do it correctly, checks begin to bounce. In this exercise, you create a model that makes the checkbook-balancing calculations for you. To keep a checkbook in balance, you start with a known balance and subtract withdrawals and add deposits. In the *chkbk.xls* workbook, you could do this with a simple formula. In cell F8 you could enter =F7-D8+E8 and copy the formula all the way down column F. However, you can make the model a little more sophisticated by using a function to enter *N/A* in the balance column for rows past the final record. When finished, your model should look like the figure "The Checkbook Model."

The Checkbook Model

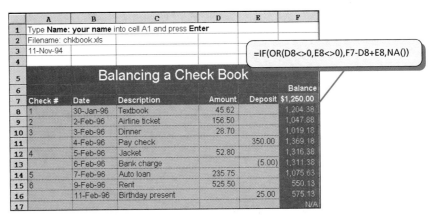

1. Open the *chkbk.xls* workbook stored in the *exercise* directory on the *Excel Student Resource Disk (Part 2)* and enter your name into cell A1.

2. Enter the dates in column B shown in the figure "The Checkbook Model."

3. In cell F8, enter the function **=IF(OR(D8<>0,E8<>0),F7-D8+E8,NA())**. The formula reads (in English) "If either cell D8 or cell E8 has any value other than zero, subtract any value in cell D8 from F7 and add cell E8; otherwise, display #N/A in cell F8."

4. Select cell F8 and use its fill handle to copy the formula from cell F8 to cells F9 through F17.

5. Save and print the workbook.

6. Explore what-ifs by changing the opening balance in cell F7, or any of the numbers in the *Amount* or *Deposit* column.

7. Close the workbook without saving your changes.

4-2. Calculating an Auto Loan

The *autoloan.xls* model is designed to make it easy to determine the monthly payments on a variety of auto loans. When finished, your model should look like the figure "The Auto Loan Model" on the following page.

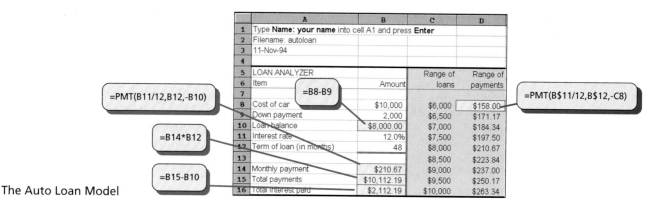

The Auto Loan Model

	A	B	C	D
1	Type **Name: your name** into cell A1 and press **Enter**			
2	Filename: autoloan			
3	11-Nov-94			
4				
5	LOAN ANALYZER		Range of	Range of
6	Item	Amount	loans	payments
7				
8	Cost of car	$10,000	$6,000	$158.00
9	Down payment	2,000	$6,500	$171.17
10	Loan balance	$8,000.00	$7,000	$184.34
11	Interest rate	12.0%	$7,500	$197.50
12	Term of loan (in months)	48	$8,000	$210.67
13			$8,500	$223.84
14	Monthly payment	$210.67	$9,000	$237.00
15	Total payments	$10,112.19	$9,500	$250.17
16	Total interest paid	$2,112.19	$10,000	$263.34

Callouts: =PMT(B11/12,B12,-B10), =B8-B9, =PMT(B$11/12,B$12,-C8), =B14*B12, =B15-B10

1. Open the *autoloan.xls* workbook stored in the *exercise* directory on the *Excel Student Resource Disk (Part 2)* and enter your name into cell A1.

2. Enter the formulas shown on the figure "The Autoloan Model." After entering the function into cell D8, select it and use its fill handle to copy the function to the cells below. Note that the two PMT functions divide the interest rate by 12 to convert it to a monthly interest rate.

3. Use the **Format**, **Cells**, **Border** commands to restore the border under cell D16.

4. Use the **Format**, **Cells**, **Number** commands to format all of the cells where you entered formulas as currency with two decimal places.

5. Save and print the workbook.

6. Explore what-ifs by changing the *Cost of car*, *Down payment*, *Interest rate*, or *Term of loan*. Then close the workbook without saving your what-if changes.

4-3. Calculating Travel Expenses

When traveling on business, you are normally reimbursed for your expenses if you work for a large company, or you can deduct your expenses from your gross income for tax purposes when working on your own. In this application, you build a model that allows you to keep track of your expenses.

The expenses that are reimbursed vary from company to company. Normally, they cover only those expenses directly related to the business trip. Side trips or entertainment while traveling are not usually covered. Obviously, you do not create a good impression by billing for things that are not covered by the company. Where possible, attach receipts for each item you are billing to support the claim. When finished, your model should look like the figure "The T&E Model."

The T&E Model

	A	B	C	D	E	F	G	H	I
1	Type **Name: your name** into ce		Enter **Sun** here and						
2	Filename: t&e		fill to the right.						
3	11-Nov-94								
4									
5	**T&E Worksheet**	Sun	Mon	Tue	Wed	Thu	Fri	Sat	Total
6		4-Jan-96	5-Jan-96	6-Jan-96	7-Jan-96	8-Jan-96	9-Jan-96	10-Jan-96	
7	**Travel**								
8	Air fare	$335.75							$335.75
9	Taxis	$26.75	$29.00						$55.75
10	Parking	$5.00	$10.00	$10.00	$10.00	$10.00	$5.00		$50.00
11	Mileage	$12.00					$12.00		$24.00
12	Meals								
13	Breakfast	$4.95	$6.00	$8.00	$12.00	$6.00	$4.00		$40.95
14	Lunch		$7.50	$21.00	$18.00	$15.00	$12.00		$73.50
15	Dinner	$16.75	$24.00	$18.00	$26.00	$13.00			$97.75
16	Total	$401.20	$76.50	$57.00	$66.00	$44.00	$33.00	$0.00	$677.70

Callouts: Enter **4-Jan-96** here and fill to the right. / Calculate this with AutoSum, then copy to the cells to the right.

1. Open the *t&e.xls* workbook stored in the *exercise* directory on the *Excel Student Resource Disk (Part 2)* and enter your name into cell A1.

2. Select the cell range I8:I15 and use the **AutoSum** button on the toolbar to enter sum functions in the column.

3. Select the cell range B16:I16 and use the **AutoSum** button on the toolbar to enter sum functions on the row.

4. Enter the text **Sun** into cell B5 and use the cell's fill handle to copy it to other cells on the row through cell H5. It automatically changes to Mon, Tue, and so on.

5. Enter the date **4-Jan-96** into cell B6 and use the fill handle to copy it to other cells on the row through cell H6. It automatically changes to 5-Jan-96, 6-Jan-96, and so on.

6. Select columns B through I and use the **Format**, **Column** commands to autofit their width to their contents.

7. Use the **Format**, **Cells** commands to format your model to match the figure "The Travel & Expense Model."

8. Use the **File**, **Page Setup** commands to turn off gridlines and row and column headings and then make a printout.

9. Save and close the workbook.

4-4. Calculating Lottery Payments

Almost all state lotteries offer huge prizes, but they spread their payment over a number of years. This stretched-out payment schedule saves the states a lot of money compared to what it would cost to pay winners a lump sum. In fact, you can say that these lotteries are guilty of false advertising. The tool you use to analyze the true value of payments over time is called present value analysis.

In this exercise, you enter a model that allows you to determine how much a lottery prize, or any other payment stretched over a period of years, is worth if you were to receive all of it today. The model shows how much a series of payments is worth in today's dollars, after accounting for interest you would have earned had you invested annual payments at a given interest rate. When finished, your model should look like the figure "The Lottery Payments Model."

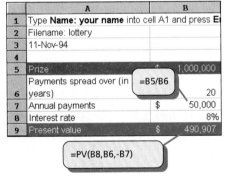

The Lottery Paments Model

1. Open the *lottery.xls* workbook stored in the *exercise* directory on the *Excel Student Resource Disk (Part 2)* and enter your name into cell A1.

3. Enter the formulas shown in the figure "The Lottery Payments Model. As you can then see, $1 million spread in equal payments over 20 years is worth only $490,907 in today's dollars. If you had $490,907 and invested it for 20 years at 8%, you would have $1 million.

4. Save the finished model and make a printout without gridlines.

5. Change the size of the prize or the interest rate, and see how the present value changes. For example, what is the present value of a $10,000 prize spread over five years with interest rates at 12%?

6. Close the workbook without saving your what-if changes.

	A	B		
1	Type **Name: your name** into		=AVERAGE(B$6:B6)	
2	Filenam	=SUM(B$6:B6)		
3	11-Nov			
4				
5	Month	Sales	Total (to date)	Average (to date)
6	Jan	100	100	100
7	Feb	110	210	105
8	Mar	120	330	110
9	Apr	130	460	115
10	May	140	600	120
11	Jun	150	750	125
12	Jul	160	910	130
13	Aug	170	1080	135
14	Sep	180	1260	140
15	Oct	190	1450	145
16	Nov	200	1650	150
17	Dec	210	1860	155

The Running Totals and Averages Model

4-5. Calculating Running Totals and Running Averages

One useful application of absolute and relative references is to anchor one end of a range while letting the other end remain relative. This way, you can enter a function that includes the first number in a range, but when you copy it, additional numbers are included. In this exercise, you use this technique to calculate running totals and averages. When finished, your model should look like the figure "The Running Totals and Averages Model."

1. Open the *running.xls* workbook stored in the *exercise* directory on the *Excel Student Resource Disk (Part 2)* and enter your name into cell A1.

2. In cell C6, enter the function **=SUM(B$6:B6)** being sure to use the correct relative and absolute addresses.

3. In cell D6, enter the function **=AVERAGE(B$6:B6)** being sure to use the correct relative and absolute addresses.

4. Select cells C6 and D6 and use the fill handle to copy the formulas down to row 17. Each cell in column C displays the cumulative total of numbers in column B and each cell in column D displays the cumulative average of numbers in that column.

5. Press Ctrl+` to display formulas in their cells and notice the results of copying the formula. Then , press Ctrl+` to display values in their cells.

6. Save, print, and close the workbook.

▶▶ REAL-WORLD PROJECTS

4-1. Buying a Home: The Cash Needed

When you buy a home, you need money for the down payment and other costs called closing costs. In this project you create a model that calculates closing costs when you purchase a new home. To begin, open the *house1.xls* stored in the *projects* directory on the *Excel Student Resource Disk (Part 2)*. This model contains all of the text you'll need but none of the numbers, formulas, or formats. The finished model is shown in the figure "The Closing Costs Model" (on the next page), and its formulas are indicated on the illustration and described below. Using these descriptions and formatting commands, make your model look just like the one illustrated. When finished, change the size of the loan to $125,000, save the workbook, and make a printout.

1. **Origination fee**, know as points, is a one-time charge used to adjust the yield on the loan to what market conditions demand. Each point is equal to 1% of the loan amount.

2. **Title insurance** protects you and the lender from other people making claims on the property. It is usually bought at a given amount per $1,000 of mortgage.

3. **Total closing costs** is the sum of all closing costs broken down above.

	A	B	C
1	Type **Name: your name** into cell A1 and press **Enter**		
2	Filename: house1		
3	11-Nov-94		
4		Examples	Your Loan
5	Size of loan		$ 100,000.00
6			
7	**Closing costs**		
8	Application fee (applied to credit and appraisal)	$ 250.00	$ 250.00
9	Origination fee (points)	1% of loan amount	$ 1,000.00
10	Appraisal fee (deducted from application fee)	$ (200.00)	$ (200.00)
11	Credit report (deducted from application fee)	$ (40.00)	$ (40.00)
12	Title insurence: lender's coverage	1.25 per 1000	$ 125.00
13	Attorney's fee/title search		$ 300.00
14	Private mortgage insurance		
15	Recording/Transfer fees		
16	Total closing costs		$ 1,435.00
17			
18	**Others costs--escrow accounts**		
19	Real estate taxes		$ 500.00
20	Property insurence		$ 300.00
21	Interest paid in advance		
22	Owner's title insurance coverage		
23	Other charges		
24	Total other costs		$ 800.00
25			
26	Total Costs		$ 2,235.00

The Closing Costs Model

4. **Total other costs** is the sum of all other costs broken down above. These include such items as money required for tax prepayments or escrow accounts.

5. **Total costs** is the sum of total closing costs and total other costs.

4-2. Buying a Home: The Mortgage

Shopping for the best mortgage credit available can save you money. Real estate mortgage loans differ in rate of interest, length of repayment period, and size. Some have penalties for prepayment. Because these factors can make a big difference in the ultimate cost of your real estate, it is worthwhile to shop for the type of loan and the terms that best suit your needs.

For each individual, there is a particular set of arrangements for down payment and length of time to repay the loan that will prove best. A desirable contract provides for payments as large as you can afford at the present time, with the right to repay the loan at a faster rate than originally agreed on if you later find that you want to.

In this project, you create a model that calculates the payments due on a home loan of any amount, for any period, at any interest rate. The emphasis is on mortgages, but the principles and calculations apply to almost any type of loan. After completing this project, you will be able to enter and describe how loan payments are calculated and how the terms affect the payments due.

The finished model is shown in the figure "The Mortgage Model" and its formulas are indicated on the illustration and described below. When finished, save the model as *house2.xls* in the *project* directory of the *Excel Student Resource Disk (Part 2)*.

1. **The loan balance** is the amount of the loan minus the down payment that you pay yourself without a bank's help. Your ability to make a large down payment can save you money on the cost of a mortgage. A large down payment usually has these advantages:

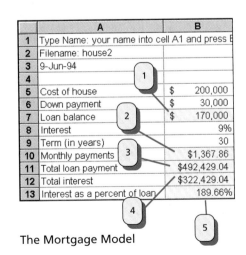

	A	B
1	Type Name: your name into cell A1 and press E	
2	Filename: house2	
3	9-Jun-94	
4		
5	Cost of house	$ 200,000
6	Down payment	$ 30,000
7	Loan balance	$ 170,000
8	Interest	9%
9	Term (in years)	30
10	Monthly payments	$1,367.86
11	Total loan payment	$492,429.04
12	Total interest	$322,429.04
13	Interest as a percent of loan	189.66%

The Mortgage Model

- ▸ You may find it easier to obtain a loan.
- ▸ You may be able to get a loan at a more reasonable rate of interest.
- ▸ Your total interest expense will be lower.
- ▸ Your equity in your home will be greater.

On a 25-year, 12-percent loan, every $1,000 of down payment decreases the amount of total interest paid by about $2,160. For example, if you make a down payment of $10,000, the cost of interest over the 25-year period amounts to about $129,580. If you make a down payment of $20,000, the total cost of interest is about $107,990.

2. **The monthly payment** is calculated by a function using the term in months instead of years and the interest rate divided by 12 so it's also in months.

   - ▸ The interest rate you agree to pay affects the total cost of your loan. Because the amount borrowed is large and repayment extends over many years, a variation of one-half of 1 percent can make a big difference. For example, on a 30-year, $50,000 mortgage, you would pay about $6,960 more in interest on a 12fi-percent loan than on a 12-percent loan.

   - ▸ The term is the length of time you take to repay a loan, and it has a bearing on the amount of interest you pay. The shorter the time taken to repay the loan, the lower the total cost of interest to you; the longer the time to repay, the higher the total cost. The advantage of spreading payments over a long period is the smaller monthly payment, which may make financing easier for you because it leaves more for current living. The disadvantage is the larger amount paid out in interest for the loan. When the annual rate is 12 percent, the total interest paid on a loan repaid in 20 years is about one-half more than the amount of the original loan, and in 25 years, it will almost double the original loan. If you take as long as 30 years to repay, the amount you pay in interest is almost triple the amount of the original loan.

3. **The total loan payment** is the monthly payment times the number of months that you must pay it.

4. **Total interest** if the *total loan payment* minus the *loan balance*.

5. **Interest as a percent of loan** is calculated the way you calculate any percentage.

4-3. The Computer System Pricing Model

Over the past few years, the power of desktop computers has increased dramatically. At the same time, the power required by newer programs such as Microsoft Windows has increased just as dramatically. Many new programs require a great deal of memory and hard disk storage, as well as a fast processor to operate well. In addition, a number of useful peripheral devices, such as scanners and CD-ROM disks, have dropped in price to where they are now affordable for many business and personal applications.

	A	B
1	Type **Name: your name** into cell A1 and press **Ent**	
2	Filename: compsys	
3	11-Nov-94	
4		
5	Computer System Quote	
6	Element	Price
7	*Hardware*	
8	Basic system	$ 1,500
9	Display monitor--upgrade to 17"	400
10	RAM-additional	400
11	Printer	600
12	Tape backup	150
13	Surge protector	25
14	Modem/fax card	100
15	Multimedia soundcard and speakers	150
16	CD-ROM drive	250
17	Scanner	900
18	Other	
19	*Software*	
20	Word processor	250
21	Spreadsheet	250
22	Graphics program	450
23	Database program	300
24	Desktop publishing program	600
25	Other	
26	*Total System Costs & Financing*	
27	Hardware and software cost	$ 6,325
28	Down payment	2,000
29	Interest rate	12.0%
30	Period (in months)	48
31	Loan balance	4,325
32	Monthly payment	113.89

The Computer System Model

Before you purchase a system, you should carefully analyze your needs over the next five years and buy a system you won't outgrow. Because new programs require more sophisticated systems, older computers can be purchased for less than $1,000. If you don't anticipate needing newer programs, one of these systems can be a great buy. However, if you plan to use the latest software, or to use your computer for applications such as graphics or desktop publishing, a more powerful and more expensive system may be cheaper in the long run.

Open the model *compsys.xls* stored in the *project* directory of the *Excel Student Resource Disk (Part 2)*. This model contains all of the text and numbers you'll need but none of the formulas or formats. The finished model is shown in the figure "The Computer Systems Model" and its formulas are indicated on the illustration and described below. Using these descriptions and formatting commands, make your model look just like the one illustrated. When finished, change the price of the basic system to $1,250, save the workbook, and make a printout.

1. **Hardware and software cost** is the sum of all of the individual costs.

2. **Loan balance** is the total hardware and software cost minus the down payment.

3. **The monthly payment** is calculated by the PMT function based on the given *Interest rate* (divided by 12), *Period (in months)*, and *Loan balance* (expressed as a negative value).

PicTorial 5

Exploring Workbooks, Charts, and Macros

After completing this PicTorial, you will be able to:

▶ Manage the sheets in a workbook

▶ Create and modify embedded charts

▶ Create and modify chart sheets

▶ Use different types of charts to best represent your data

▶ Record and play back macros

Entering data on a single sheet gives you a powerful analytical tool. However, Excel allows you to store a number of related sheets together in the same workbook and to chart that data on those worksheets. Finally, you can record keystrokes and play them back to automate repetitive tasks. These features greatly expand on the power and ease of use of the program.

5-1. MANAGING A WORKBOOK

When building models, it's important for you to know how to manage workbooks. You can rename sheets, add and delete them, or copy and move them. Normally, only one sheet is selected. This is called the *active sheet*. Any data that you type is entered into the active sheet. You can select another sheet by clicking its tab with the mouse.

QUICKSTEPS: MANAGING A WORKBOOK
Opening New Workbooks

▶ To open a new workbook, pull down the **File** menu and click the **New** command.

Renaming Sheets

▶ To rename a sheet, double-click its tab to display the Rename Sheet dialog box. Type the new name into the **Name** text box and click the **OK** command button.

Moving Around a Workbook with the Keyboard

▶ Press [Ctrl]+[PageDown] to move to the next sheet.

▶ Press [Ctrl]+[Page Up] to move to the previous sheet.

Moving Around a Workbook with the Tab Scrolling Buttons

▶ Click the two end buttons to move to the first and last sheets.

▶ Click the two middle buttons to move forward or backward one sheet.

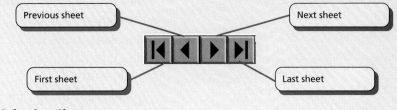

Selecting Sheets

▶ Click a sheet's tab to select it.

(continued on next page)

QUICKSTEPS: MANAGING A WORKBOOK (CONTINUED)

▶ To select a series of adjacent sheets, click the first and then hold down ⇧Shift while you click the last.

▶ To select a series of nonadjacent sheets, click the first and then hold down Ctrl while you click others.

Inserting and Deleting Sheets

▶ To insert a sheet, click the tab on the sheet to the right of where you wanted it inserted, pull down the **Insert** menu, and click the **Worksheet** command.

▶ To delete a sheet, click its tab to make it the active sheet, then pull down the **Edit** menu and click the **Delete Sheet** command. A dialog box warns you that the sheet will be permanently deleted. Click **OK** to delete it or **Cancel** to leave it undeleted.

Copying and Moving Sheets by Dragging and Dropping

▶ To copy a sheet, point to its tab, hold down Ctrl and the left mouse button, and drag the page icon to the tab you want it to be copied in front of. Release the mouse button to copy the sheet. The new sheet will have the same name as the original, but it will be followed by a number indicating which copy it is.

▶ To move a sheet, point to its tab, hold down the left mouse button, and drag the page icon to the tab you want it to be moved in front of. Release the mouse button to move the sheet.

TUTORIAL

In this tutorial you are introduced to managing a workbook and tasks such as renaming, moving, copying, and deleting sheets. The model you use is a master budget where one sheet summarizes a number of regional budgets.

Getting Started

1. Open the *mstbudgt.xls* workbook stored in the *tutorial* directory on the *Excel Student Resource Disk (Part 1)* and enter your name into cell A1.

Changing the Active Sheet

2. Click each of the first five sheet tabs (*Sheet1* through *Sheet5*) one after the other to make each sheet active so you can see what's on it. Then click the *Sheet1* tab to again make that the active sheet.

Renaming Sheets

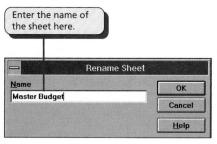

Step 3

3. Double-click the tab for *Sheet1* to display the Rename Sheet dialog box, type **Master Budget** into the **Name** text box, and then click the **OK** command button. The name appears on the sheet tab (see the margin illustration).

4. Double-click the tab for *Sheet2* to display the Rename Sheet dialog box, type **East** into the **Name** text box, and then click the **OK** command button.

5. Double-click the tab for *Sheet3* to display the Rename Sheet dialog box, type **West** into the **Name** text box, and then click the **OK** command button.

6. Double-click the tab for *Sheet4* to display the Rename Sheet dialog box, type **Southeast** into the **Name** text box, and then click the **OK** command button.

7. Double-click the tab for *Sheet5* to display the Rename Sheet dialog box, type **Southwest** into the **Name** text box, and then click the **OK** command button.

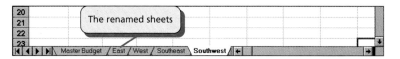

Moving Sheets

8. Point to the *East* tab and hold down the left mouse button. A downward pointing arrowhead appears on the tab, and a sheet of paper appears on the mouse pointer.

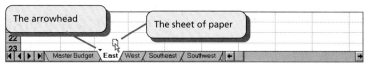

9. Drag the mouse pointer to the left side of the *Southwest* tab (the downward pointing arrowhead shows where the sheet will move to—between the *Southeast* and *Southwest* sheets) and release the mouse button.

Copying Sheets

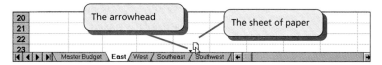

10. Point to the *East* tab again, hold down Ctrl and the left mouse button (the sheet of paper attached to the mouse pointer displays a plus sign to indicate you are copying). Drag a copy of it back to its original position—release the mouse button with the downward pointing arrowhead positioned between the *Master Budget* and *West* tabs. The copy is named *East (2)*.

Using Tab Scrolling Buttons

11. Explore moving through the 16 sheets using the tab-scrolling buttons. Click the two end buttons to move to the first and last sheets and the two middle buttons to move forward or backward one sheet.

Deleting a Sheet

12. Click the *Sheet6* tab, pull down the **Edit** menu, and click the **Delete Sheet** command. A dialog box asks you to confirm the deletion (see the margin illustration).

13. Click the **OK** command button to delete the sheet.

Selecting and Deleting Multiple Sheets

14. *Sheet7* should already be selected, but if it isn't, click its tab.

15. Click the right end tab-scrolling button to move to the last sheet, hold down ⇧ Shift, and click the *Sheet16* tab. Sheets 7 through 16 are now selected and have white tabs (see the illustration on the next page).

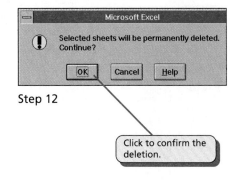

Step 12

Click to confirm the deletion.

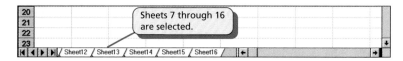

16. Pull down the **Edit** menu and click the **Delete Sheet** command. A dialog box asks you to confirm the deletion.

17. Click the **OK** command button to delete the selected sheets.

Finishing Up

18. Save the workbook to save the names you assigned to sheets, and then close it.

5-2. CREATING EMBEDDED CHARTS

Excel can create charts of the data on your worksheets. The power of a chart is that it plots the values stored in a range of cells and remains linked to those cells. This way, when any of the values in those cells are changed, the chart immediately and automatically reflects those changes. This makes charts powerful analytical tools since you can explore changes in your model graphically instead of trying to interpret columns or rows of numbers.

When you create a chart, you can embed it on the same sheet as the data that it's based on or put it on a page by itself. The first type of chart is called an embedded chart and the second a chart sheet. In this section, we introduce the embedded chart. To create an embedded chart, you use Excel's ChartWizard. After you select the data you want to plot, the ChartWizard guides you through the process of creating the chart.

SELECTING CHART RANGES

Since the only step where the ChartWizard doesn't guide you is in selecting the data, let's look at this procedure. Data that you chart on most charts has two axes—a value axis against which numbers are plotted, and a category axis that contains the labels for the data being plotted. For many charts the value axis is what is called the Y or vertical axis, and the category axis is called the X or horizontal axis.

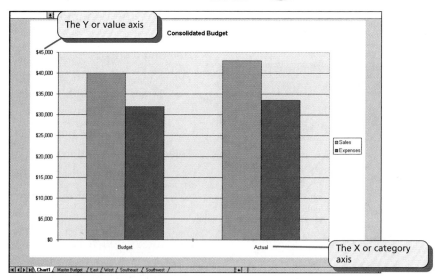

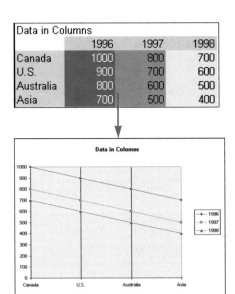

Data in Columns

	1996	1997	1998
Canada	1000	800	700
U.S.	900	700	600
Australia	800	600	500
Asia	700	500	400

When you specify that data is in columns, the first column is used to label the category axis (the countries), and data from each of the three data columns is plotted against those labels. The first cell in each column is used as a label in the legends box to identify the data series.

The data that is plotted is taken from cells on rows or in columns. The data in each row or column forms a data series, and all of the points in a data series are shown on the chart in the same color or pattern. Different data series are shown in different colors or patterns so they can be distinguished from one another. A data series can be best seen in a line chart since a line connects each of the points that represents one of the values in the series.

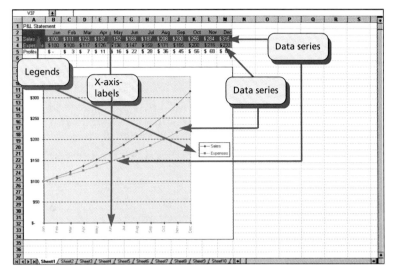

When you create a model to be used for a chart, the data normally takes the form of a table. When you chart this data, you can select which way the data series are oriented—whether they are in columns or rows. When you are creating the chart, Excel will guess at which way the data series run, but you can change its guess.

If you tell Excel the data series are in columns, it uses the top cell in each column as a legend and the text or values in the leftmost column as category axis labels. If you tell Excel the data series are in rows, it uses the left cell on each row as a legend and the text or values in the top row as category axis labels (see the margin illustration).

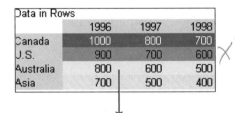

Data in Rows

	1996	1997	1998
Canada	1000	800	700
U.S.	900	700	600
Australia	800	600	500
Asia	700	500	400

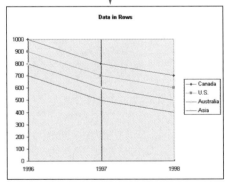

When you specify that data is in rows, the first row is used to label the category axis (the years) and data from each of the four data rows is plotted against those labels. The first cell in each row is used as a label in the legends box to identify the data series.

TIPS: SELECTING CHART RANGES

▶ Include row and column headings in the selection if you want category axis labels and legends.

▶ Select nonadjacent rows or columns by selecting the first, then holding down Ctrl while you select each of the others. Each row or column to be plotted must have the same number of cells.

▶ If there are rows or columns that you do not want included in a chart, you can set their height or width to zero to hide them. (See Section 2-10, "Adjusting Column Widths and Row Heights.")

USING THE CHARTWIZARD

After selecting the ranges to be plotted, you can use the ChartWizard to lead you step by step through a series of dialog boxes. In each of these boxes, you can check, and if you want to, change any of Excel's guesses about how your chart should be presented. In addition, you can add optional items such as legends and titles to make your chart more understandable to yourself and others. As you create the chart, a sample of it is shown in the dialog box so you have a preview of the finished chart.

The ChartWizard button

QUICKSTEPS: CREATING EMBEDDED CHARTS

1. Select the ranges for the chart as described in the section "Selecting Chart Ranges."

2. Click the **ChartWizard** button on the toolbar, or pull down the **Insert** menu, click the **Chart** command to cascade the menu, and then click **On This Sheet** to display the mouse pointer as a cross hair with a chart attached.

3. Point to the upper-left corner of where you want the chart to appear. Hold down the left mouse button, and drag the box to the size and shape that you want the chart to be. Release the mouse button to display the first ChartWizard dialog box.

4. Follow the instructions as you proceed through the ChartWizard dialog boxes described in the box "Understanding the ChartWizard."

5. When the chart is finished, click anywhere outside of the chart to unselect it and return the menu bar commands to normal (they change to chart-specific commands when a chart is selected).

UNDERSTANDING THE CHARTWIZARD

Excel's ChartWizard makes creating charts a simple-to-follow step-by-step process. When the ChartWizard dialog boxes are displayed, click the <**Back** or **Next**> command buttons to move through the series of dialog boxes and make choices as you go. When the chart is the way you like it, click the **Finish** button. If you want to quit at any point, click **Cancel** or click **Help** for help.

Step 1 of 5 is where you confirm that you selected the correct range.

Step 2 of 5 is where you select a chart type by clicking a graphic image of it. The default chart type is a column chart.

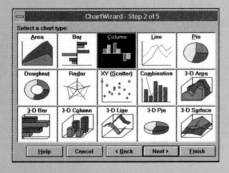

Step 3 of 5 is where you select a format by clicking a graphic image of it. The choices on this dialog box vary depending on the type of chart you selected in Step 2. The default format has gridlines.

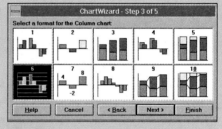

Step 4 of 5 is where you confirm or change Excel's guess about your data.

▸ **Data series in** specifies if the data series run along **Rows** or down **Columns**.

▸ **Use First Row(s)** and **Use First Column(s)** specifies what rows or columns are to be used for such chart elements as titles, legends, and category axis labels. The choices vary with the chart type.

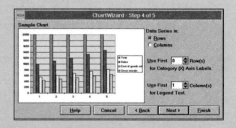

Step 5 of 5 is where you specify if the chart is to have a legend and where you type in titles for the chart and the category and value axes. The default chart has legends added.

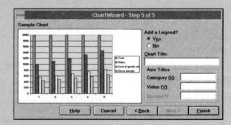

TUTORIAL

In this tutorial you use the ChartWizard to create an embedded chart of the five-year plan model. The chart will show the relationship between cost of goods and gross margin.

Getting Started

1. Open the *5yrplan.xls* workbook stored in the *tutorial* directory on the *Excel Student Resource Disk (Part 1)*.

2. Change the numbers in the variables section if they are not $1,000 as the initial sales (cell B6), 10% as the sales growth rate (cell B7), and 56% as cost of goods sold (cell B8).

Creating the Chart

3. Select cells A11 to F11, then hold down Ctrl and select cells A13 to F14. Release Ctrl and the mouse button, and the selected cells remain highlighted.

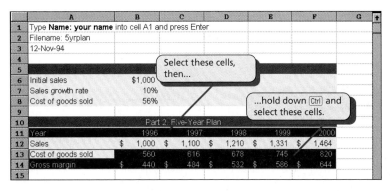

4. Click the **ChartWizard** button on the toolbar. The selected cells are highlighted by moving borders, and the mouse pointer turns into a cross hair with a chart symbol.

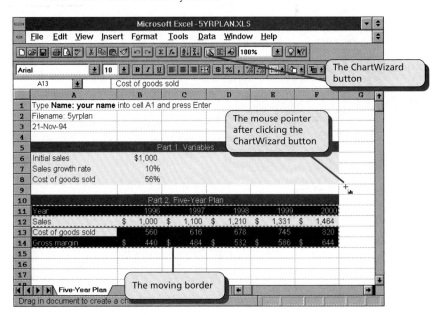

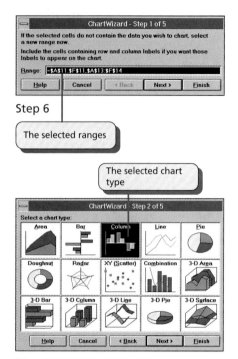

Step 6

The selected ranges

The selected chart type

Step 7

The selected format

Step 8

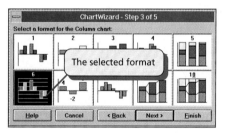

Three data series are plotted.

Step 9

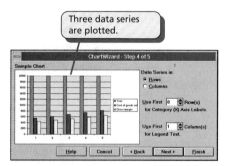

Two date series

Set to 1.

Step 10

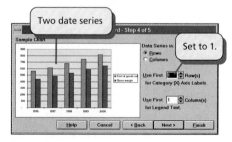

5. Point to the upper-left corner of cell A16 and hold down the left mouse button. Drag the mouse pointer to the lower right corner of cell D30 to draw a box where you want the chart to appear. (The screen will scroll for you when you drag against the lower window border.)

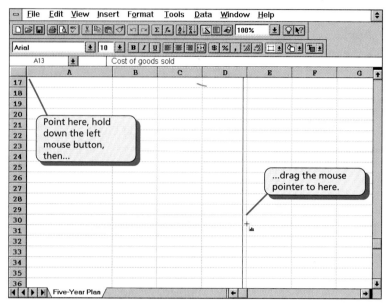

Point here, hold down the left mouse button, then...

...drag the mouse pointer to here.

6. Release the mouse button to display the ChartWizard *Step 1 of 5* dialog box. The **Range** text box lists the two ranges that you selected for the chart (see the margin illustration).

7. Click the **Next>** command button to display the *Step 2 of 5* dialog box illustrating chart types you can use; the **Column** type should be selected.

8. Click the **Next>** command button to display the *Step 3 of 5* dialog box illustrating formats you can use; number 6 should be selected.

9. Click the **Next>** command button to display the *Step 4 of 5* dialog box illustrating a sample chart. It shows three data series when you only selected two.

10. Click the up spin arrow (⬆) on the box for **Use First 0 Row(s) for Category [X] Axis Labels** to change it to 1. Immediately, the Y-axis changes and only two bars are plotted for each period.

11. Click the **Next>** command button to display the *Step 5 of 5* dialog box. Click in the **Chart Title** text box to move the insertion point there, and type **Five-Year Plan**.

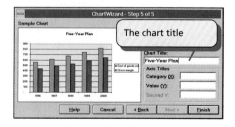

The chart title

12. Click the **Finish** command button to display the chart on the worksheet, as shown on the next page.

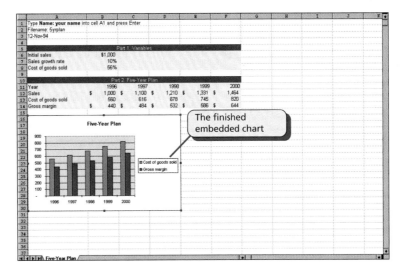

The finished embedded chart

Finishing Up

13. Click the **Save** button on the toolbar to save your changes.

14. Click the **Print Preview** button on the toolbar to see how the table and chart will appear when printed. (Displaying this preview may take a few moments.)

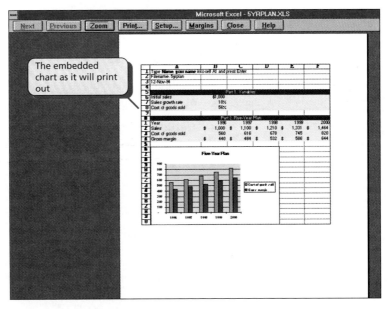

The embedded chart as it will print out

15. If you have time to print the sheet (this can take a long time on some systems), click the **Print** button on the preview screen; or click the **Close** command button to return to the document.

16. Close the workbook.

5-3. MOVING, SIZING, AND DELETING EMBEDDED CHARTS

After embedding a chart on a worksheet, you may find that it isn't the right size or in the right place. To refine its layout, you can drag it to a new position or drag one of its corners or sides to shrink or enlarge it. To

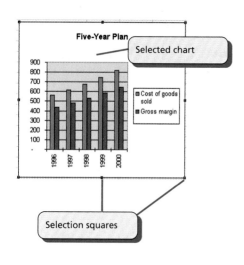

Five-Year Plan

Selected chart

Selection squares

move, size, or even delete a chart, you must first select it. To do so, click anywhere in the chart. When you do so, *selection squares* appear on the top and bottom, sides, and corners of a frame around the chart.

QUICKSTEPS: MOVING, SIZING, AND DELETING EMBEDDED CHARTS

▸ To move a selected chart, point anywhere in the chart, hold down the left button, and drag the chart to where you want it. As you drag it, a dotted border indicates its new position. To drop the box into position, release the mouse button.

▸ To size a selected chart (and retain its proportions), point to any corner selection square until the mouse pointer turns into a diagonal two-headed arrow. Then hold down ⇧Shift and the mouse button, and drag the corner in and up or out and down to shrink or expand the size of the chart. When the chart is the size you want it, release the mouse button.

▸ To change a selected chart's proportions, point to any selection square until the mouse pointer turns into a two-headed arrow. Then hold down the mouse button, and drag the top or bottom up or down or a corner or side in and out. When the chart is the shape you want it, release the mouse button.

▸ To deleted a selected chart, press Delete. (If you find you have made a mistake, immediately click the **Undo** button on the toolbar.)

TUTORIAL

In this tutorial you size and move the embedded chart that you created on the five-year plan in the previous section.

Getting Started

1. Open the *5yrplan.xls* workbook stored in the *tutorial* directory on the *Excel Student Resource Disk (Part 1)*.

Sizing the Chart

2. To change the size and proportions of the chart, point to the lower-right corner of the chart until the mouse pointer turns into a diagonal two-headed arrow. Then hold down the mouse button, and drag the corner in and up or out and down to shrink or expand the size of the chart. When it's a size and shape you like, release the mouse button. Then click the **Undo** button on the toolbar to undo the change.

3. To change the size but retain the proportions of the chart, point to the lower-right corner of the chart until the mouse pointer turns into a diagonal two-headed arrow. Then hold down ⇧Shift and the mouse button, and drag the corner in and up or out and down to shrink or expand the size of the chart while retaining its proportions. When it's a size about four columns wide, release the mouse button.

Moving the Chart

4. Point anywhere in the chart, hold down the left mouse button, and drag the outline of the chart so it's centered under the model.

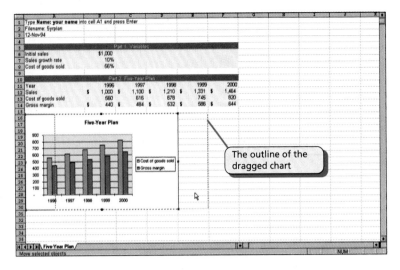

5. Release the mouse button to drop the chart into position.

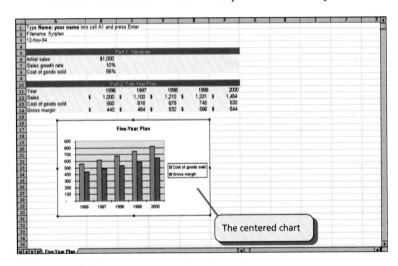

Finishing Up

6. Click the **Save** button on the toolbar to save your changes.

7. Click the **Print Preview** button on the toolbar to see how the resized and moved chart will appear when printed. (Displaying this preview may take a few moments.)

8. If you have time to print the sheet (this can take a long time on some systems), click the **Print** button on the preview screen; or click the **Close** command button to return to the document without printing the chart.

9. Close the workbook.

5-4. CREATING CHART SHEETS

When you don't want a chart embedded on the same worksheet as the data it is based on, you can create it on its own sheet in the workbook. You create a chart sheet the same way you create an embedded chart, with one exception: you must use the **Chart** command on the **Insert** menu and specify that the chart be on a new sheet.

Chart sheets are initially named Chart1, Chart2, and so on, but you can change the name. To do so, double-click the sheet's tab to display the Rename Sheet dialog box. Type the new name into the **Name** text box and click the **OK** command button

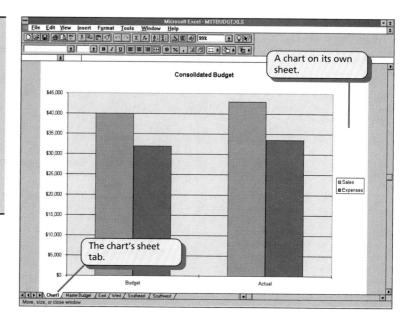

A chart on its own sheet.

The chart's sheet tab.

TIP: CREATING A NEW CHART SHEET— FASTER THAN A SPEEDING BULLET

After selecting the ranges to be plotted, press F11 to create a new chart sheet immediately. The ChartWizard appears only when Excel needs more information to create the chart.

QUICKSTEPS: CREATING CHART SHEETS

1. Select the ranges for the chart as described in the section "Selecting Chart Ranges" in Section 5-2, "Creating Embedded Charts."
2. Pull down the **Insert** menu, click **Chart** to cascade the menu, and then click **As New Sheet** to display the first ChartWizard dialog box.
3. Follow the instructions as you proceed through the ChartWizard dialog boxes described in the box "Understanding the ChartWizard" in Section 5-2, "Creating Embedded Charts."

QUICKSTEPS: DELETING A CHART SHEET

1. Click the sheet's tab to make it active.
2. Pull down the **Edit** menu and click the **Delete Sheet** command. When a dialog box asks you to confirm the deletion, click the **OK** command button.

TUTORIAL

In this tutorial you create a chart of the master budget on its own sheet. The chart will show the relationship between budgeted and actual sales and expenses so you can easily compare them.

Getting Started

1. Open the *mstbudgt.xls* workbook stored in the *tutorial* directory on the *Excel Student Resource Disk (Part 1)*.

Creating the Chart

2. With the *Master Budget* sheet active (click its sheet tab if necessary), select cells A6 through C8, then pull down the **Insert** menu, and click the **Chart** command to cascade the menu.

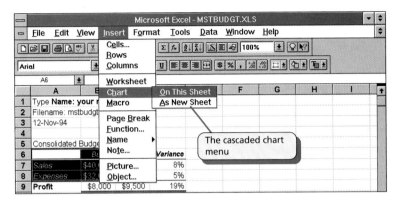

Step 3

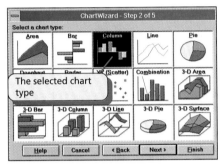

Step 4

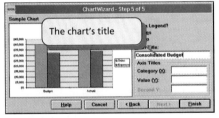

Step 7

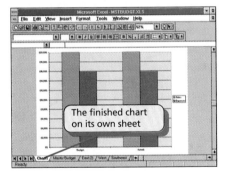

Step 8

3. Click the **As New Sheet** command to display the ChartWizard *Step 1 of 5* dialog box. The **Range** text box lists the range that you selected for the chart (see the margin illustration).

4. Click the **Next>** command button to display the *Step 2 of 5* dialog box illustrating chart types you can use; the **Column** type should be selected (see the margin illustration).

5. Click the **Next>** command button to display the *Step 3 of 5* dialog box illustrating formats you can use; number 6 should be selected.

6. Click the **Next>** command button to display the *Step 4 of 5* dialog box showing a sample chart.

7. Click the **Next>** command button to display the *Step 5 of 5* dialog box showing a sample chart again. Click in the **Chart Title** text box to move the insertion point there, and type **Consolidated Budget** (see the margin illustration).

8. Click the **Finish** command button to display the chart on the worksheet (see the margin illustration).

Finishing Up

9. Click the **Save** button on the toolbar to save your changes.

10. Click the **Print Preview** button on the toolbar to see how the sheet and chart will appear when printed. (Displaying this preview may take a few moments.) Notice how the chart has automatically incorporated the text you selected in the model along with the numbers.

11. If you have time to print the sheet (this can take a long time on some systems), click the **Print** button on the preview screen; or click the **Close** command button to return to the document.

12. Close the workbook.

5-5. EDITING AND REVISING CHARTS

Excel offers you a lot of control over the way your data is presented on a chart. You can add new elements, revise existing ones, or add formats such as font changes, boxes, and borders.

ACTIVATING A CHART

To make any changes to a chart you have created, you must first activate it. This allows you to select elements within the chart and changes the

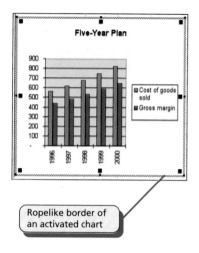

Ropelike border of an activated chart

menus to list chart commands. To activate an embedded chart, double-click it. When it is activated, its border changes from a thin line to a ropelike blue border. To activate a chart page, click its tab. It's activated when it's displayed and its tab is white.

When a chart is active, the menu bar and menu commands change to those you use to work with charts. (To deactivate a chart and return the menu bar to normal, click anywhere outside of an embedded chart or click any other tab in the workbook.)

ADDING ELEMENTS TO AN ACTIVATED CHART

Once you have activated a chart, you can add elements to it that may be missing. These include titles, data labels, legends, axes, and gridlines.

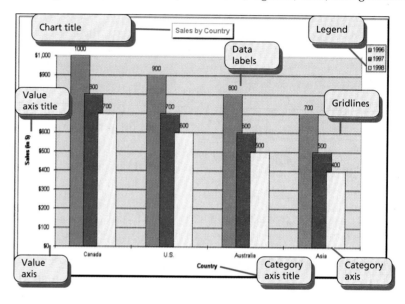

QUICKSTEPS: ADDING ELEMENTS TO AN ACTIVATED CHART

1. Activate the chart and then pull down the **Insert** menu.
2. Select any of the commands described in the box "Understanding the Insert Menu."

TIP: TRANSFERRING TITLES FROM THE WORKSHEET TO A CHART WITH CELL REFERENCES

You can use text that you enter into worksheet cells as titles for your chart or as legends. This makes it easy to revise the chart because changing the labels in the worksheet cells changes the chart automatically. To refer to cells, select the text box on the chart and then type the reference to the sheet name and cell on the formula bar. For example, to refer to text in cell A1 or a sheet named Sheet1, type **=Sheet!A1** and press [Enter ↵]. Once you establish such a link, you can only edit the text in the cell it's linked to—not on the chart itself.

UNDERSTANDING THE INSERT MENU

To add elements to a chart, pull down the **Insert** menu and then click any of the following commands:

Titles displays the Titles dialog box. When you turn the check boxes on (⊠) and then click the **OK** command button, the placeholder terms *Title*, *X*, and *Y* appear on the chart. Click one to select it, and then click again to delete it and enter your own title.

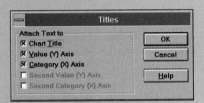

Axes displays the Axes dialog box. Check either or both Axes check boxes to turn them on (⊠) or off (☐) and then click the **OK** command button. When they are off, tick marks and labels are not displayed.

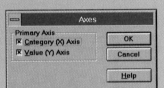

Data Labels displays the Data Labels dialog box. Click any of the available option buttons (◉) and then click the **OK** command button. The selected data labels will appear above the data points they refer to.

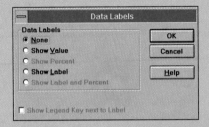

Legend inserts the legend to the right of the chart area.

Gridlines displays the Gridlines dialog box. Click any check boxes to display major or minor gridlines extending from the category or value axis, and then click the **OK** command button.

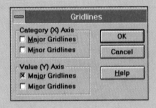

EDITING AND FORMATTING ELEMENTS OF AN ACTIVATED CHART

Once you have activated a chart, you can click any element in it to select it. The parts you can select include those shown in box "Chart Parts You Can Select" on the next page. The name of the selected element is displayed in the Name box on the formula bar. Selection handles will also appear on the element within the chart.

To edit a text item, click it once to select it and then click it again to move the insertion point into it. Then edit it just as you would any other text.

To format an item, double-click it to display a relevant dialog box. You can also click it to select it, and then pull down the **Format** menu. On this menu, click the topmost command that begins **Selected** followed by the name of the item you have selected. This displays a tabbed dialog box containing the formatting commands you can use (the commands vary depending on what you have selected).

 TIP: SELECTING WITH THE KEYBOARD

Press the arrow keys to move the selection from item to item on the chart. Press ⬆ and ⬇ to move from item to item. Press ⬅ and ➡ to move between items within a group.

CHART PARTS YOU CAN SELECT

When a chart is activated, you can click any of its elements to select it for formatting or revision. (To undo a selection, press [Esc].) To format the selected element, pull down the **Format** menu and click the **Selected** command. This command is always followed by the name of the selected element.

Selected Chart Area can have a border or pattern added, or you can change its fonts. To select the entire chart, click the chart when not pointing to a specific item.

Selected Plot Area can have a border or pattern added. To select the plot area to change its size or formatting, click anywhere in it except on a data marker.

Selected Data Series allows you to change patterns and add or remove data labels. You can also change the ranges plotted on the chart. To select a data series, click a data marker. Changes you then make affect the entire series. To select a single data marker in a series, select the series, and then click the data marker. Changes you then make affect only the selected marker.

Selected Chart Title or **Selected Axis** can have their pattern, font, or alignment changed. To select one of the titles, click it.

Selected Value Axis or **Category Axis** can have their pattern, font, number format, alignment, or scale changed. To select one of the axes, click it.

Selected Gridlines can have their pattern or scale changed. To select a gridline, click it.

Selected Legend can have its pattern, font, or placement changed. To select a legend box, click the box. To select a specific legend, select the legend box and then click the legend.

Selected Data Labels can have their pattern, font, number format, or alignment changed. To select data labels, click one.

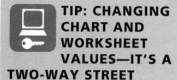

TIP: MOVING ACTIVATED EMBEDDED CHARTS

When you activate an embedded chart, you can only move it by dragging it by its border. However, if you drag one of the selection squares, you'll change its size rather than its position.

TIP: CHANGING CHART AND WORKSHEET VALUES—IT'S A TWO-WAY STREET

The values plotted on a chart are taken from the values in the worksheet cells to which the chart's data series are linked. Normally, to change a chart value, you would enter a revised number into the worksheet, and the chart would immediately change to reflect the new value. However, you can also select the data marker on the chart that you want to change and drag it up or down in value. As you do so, the corresponding number in the worksheet cell to which it's linked also changes.

ADDING DATA SERIES AND DATA POINTS

To add data series or data points to a chart, select the cells on the worksheet, drag them onto the chart, and release them.

TUTORIAL

In this tutorial you edit and revise the chart you created for the five-year plan. In doing so, you will revise the chart title and format the Y-axis values to display them as currency.

Getting Ready

1. Open the *5yrplan.xls* workbook stored in the *tutorial* directory on the *Excel Student Resource Disk (Part 1)*.

Revising the Chart Title

2. Double-click the embedded chart to activate it. When activated, it has a blue rope-like border around it.

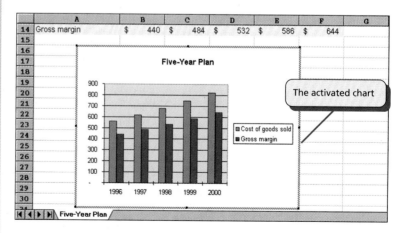

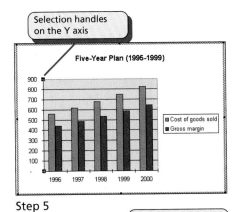

Selection handles on the Y axis

Step 5

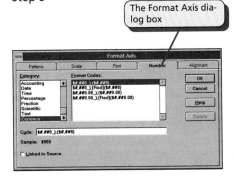

The Format Axis dialog box

Step 8

3. Click the chart title (*Five-Year Plan*) to select it and then click it again to move the insertion point into it. *Title* is displayed in the Name box on the formula bar indicating that is the chart element you have selected.

4. Press End to move the insertion point to the end of the title, press Spacebar, and type **(1995-1999)**.

Formatting the Y-Axis Values

5. Click the Y-axis (the vertical axis) to select it, and selection squares appear at the top and bottom of the axis. *Axis 1* is displayed in the Name box on the formula bar (see the upper margin illustration).

6. Press ↑ to scroll the selection handles through all of the selectable items in the chart. As you do so, watch the name of the selected items change in the Name box on the formula bar. When finished, press ↑ or ↓ to again display *Axis 1* in the Name box.

7. Pull down the **Format** menu and click the **Selected Axis** command to display the Format Axis dialog box.

8. Click the *Number* tab to display that dialog box, and then click *Currency* in the **Category** list (you'll have to scroll to see it—see the lower margin illustration).

9. Click *$#,##0_);($#,##0)* on the **Format Codes** list, and then click the **OK** command button to format the axis with dollar signs.

10. Click the **Save** button on the toolbar to save your changes.

11. Click the **Print Preview** button on the toolbar to see how the resized and moved chart will appear when printed. (Displaying this preview may take a few moments.)

12. If you have time to print the sheet (this can take a long time on some systems), click the **Print** button on the preview screen; or click the **Close** command button to return to the document.

PAUSING FOR PRACTICE

Continue selecting other elements on the chart, then pull down the **Format** menu and click the **Selected** command to change formats for the element. Don't worry about making mistakes since you'll close the workbook without saving it. Explore how the various formats affect the look of the chart.

Finishing Up

13. Close the workbook without saving your changes.

5-6. EXPLORING CHART TYPES AND AUTOFORMATS

One of the most important decisions you make when creating charts is what chart type to use. Excel has fifteen basic chart types and many subtypes. Choosing the right type determines how well your data is conveyed. Many chart types include normal 2-D versions and more graphic 3-D versions that use depth to add emphasis.

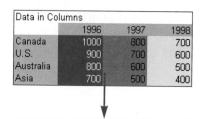

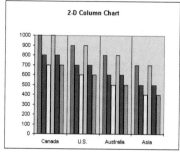

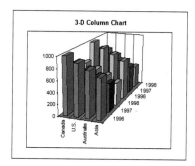

2-D and 3-D Charts

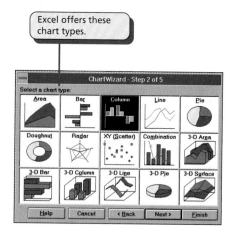

There are two ways to change a chart type: using the **Chart Type** or **AutoFormat** commands on the **Format** menu.

> **QUICKSTEPS: CHANGING CHART TYPES WITH THE FORMAT MENU**
>
> 1. Double-click an embedded chart to activate it or click the tab of a chart sheet to make it active.
> 2. Pull down the **Format** menu and click the **Chart Type** command to display the Chart Type dialog box.
>
>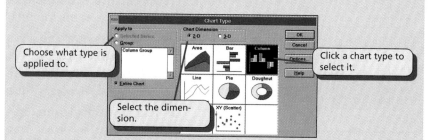
>
>
> 3. Click a type to select it, and then click the **OK** command button. If you select one or more data series in the chart before using this command, the **Selected Series** option button will be turned on (◉) in the dialog box and the chart type you select will be applied only to the selection.

Excel's AutoFormat command recognizes various parts of a chart and applies stored formats to them automatically.

> **QUICKSTEPS: CHANGING FORMATS AND CHART TYPES WITH THE AUTOFORMAT COMMAND**
>
> 1. Double-click an embedded chart to activate it or click the tab of a chart sheet to make it active.
> 2. Pull down the **Format** menu and click the **AutoFormat** command to display the AutoFormat dialog box.
>
>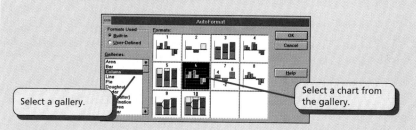
>
> 3. Click any chart type on the **Galleries** list to display the **Formats** palette of subtypes. Click the format you want to use, and then click the **OK** command button to apply it to the activated chart. The format you apply with this command does not affect the data in the chart, but it changes the look of the chart and overrides any chart formatting you may have already applied.

STANDARD TYPES OF CHARTS

Excel has fifteen basic chart types with a number of variations of each.

The chart type you choose should depend on the kind of data you are plotting. Normally it will be one of two types: discrete or continuous data.

Discrete data are values representing specific periods of time or other units.

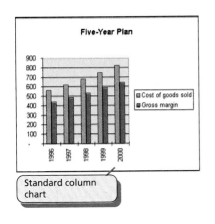

Standard column chart

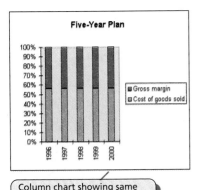

Column chart showing same data as parts of the whole

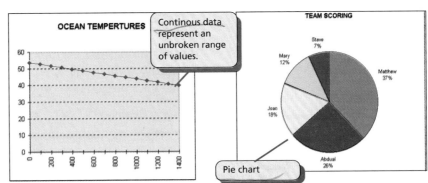

Continuous data represent an unbroken range of values.

Pie chart

Discrete data consist of values measured at a series of selected points. When plotted on a chart, all data between those points are meaningless. Charts of this kind are frequently called time-series charts and are used in business to plot sales, profits, inventory, and other important financial values. The best chart types to use for this kind of data include bar and column charts.

Continuous data occur when measurements have been sampled to determine a trend. Although each data point is a discrete value, the points are sampled so that when plotted, values between the measured data points can be estimated from the chart. This estimation of values falling between the points that were actually measured and plotted is called interpolation. When charting continuous data, a general rule is that the more data points you measure and plot, the more accurate the chart is. The best chart types to use for this kind of data include line and area charts.

Percentages of a whole data are those where you have a data series that contains parts equaling a significant whole such as sales of various products in a product line and market shares. When you have only one data series, the best chart for this kind of data is a pie chart where the pie represents "the whole" or 100 percent, and the individual slices represent parts of the whole. The relative sizes of the parts are indicated by the sizes of the pie slices.

When you have more than one data series, you can create a pie chart for each series or plot them on a 100% bar or column chart where Excel will convert each data point to a percentage of the whole. You can also use a doughnut chart which plots data series in concentric circles.

TIP: LOGARITHMIC SCALES

Logarithmic scales on charts allow you to plot very large and very small values on the same chart. To create a log scale, double-click the value axis to display the Format Axis dialog box. Click the *Scale* tab, click the **Logarithmic Scale** check box to turn it on (⊠), and then click the **OK** command button.

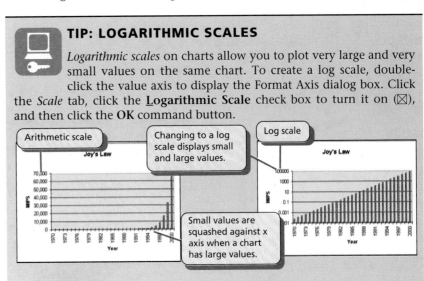

Arithmetic scale

Changing to a log scale displays small and large values.

Log scale

Small values are squashed against x axis when a chart has large values.

TUTORIAL

In this tutorial you explore how to change chart types and how to automatically format charts. Both of these procedures make it possible to refine your presentation so your data is best illustrated.

Getting Ready

1. Open the *5yrplan.xls* workbook stored in the *tutorial* directory on the *Excel Student Resource Disk (Part 1)*.

Changing The Chart Type

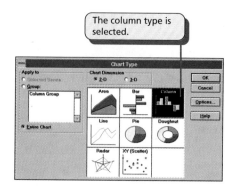

The column type is selected.

Step 3

2. Double-click the chart to activate it, and its border changes to a blue ropelike pattern.

3. Pull down the **Format** menu and click the **Chart Type** command to display the Chart Type dialog box. The *Column* chart type should be selected (see the top margin illustration).

4. Click the **Options** command button to display the Format Column Group dialog box. Click the *Subtype* tab to display that dialog box, then click the second type from the left (stacked columns) in the **Subtype** window (see the middle margin illustration).

5. Click the **OK** command button to close the dialog box and display the chart in the new format.

Exploring AutoFormats

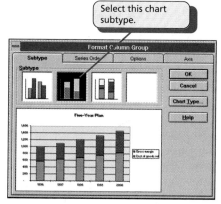

Select this chart subtype.

Step 4

6. With the chart still activated, pull down the **Format** menu and click the **AutoFormat** command to display the AutoFormat dialog box.

7. Click the *Bar* choice in the **Galleries** list to display a variety of bar chart types in the **Formats** section (see the bottom margin illustration).

8. Click number *4* to select it and then click the **OK** command button to change the chart.

9. Repeat Steps 6 through 8 but select these chart types:

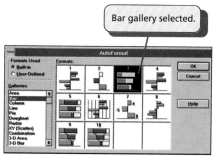

Bar gallery selected.

Step 7

Galleries	Formats
Bar	9
Area	4
3-D Bar	4
3-D Column	4

Finishing Up

10. Save, print, and close the workbook.

5-7. RECORDING AND PLAYING BACK MACROS

Macros are simply a way to store commands so that they can be played back later. They can save you from having to rekey repetitive data or commands. It is like making a piano into a player piano; the only difference is the computer's keys do not move up and down and the mouse doesn't move about—it is all done electronically. You use macros to quickly execute any sequence of commands that you find yourself doing over and over again. These might include such procedures as:

▸ Entering a heading (for example, entering your name in cell A1 on each new model that you retrieve).

▸ Formatting a range of cells as currency with zero decimal places

▸ Querying a list (lists are the subject of PicTorial 6)

▸ Adding borders and patterns to headings or changing their font

▸ Widening columns

To use a macro, you must first record it. You can then play it back by selecting its name from a menu or by clicking a button. To record a macro, you use Excel's Macro Recorder to create Visual Basic code. This code, like that used to create any program, contains commands that Excel can interpret and execute.

RECORDING MACROS

To record a macro, you turn recording on, enter the keystrokes or commands you want recorded, and then turn recording off.

The Stop button

QUICKSTEPS: RECORDING MACROS

1. Pull down the **Tools** menu and click the **Record Macro** command to cascade the menu.

2. Click the **Record New Macro** command to display the Record New Macro dialog box and begin recording.

3. Enter any of the commands described in the box "Understanding the Record New Macro Dialog Box."

4. Click the **OK** command button to begin recording the macro. The status bar reads *Ready Recording*, and the **Stop** button from the Visual Basic toolbox is displayed on the screen.

5. Execute the commands you want recorded.

6. Click the **Stop** button from the Visual Basic toolbox, or, pull down the **Tools** menu, click the **Record Macro** command to cascade the menu, and then click the **Stop Recording** command to end macro recording.

UNDERSTANDING THE RECORD NEW MACRO DIALOG BOX

When you use the command to record a macro, the Record New Macro dialog box appears. All of the settings in this box are optional, but it is recommended that you assign a name to the macro so you'll be able to recognize it later.

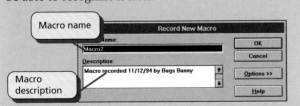

Macro Name text box is where you enter the name that will be listed when you use the command that runs macros. If you don't enter a name here, Excel will give

the macro a sequential name such as Macro1, Macro2, Macro3, and so on.

Description text box is where you enter a description of the macro so you'll know what it does when you look it up later. If you don't enter a description, Excel gives just the date and the name of the person who recorded it.

Command Buttons

Options button expands the dialog box to offer these choices.

Assign To Section

Menu Item on Tools Menu check box is where you click to add the macro to the **Tools** menu. (You can also do this later.) After clicking the check box, type the name of the macro as you want it to appear on the menu.

(Continued on next page)

UNDERSTANDING THE RECORD NEW MACRO DIALOG BOX (CONTINUED)

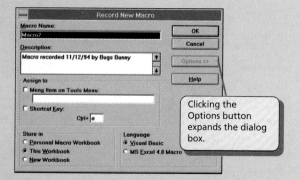

Clicking the Options button expands the dialog box.

Shortcut Key check box is where you click if you want to be able to execute the macro by holding down Ctrl while pressing one of the letter keys on the keyboard. After turning the check box on (⊠), enter the letter you want to assign the macro to in the **Ctrl+** text box.

Store In Section

Personal Macro Notebook option button, when on (◉), stores macros all on the same sheet in a hidden workbook. To see it, pull down the **Window** menu and click the **Unhide** command to display a list of hidden workbooks.

This Workbook option button, when on (◉), stores the macro's code on a sheet in the same workbook named Module1, Module2, and so on.

New Workbook option button, when on (◉), stores the macro's code in a separate workbook. To see it, pull down the **Window** menu and click its name at the bottom of the menu.

Language Section

Visual Basic option button, when on (◉), generates the macro using Visual Basic code and stores it on a sheet named *Module1, Module2,* and so on.

MS Excel 4.0 Macro option button, when on (◉), generates the macro in Excel's own specific language and stores it on a sheet named *Macro1, Macro2,* and so on.

PLAYING BACK MACROS

Once a macro has been recorded, you can play it back by selecting its name from a menu or by holding down Ctrl and pressing the letter you assigned it to if you specified a shortcut key in the **Ctrl+** text box when recording the macro.

QUICKSTEPS: PLAYING BACK MACROS

1. Pull down the **Tools** menu and click the **Macro** command to display the Macro dialog box.
2. Click the name of the macro you want to run in the **Macro Name/Reference** list to select it.
3. Click the **Run** command button.

TUTORIAL

In this tutorial you record and play back a macro that enters the three-line heading found at the top of all workbooks included with this text. You see how to run the macro using menu commands and also how to assign it to a keyboard key so you can execute it by holding down Ctrl while pressing that key.

Getting Started

1. Click the **New Worksheet** button on the toolbar to open a new document.

Recording a Macro

2. Pull down the **Tools** menu and click the **Record Macro** command to cascade the menu.

TIP: INTERRUPTING A RUNNING MACRO

If you find you are running the wrong macro, or want to stop it for some other reason, you can do so by pressing Esc. This will display the Macro Error dialog box. To close the dialog box, press Esc again or click the **End** command button.

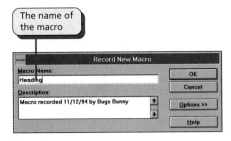

The name of the macro

Step 3

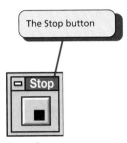

The Stop button

Stop

Step 6

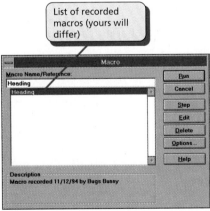

List of recorded macros (yours will differ)

Step 9

3. Click the **Record New Macro** command to display the Record New Macro dialog box (see the margin illustration).

4. Type **Heading** in the **Macro Name** text box, and then click the **OK** command button to begin recording the macro. The status bar reads *Ready Recording*, and the **Stop** button from the Visual Basic toolbox is displayed on the screen.

5. Execute the following commands so they are recorded.

   ▸ Press ⌊Ctrl⌋+⌊Home⌋ to select cell A1 (even if it is already selected).

   ▸ Type **Name:** press ⌊Spacebar⌋ and type your name.

   ▸ Press ⌊Enter ↵⌋ to select cell A2, and type **Filename: macro.xls**

   ▸ Press ⌊Enter ↵⌋ to select cell A3 and type **=NOW()** and press ⌊Enter ↵⌋.

   ▸ With cell A3 selected, pull down the **Format** menu and click the **Cells** command to display the Format Cells dialog box.

   ▸ Click the *Number* tab to display that dialog box, then click *Date* in the **Category** list.

   ▸ Click *d-mmm-yy* in the **Format Codes** list, and then click the **OK** command button.

6. Click the **Stop** button from the Visual Basic toolbox to end macro recording.

Displaying the Macro

7. Scroll the sheet tabs till you see *Sheet16*, and the one following it is named *Module1*. Click that tab to display the macro you just recorded.

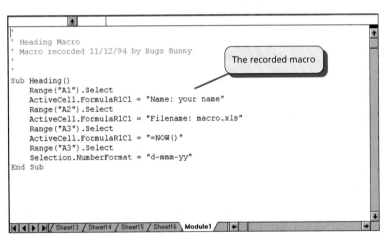

The recorded macro

Playing Back a Macro from the Menu

8. Scroll the sheet tabs till you see *Sheet2*, and click that tab to display a blank sheet.

9. Pull down the **Tools** menu and click the **Macro** command to display the Macro dialog box (see the margin illustration).

10. Click the macro named *Heading* to select it in the **Macro Name/Reference** list, and then click the **Run** command button. The macro automatically enters the three-line heading at the top of the sheet.

Assigning a Macro to Shortcut Keys

11. Pull down the **Tools** menu and click the **Macro** command to display the Macro dialog box.

12. Click the *Heading* macro on the **Macro Name/Reference** list and then click the **Options** command button to display the Macro Options dialog box.

13. Click the **Shortcut Key** check box to turn it on (⊠), then type **h** in the **Ctrl+** text box.

14. Click the **OK** command button to close the Macro Options dialog box.

15. Click the **Close** command button to close the Macro dialog box.

Playing Back a Macro from the Shortcut Keys

16. Click the sheet tab for *Sheet3* to display a blank sheet.

17. Press ⌈Ctrl⌉+⌈H⌉ to play back the macro and enter the heading.

Finishing Up

18. Click the **Save** button on the toolbar, and save your workbook as *macro.xls* in the *tutorial* directory on the *Excel Student Resource Disk (Part 1)*.

19. Click the *Module1* sheet to make it active, and then click the **Print** button on the toolbar to print the sheet.

20. Close the workbook.

PicTorial 5 Review Questions

True-False

T F **1.** If you double-click an embedded chart, you select it.

T F **2.** Text in worksheet cells can be used as titles for a chart.

T F **3.** Excel has 18 basic chart types.

T F **4.** A chart is linked to data in a worksheet.

T F **5.** When creating a chart, select the data before activating the ChartWizard.

T F **6.** If after creating an embedded chart, you change the data in the worksheet, the graph must be recreated.

T F **7.** All charts must have a data range.

T F **8.** An embedded chart is displayed and printed on the same sheet as the data on which it is based.

T F **9.** If you tell Excel the data series are in rows, it uses the text or values in the topmost row as category axis labels.

T F **10.** To select nonadjacent sheets, click the first sheet tab and then hold down ⌈⇧ Shift⌉ and click another sheet.

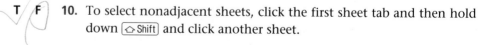

Multiple Choice

1. Bar and column charts are best suited for _____ data.

a. Continuous

b. Percentages of whole

c. Discrete

d. Placid

2. On a chart, the _____ axis contains the labels for the data being plotted.

a. Value

b. Topic

c. Category

d. Topical

3. When you have only one data series, the best chart to use is a _____ chart.

a. Pie

b. Bar

c. Line

d. Area

4. To stop a macro while it is running, press _____.

a. Esc

b. **Pause**

c. Ctrl + Break

d. End

5. The number of items in a legend on a chart is based upon the number of _____.

a. Titles

b. Data series

c. Labels

d. Bars

6. _____ identify the symbols or patterns used to plot charts so that data series can be distinguished from one another.

a. Titles

b. Legends

c. Scales

d. Data labels

7. Area and line charts are best suited for _____ data.

a. Continuous

b. Percentages of whole

c. Discrete

d. Placid

8. On a chart, the axis against which numbers are plotted is called the _____ axis.

a. Value

b. Topic

c. Category

d. Topical

9. To copy a sheet, point to its tab, hold down _____ and the left mouse button and drag the page icon to the tab you want it to be copied in front of.
   a. Ctrl
   b. Alt
   c. Ctrl + Shift
   d. Shift

10. To select adjacent sheets, click the first sheet tab and then hold down _____ and click the next one.
   a. Ctrl
   b. Alt
   c. Ctrl + Shift
   d. Shift

Fill In the Blank

1. If you want category axis labels and legends on a chart, include _row & column headings_ in the data selection range.

2. When you select a chart, _selection squares_ appear on the top and bottom, sides, and corners of a frame around the chart.

3. _Continuous_ data occurs when measurements have been sampled to determine a trend.

4. For many charts the value axis is what is called the Y or _vertical_ axis. _X – horizontal_

5. When creating a pie chart, you can have _one_ data series(s).

6. _Logarithmic_ scales on charts allow you to plot very large and very small values on the same chart.

7. Data that you chart on most charts has _two_ axis.

8. _Percentages of whole_ data are those where you have a data series that contains parts equaling a significant whole.

9. If you tell Excel the data series are in rows, it uses the leftmost cell on each row as a _legend_.

10. _Discrete_ data consists of values measured at a series of selected points.

PicTorial 5 Lab Activities

▶▶ COMPUTER-BASED TUTORIALS

We suggest you complete the following computer-based lessons to learn more about the features discussed in this PicTorial. To do so, pull down the **Help** menu and click the **Examples and Demos** command, click the *Topic* listed in the table "Suggested Examples and Demos to Complete" and then click the *Subtopic* listed in that same table. (If you need more help on using the system, see the "Computer-Based Tutorials" section at the end of PicTorial 1.)

Suggested Examples and Demos to Complete	
Topic	**Subtopic**
☐ Working in Workbooks	Inserting, Deleting, and Renaming Sheets in a Workbook
☐ Working in Workbooks	Moving and Copying Sheets in a Workbook
☐ Creating a Chart	What is a Chart?
☐ Creating a Chart	Creating a Chart with the ChartWizard
☐ Creating a Chart	Plotting a Chart Using Nonadjacent Selections
☐ Creating a Chart	Adding Data Labels
☐ Creating a Chart	Setting the Default Chart
☐ Creating a Chart	Adding Data to a Chart
☐ Creating a Chart	Changing Chart Text
☐ Formatting a Chart	Arranging and Sizing Chart Items
☐ Formatting a Chart	Formatting Data Markers
☐ Formatting a Chart	Changing the Number Format and Scale of an Axis
☐ Formatting a Chart	Changing and Combining Chart Types

▶▶ QUICKSTEP DRILLS

5-1. Managing a Workbook

The advantage of workbooks is that they contain many sheets, each of which you can use for a related model. In this drill, you practice naming, deleting, copying, and moving sheets.

1. Open a new workbook.

2. Double-click on the sheet tab for the sheet labeled *Sheet 1* to display the Rename Sheet dialog box, enter the name **Master Budget**, and click the **OK** button.

3. Double-click on the sheet tab for the sheet labeled *Sheet 2* to display the Rename Sheet dialog box, enter the name **Income Budget**, and click the **OK** button.

4. Double-click on the sheet tab for the sheet labeled to display the Rename Sheet dialog box, enter the name **Expense Budget**, and click the **OK** button.

5. Select sheets 4 through 16, then delete them with the **Edit**, **Delete Sheet** commands.

6. Drag the *Expense Budget* sheet in front of the *Income Budget* sheet.

7. Use Ctrl to drag a copy of the *Expense Budget* sheet so it is the last sheet.

8. Delete the duplicate *Income Budget* sheet using the **Edit**, **Delete Sheet** command.

9. Close the workbook without saving your changes.

5-2. Creating Embedded Charts

Charts allow you to view data in a new way, making some things stand out better for analysis. In this drill, you create a chart that illustrates the sales for all of the regions to see how they compare. When finished, your chart should look like the one shown in the figure "Sales by Region" on the following page.

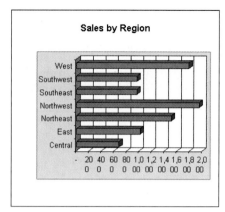

Sales by Region

1. Open the *stat.xls* workbook stored in the *drill* directory on the *Excel Student Resource Disk (Part 1)*.

2. Select the cell range A5:B12 and click the **ChartWizard** button. Draw an outline showing where you want the chart, starting in the upper-left corner of cell A1 and ending in the lower-right corner of cell F18.

3. Click the **Next>** command button to display the ChartWizard *Step 2 of 5* dialog box, and click the **3-D Bar** chart type to select it.

4. Click the **Next>** command button three times to display the *Step 5 of 5* dialog box, then:

   ▶ Click on the **No** option button (◉) under the heading *Add A Legend?* to turn it off.

   ▶ Enter the title **Sales by Region** in the **Chart Title** text box.

5. Click the **Finish** command button to display the chart. Don't worry that the chart covers the model, you'll fix that in the next drill.

6. Save, print, and close the workbook.

5-3. Moving, Sizing, and Deleting Embedded Charts

Once you have created an embedded chart, you can easily move, size, or delete it. In this drill you practice those procedures. When finished, your chart should be the size and in the position shown in the figure "The Sized Chart."

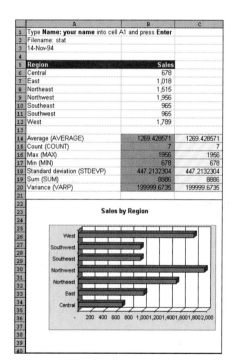

The Sized Chart

1. Open the *stat.xls* workbook stored in the *drill* directory on the *Excel Student Resource Disk (Part 1)*.

2. Drag the chart below the model then scroll the screen so you can see the entire chart or at least the lower right corner of it.

3. Use the lower-right selection square to make the chart as wide as the model above it. Be sure to hold down ⬆Shift so it is sized proportionally. When you release the mouse button, notice how not all of the Y-axis labels are displayed now. Also, the X-axis labels are not displayed correctly. We'll fix the Y-axis labels now and then fix the X-axis labels in a later drill.

4. Use the selection square on the bottom of the chart to drag it down until all seven Y-Axis labels are displayed. (It may take a few tries.)

5. Save, print, and close the worksheet.

5-4. Creating Chart Sheets

Unlike embedded charts, chart sheets are on their own sheet in the workbook. In this drill you create a chart sheet that illustrates the sales for all of the regions using the same model on which you created an embedded chart. When finished, your chart should look like the figure "The Stat Chart Sheet" on the following page.

1. Open the *stat.xls* workbook stored in the *drill* directory on the *Excel Student Resource Disk (Part 1)*.

2. Select the cell range A5:B12, then use the **Insert**, **Chart**, **As New Sheet** commands to display the ChartWizard *Step 1 of 5* dialog box.

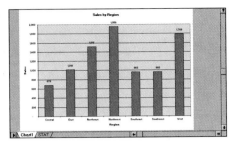

The Stat Chart Sheet

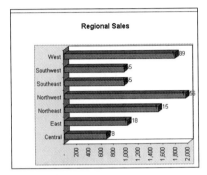

The Revised Sales Chart

3. Click the **Next>** command button four times to display the ChartWizard *Step 5 of 5* dialog box:

   ▸ Click to turn on the **No** options button (◉) under the heading *Add A Legend?*

   ▸ Enter the three titles **Sales by Region**, **Region**, and **Sales** in the appropriate text boxes.

4. Click the **Finish** command button to display the chart on its own sheet.

5. Insert data labels on the chart by selecting the **Insert**, **Data Labels** command. When the Insert Data Labels dialog box appears, click on the **Show Value** option button (◉), then click the **OK** command button.

6. Save the workbook, print the chart sheet, and then close the workbook.

5-5. Editing and Revising Charts

In this drill you revise the embedded chart you created in Drill 5-2 by changing its title and removing gridlines. When finished, your chart should look like the one shown in the figure "The Revised Sales Chart."

1. Open the *stat.xls* workbook stored in the *drill* directory on the *Excel Student Resource Disk (Part 1)* and click the sheet tab labeled *STAT*.

2. Double-click the embedded chart to activate it (it's the one on the same sheet as the model).

3. Click the chart title to select it, then click it again and change the title to *Regional Sales*. Click anywhere outside of the title area so it isn't selected.

4. Remove the gridlines with the **Insert**, **Gridlines** command and click off the **Major Gridlines** check box under the heading *Value (Z) Axis*. Click the **OK** command button to close the dialog box.

5. Insert data labels on the chart using the **Insert**, **Data Labels** commands, and click on the **Show Value** option button (◉).

6. Double-click the X axis (the horizontal axis) to display the Format Axis dialog box. (If the wrong dialog box appears, click its **Cancel** command button and try again.). On the **Alignment** tab select the middle choice under the **Orientation** heading and click the **OK** command button. Notice how the X-axis labels now run vertically so there is room for all of them to be displayed. Also notice that the X-axis labels are again not displayed correctly.

7. Click outside the chart so it is no longer activated, then click it one to select it. Use the selection square on the bottom of the chart to drag it down until all seven Y-axis labels are displayed. (It may take a few tries.)

8. Save the workbook, print the worksheet, and then close the workbook.

5-6. Exploring Chart Types and AutoFormats

The type of chart you choose determines how easy it is to interpret your data. One nice thing about spreadsheet graphics is that you can display

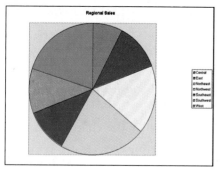

The Pie Chart

the same data in a variety of ways to see which chart type best represents the data you are presenting. When finished, your chart should look like the figure "The Pie Chart."

1. Open the *stat.xls* workbook stored in the *drill* directory on the *Excel Student Resource Disk (Part 1)*.

2. On the sheet named *STAT*, double-click the embedded chart to activate it. Then use the **Format**, **Chart Type**, **2-D**, **Pie** commands to change it to a pie chart.

3. Insert legends on the chart using the **Insert**, **Legend** command.

4. Save the workbook, print the worksheet, and then close the workbook.

5-7. Recording and Playing Back Macros

When creating models, you often want to print them out with row and column headings and cell gridlines so you can trouble-shoot them or have a record of their final form. Here you record a macro that includes directions for turning off row and column headings and turning off gridlines. You then record another that turns them on.

1. Open the *loan.xls* workbook stored in the *drill* directory on the *Excel Student Resource Disk (Part 1)*.

2. Turn on macro recording by selecting **Tools**, **Record Macro**, **Record New Macro**. In the Record New Macro dialog box, enter the macro name **heads_grids_off**.

3. To turn off row and column headings on your printouts, use the **File**, **Page Setup**, **Sheet** commands. Click off the **Gridlines** and **Row & Column Headings** check boxes.

4. Turn off macro recording by clicking the **Stop** button displayed in the screen area.

5. Repeat Steps 2 through 4 but name the macro **heads_grids_on** and click on both **Gridlines** and **Row & Column Headings** settings.

6. Save the worksheet.

7. Execute each macro using the **Tools**, **Macro** commands. Select the name of the macro, and click the **Run** command button.

8. Make printouts after executing each macro.

9. Close the workbook.

5-1. The Pennies Model

The rate of growth of doubling a penny every day is amazing. In this exercise you create an embedded area chart that plots this growth. When finished, your chart should look like the one shown in the figure "The Pennies Chart."

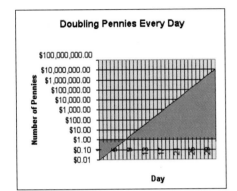

The Pennies Chart

1. Open the *pennies.xls* workbook stored in the *exercise* directory on the *Excel Student Resource Disk*.

2. Select the range A5:B36, click the **ChartWizard** button on the toolbar, and highlight the range for the chart as C1 to F14.

3. Click the **Next>** command button to display the *Step 2 of 5* dialog box and select the **Area** chart.

4. Click the **Next>** command button twice to display the *Step 4 of 5* dialog box and click the up spin arrow (⬍) in the **Use First X Column(s) for Category (X) Axis Labels** so it reads *1*.

5. Click the **Next>** command button to display the *Step 5 of 5* dialog box and click on the **No** option button (◉) under the heading *Add A Legend?*.

6. Enter the three titles **Doubling Pennies Every Day**, **Day**, and **Number of Pennies** and click the **Finish** command button to display the finished embedded chart. Notice how the chart of the first days is squashed against the category axis.

7. Double-click the chart to activate it, then double-click the value axis to display the Format Axis dialog box.

8. Click the **Scale** tab, click to turn on the **Logarithmic Scale** check box, and then click the **OK** command button to return to the worksheet. The chart is now displayed using a logarithmic scale.

9. Save, print, and close the workbook.

5-2. Birthday Probabilities

In this exercise, you create an embedded 3-D chart of the probabilities that two people might share the same birth date. When finished, your chart should look like the one shown in the figure "The Birthday Chart."

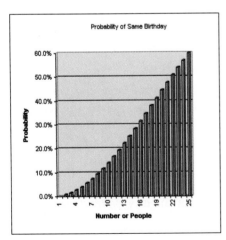

The Birthday Chart

1. Open the *birthday.xls* workbook stored in the *exercise* directory on the *Excel Student Resource Disk (Part 2)*.

2. Select the A5:A30 range and then hold down [Ctrl] key while selecting the range E5:E30.

3. Click the **ChartWizard** button on the toolbar and specify the chart area as A32 through E50.

4. Click the **Next>** command button to display the ChartWizard *Step 2 of 5* dialog box, and select **3-D Column** chart.

5. Click the **Next>** command button twice to display the *Step 4 of 5* dialog box, and click the up spin arrow (⬍) in the **Use First X Column(s) for Category (X) Axis Labels** so it reads *1*.

6. Click the **Next>** command button to display the dialog box titled *Step 5 of 5*, and click on the **No** option button (◉) under the heading *Add A Legend?*

7. Enter the three titles **Probability of Same Birthday**, **Number of People**, and **Probability**, then click the **Finish** command button to display the finished embedded chart.

8. Save, print, and close the workbook.

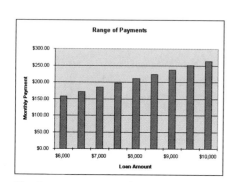

The Loan Payments Chart

5-3. Loan Payments

In this exercise you create a 2-D Column chart that shows how payments change depending on the amount of a loan. When finished, your chart should look like the one shown in the figure "The Loan Payments Chart."

1. Open the *autoloan.xls* workbook stored in the *exercise* directory on the *Excel Student Resource Disk (Part 2)* and enter your name into cell A1.

2. Select the range C5:D16 to be charted, click the **ChartWizard** button on the toolbar, and drag the pointer to specify the chart range as cells A20 through D40.

3. Click the **Next>** command button twice to display the ChartWizard *Step 4 of 5* dialog box, and click the up spin arrow (⬍) in the **Use First X Column(s) for Category (X) Axis Labels** so it reads *1*. Notice how there is no bar for the first amount in the sample graph.

4. Click the up spin arrow (⬍) in the **Use First X Row(s) for Legend Text** so it reads *3*.

5. Click the **Next>** command button to display the *Step 5 of 5* dialog box, and click on the **No** option button (◉) under the heading *Add A Legend?*.

6. Enter the three titles **Range of Payments**, **Loan Amount**, and **Monthly Payment**, then click the **Finish** command button to display the finished embedded chart.

7. Save, print, and close the workbook.

5-4. Charting the Series Model

One thing you should avoid doing is plotting very large and very small data ranges on the same chart. In this exercise, you chart the *series.xls* model to demonstrate the problems this can cause. You then use a log axis to correct the problem. When finished, your line chart should look like the one shown in the figure "The Number Series Chart" on the following page.

1. Open the *series.xls* workbook stored in the *exercise* directory on the *Excel Student Resource Disk (Part 2)*.

2. Select the range A5:C11 to be charted and use the **Insert**, **Chart** commands to specify a chart sheet for the graph and display the ChartWizard *Step 1 of 5* dialog box.

3. Click the **Next>** command button to display the *Step 2 of 5* dialog box, and select **Line** as the chart type.

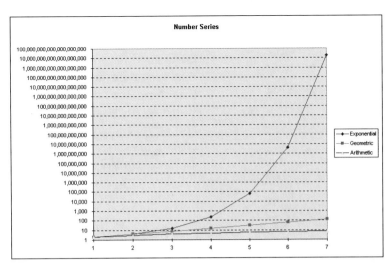

The Number Series Chart

4. Click the **Next>** command button three times to display the *Step 5 of 5* dialog box, enter the chart title **Number Series**, then click the **Finish** command button to display the embedded chart. Notice how the lines for two of the series are pressed against the category axis because the values on the other series are so large.

5. Double-click the Y-axis scale to select it and display the Format Axis dialog box. On the **Scale** tab turn on the **Logarithmic Scale** check box. The chart is now displayed using a logarithmic scale and all three lines are clearly visible.

6. Save, print, and close the workbook.

▶▶ REAL-WORLD PROJECTS

5-1. A Balance Sheet

Using the *balance.xls* workbook you created earlier, create the chart shown in the figure "The Balance Sheet Chart," and add titles and legends to match the illustration. The chart plots total assets, total liabilities, and total owner equity for this year and last year. The category axis is the range that includes the column headings on row 8. When you are finished, save the workbook, and make a printout of the chart.

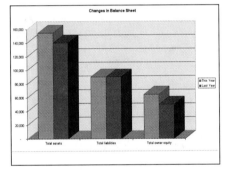

The Balance Sheet Chart

5-2. An Income Statement

Using the *income.xls* workbook you created earlier, create the chart shown in the figure "The Income Statement Chart," and add titles and legends to match the illustration. The chart plots total cost of goods and gross profits over the three-year period covered by the statement. The category axis includes the labels that head the yearly columns. When you are finished, save the workbook, and make a printout of the chart.

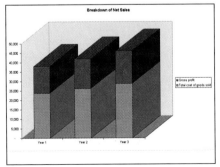

The Income Statement Chart

5-3. The Cost of Smoking

Everyone but the tobacco company management's knows that smoking is not good for you. No one knows this better than insurance companies that vary their rates for smokers and nonsmokers. Here is a worksheet that shows the rates from one company. Open the *smoking.xls* workbook stored in the *project* directory of the *Excel Student Resource Disk (Part 2)* and create the chart shown in the figure "One Cost of Smoking." The chart makes it easier to see the difference between males and females and smokers and nonsmokers.

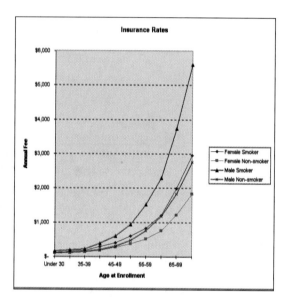

One Cost of Smoking

PicTorial 6

MANAGING LISTS

After completing this PicTorial, you will be able to:

▶ Define the terms *field*, *record*, *list*, and *database*

▶ Create lists of data so they can be used as a database of information

▶ Sort the data in a list into ascending or descending order

▶ Use criteria to find specific records in the list

▶ Filter a list to hide all records that don't match the specified criteria

▶ Use database functions to summarize data

▶ Automatically subtotal related groups of records

Much information can be arranged in the form of a table called a *list* or *database*. Once a list has been set up correctly, Excel can quickly find information in the list, sort it into any desired order, and subtotal groups of related records. These capabilities are ideal for analyzing lists containing sales figures, inventory, mailing or distribution lists, customer accounts, check registers, or any other data that needs to be collected, sorted, and analyzed. Lists are created with most of the same commands used to create a model. In fact, a *list* is just a model organized into fields and records.

6-1. THE ANATOMY OF A LIST

When creating or working with a list, you need to understand the three parts of which it is constructed:

▶ *Column labels* (also called *field names*) are entered on the first row of the list and identify the contents of the columns where data are entered. These cells must be formatted differently from the records below them so Excel can recognize them as headings.

▶ *Records* are entered on the second and subsequent rows of the list. Each record is a set of related data, much like a Rolodex™ card that contains a person's name, address, and phone number.

▶ *Fields* are the columns of information that make up a record. Each column forms a separate field like an individual item on a Rolodex™ card—the person's name, street address, city, state, ZIP code, or phone number.

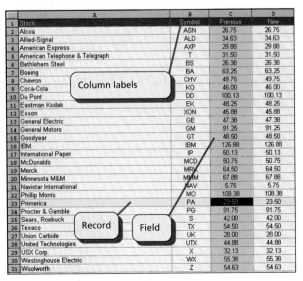

You must enter a list in such a way that Excel can recognize it as a list. This allows many of Excel's list management procedures to work automatically. The rules that you must follow are described in the box "Guidelines for Creating a List."

GUIDELINES FOR CREATING A LIST

When creating a list, here are the most important rules you must follow.

General Guidelines

▸ Have only one list on a worksheet, since some list management procedures can only work with a single list.

▸ Leave at least one blank row or column between a list and any other data on the worksheet so Excel can automatically identify the list when you select just a single cell within it. (If Excel can't recognize the list, you must select the entire list with the mouse before using list management procedures.)

▸ Avoid entering important data on the same rows on the sheet as the list. Some rows may be hidden during some list management operations, and this data would be hidden from view.

Column Label Guidelines

▸ The column labels (field names) must be entered as the first row of the list.

▸ When Excel sorts or otherwise manipulates the data in a list for you, it needs to be able to tell the difference between the column labels (which shouldn't be sorted) and the records in the list. To allow it to identify these separate parts of the list, format the column labels differently than the records below them. To do so, use a different font, data type, alignment, format, pattern, border, or capitalization style.

Row and Column Layout Guidelines

▸ Don't leave blank rows between column labels and records.

▸ Apply the same formats to all cells in a column (except the column label).

Data Entry Guidelines

▸ A list must have the same type of data in each field (column). For example, do not enter text in a field in some records and numbers, formulas, or dates in the same field of other records.

▸ All text or numbers in a column should have the same format.

▸ When entering numbers as text (as in phone numbers or ZIP codes) or combinations of numbers and text (as in 1, 2, 2a, 2b, 3, 3b, and so on), make sure they are all in a text format (type an apostrophe (') as the first character).

▸ Don't insert a space as the first character since it will be treated as a character and will affect sorting and searching.

▸ Be consistent with case since Excel can differentiate between lowercase and uppercase characters if you ask it to when sorting. (Normally Excel will ignore the case of characters. For example, it will treat *Product*, *product*, and *PRODUCT* the same during sorting.)

TIP: WRAPPING COLUMN LABELS TO NARROW COLUMNS

To fully display long column labels, you may widen a column. However, there is no need to have a column wider than the data that it contains. To narrow a column that is too wide just because of the column label, wrap the long heading into two or more lines in the same cell. (To do so, select the cell, pull down the **Format** menu and click the **Cells** command to display the Format Cells dialog box. Click the *Alignment* tab, click the **Wrap** Text check box to turn it on (⊠), and then click the **OK** command button.)

QUICKSTEPS: CREATING DATABASE LISTS

1. Enter column labels for the list following the guidelines listed in the box "Guidelines for Creating a List."

2. Type data into the rows below the column labels following the guidelines listed in the box "Guidelines for Creating a List."

TUTORIAL

In this tutorial you create a list and format the column labels so Excel recognizes them as list headings.

Getting Started

1. Open the *salelst1.xls* workbook stored in the *tutorial* directory on the *Excel Student Resource Disk (Part 1)* and enter your name in cell A1.

Entering Column Labels

2. Enter the column labels and records shown here just as you would type them into a regular model.

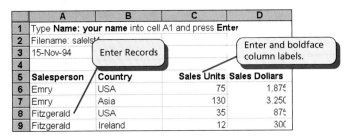

	A	B	C	D
1	Type **Name: your name** into cell A1 and press **Enter**			
2	Filename: salels			
3	15-Nov-94			
4				
5	**Salesperson**	**Country**	**Sales Units**	**Sales Dollars**
6	Emry	USA	75	1,875
7	Emry	Asia	130	3.250
8	Fitzgerald	USA	35	875
9	Fitzgerald	Ireland	12	300

Enter Records

Enter and boldface column labels.

3. Select the column headings on row 5 and click the **Bold** button on the toolbar to boldface them. Then use the **Align Right** button on the toolbar to align the text in cells C5 and D5.

Finishing Up

4. Save, print, and close the workbook.

6-2. ENTERING AND EDITING DATA USING A DATA FORM

When you work with a list, you can display it using a special dialog box called the *data form* that displays all of the fields for a single record. The parts of a data form are described in the box "Understanding the Data Form."

To enter or edit data in a data form, you use the form's edit boxes. Each of the edit boxes is labeled with a field name automatically taken from the list's column labels. Data you enter into an edit box is inserted into the list in the column of the same name, as illustrated in this sample from a workbook listing the stocks that make up the Dow Jones Industrials.

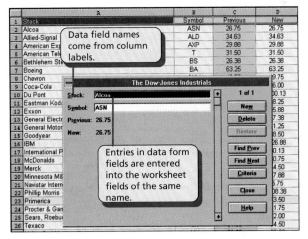

Data field names come from column labels.

Entries in data form fields are entered into the worksheet fields of the same name.

If you make mistakes when entering data, or if you want to modify a previously entered record, you can display it in the form and then edit it. You edit the contents of edit boxes the same way you edit the contents of text boxes in dialog boxes. For example, click to move the insertion point where you want it in an edit box, and then insert or delete characters. Double-click the edit box to select the entire entry, and then type a new entry or press Delete to delete the existing one.

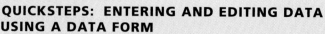

UNDERSTANDING THE DATA FORM

When you pull down the **Data** menu and click the **Form** command, the data form is displayed.

The *title bar* at the top of the dialog box displays the name of the worksheet.

Data form fields display the contents of the fields from a single record (up to 32). Those you can edit are displayed in edit boxes. Those you can't edit (computed fields containing formulas) are displayed without an edit box. The width of the widest column in the list determines the length of edit boxes.

Field names taken from the list's column labels identify the contents of each data form field. (To change these names, you must change the list's column labels.)

A *scroll bar* allows you to quickly scroll through records in the list. (See the Tip box "Using the Data Form's Scroll Bar.")

The *record number indicator* lists the number of the displayed record and the total number of records in the list.

Command buttons execute the following commands:

New enters any data currently display in the data form into the list on the worksheet and displays a new blank form.

Delete deletes the record displayed in the form and also deletes it from the list on the worksheet. When you click this command, a dialog box asks you to confirm the deletion. When you use this command to delete a record from the worksheet, all records below it move up to fill the gap left in the list.

Restore cancels any changes you have made to the record that is currently displayed. (This button is dimmed until you enter or change data in an edit box.)

Find Prev displays the previous record, if any.

Find Next displays the next record, if any.

Criteria searches for any records on the list that match the criteria you specify. (See Section 6-5, "Filtering Records.")

Close closes the data form dialog box.

TIP: USING THE DATA FORM'S SCROLL BAR

You can use the scroll bar to scroll through the records in the list.

▶ To move to the same field in the previous or next record, click the up or down scroll arrows.

▶ To move to the same field in a record 10 before or 10 after the current record, click above or below the scroll box.

▶ To move to the first or last record, drag the scroll box to the top or bottom of the scroll bar and release it.

COMMON WRONG TURNS: THINGS THAT COULD GO WRONG

When you use a data form, dialog boxes are displayed by Excel when it wants to inform you of a problem or when it wants you to take some action.

Excel Cannot Identify the Column Labels

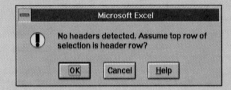

When you pull down the **Data** menu and click the **Form** command, a dialog box may appear that reads *No headers detected. Assume top row is header row?* Click the **OK** command button if it is a header row. Otherwise, click the **Cancel** command button, select the list manually (including the headings), and repeat the command. To permanently fix the problem, format the headings differently in some respect from the records that follow them and be sure they are not separated from the records by one or more blank rows.

Column Labels Not Selected

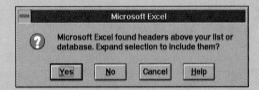

When you pull down the **Data** menu and click the **Form** command, a dialog box may appear that reads *Microsoft Excel found headers above your list or database. Expand selection to include them?* Click the **Yes** command button if it is a header row, or the **No** command button if it isn't. Or click the **Cancel** command button.

Row Below the List Contains Data

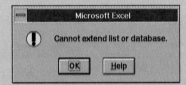

When Excel finds data on the row beneath the last row of the list, it displays the message *Cannot extend list or database.* Click the **OK** command button, insert some blank rows beneath the list, and repeat the command.

TUTORIAL

In this tutorial you open an existing list and then use a data form to add records to the list. As you do so, the records are added to the end of the list.

Step 2

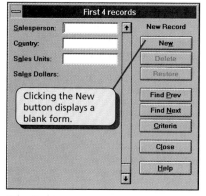

Step 3

The Revised Sales List Model

Getting Started

1. Open the *salelst1.xls* workbook stored in the *tutorial* directory on the *Excel Student Resource Disk (Part 1)*.

Entering Data

2. Select any cell in the list on rows 5 through 9, pull down the **Data** menu, and click the **Form** command to display a data form. The first record in the list is displayed in the form's edit boxes.

3. Click the **New** command button to display a blank form for a new record.

4. Enter the records shown here with the light yellow background as follows (as you enter each, it is added to the end of the list):

   ▶ Type data into each edit box, pressing Tab↹ to move the insertion point to the next edit box.

   ▶ Click the **New** command button to enter the data into the list as a new record and display a blank form for another record.

	A	B	C	D	E	F	G
1	Type **Name: your name** into cell A1 and press **Enter**						
2	Filename: salelst1						
3	15-Nov-94						
4							
5	**Salesperson**	**Country**	**Sales Units**	**Sales Dollars**			
6	Emry	USA	75	1,875			
7	Emry	Asia	130	3,250			
8	Fitzgerald	USA	35	875			
9	Fitzgerald	Ireland	12	300			
10	Henderson	USA	25	625			
11	Henderson	Asia	225	5,625			
12	Kendall	USA	100	2,500			
13	Kendall	Asia	75	1,875			
14	Moreau	Australia	100	2,500			
15	Moreau	Asia	90	2,250			
16							
17							

Enter these records into the data form.

Finishing Up

5. After entering the last record, click the **Close** command button to close the data form dialog box.

6. Save, print, and close the workbook.

6-3. PERFORMING SIMPLE SORTS

Sorting arranges entire rows in a list based on the contents of a single column—called the *Sort By* column. Sorting arranges the contents of the Sort By column in alphabetic or numeric order. (Column labels are not sorted.)

SORT ORDERS

Lists can be sorted into ascending or descending order. In an ascending sort, Excel puts numbers before dates before text before blank cells. It puts numbers in the order of smallest to largest, dates in the order of earliest to latest, and text in alphabetical order. In the default sort, Excel doesn't distinguish uppercase from lowercase letters. But if you check the Case Sensitive box in the Sort Options dialog box, it will sort in this order: SORT, Sort, sort. In a descending sort, all of this is reversed except that blank cells are still put last.

Sort orders

Ascending Sort of Categories	Subsorting within Categories
Numbers	Smallest to largest (for example -99 to 99)
Date	Earliest to latest (for example 1/1/96 to 12/1/96)
Text	A to Z

SORTING BY SINGLE COLUMNS

When you need to sort a list based on the contents of a single column, you can do so with just a couple of mouse clicks. For example, to sort a list so it's arranged by people's last names, click anywhere in the column where last names are listed and then click one of the **Sort** buttons on the toolbar.

In some cases, you may want to sort based on more than one column. To do so, sort the least important column first and the most important column last. For example, if you sort a list just by last names, the people with the same last name will be listed in the order in which their first names were entered. To have both first and last names listed alphabetically, first sort by the first name column and then sort by the last name column.

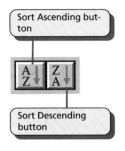

Sort Ascending button

Sort Descending button

QUICKSTEPS: SORTING BY SINGLE COLUMNS
1. Select any cell in the column you want to sort by.
2. Click the **Sort Ascending** or **Sort Descending** buttons on the toolbar.

SORTING BY MULTIPLE COLUMNS

You can sort a list by more than one field at a time whenever you want related items to be subsorted. For example, if you were sorting a database by name, you would want to sort first by the *Last Name* field and then by the *First Name* field. This way, the name Jones, Smith would follow the name Jones, Alice. To subsort like this, specify the *Last Name* field as the field to **Sort By** and the *First Name* field as the **Then By** field to sort. If you wanted to subsort the second field, perhaps by department, you would specify that field as the second **Then By** field to sort.

TIP: RETURNING A LIST TO ITS ORIGINAL ORDER

You can always sort a list back into its original order if you plan ahead. Before sorting the list, label one column *Original Order*. Then enter the number **1** in that field of the first record, hold down [Ctrl] and drag the fill handle down the column to the last record and release it. The column will be filled with a series of sequential numbers you can use to sort the list back into its original order at any time.

	A	B
1	Original Order	
2		
3		
4	**Last Name**	**First Name**
5	Henderson	Carolyn
6	Fitzgerald	Liz
7	Emry	Barbara
8	Fitzgerald	Dennis
9	Emry	Alonzo
10	Emry	Judy
11	Henderson	Richard
12	Henderson	Ann
13	Fitzgerald	Frank
14	Fitzgerald	Jackie
15	Emry	Matthew

The original order of first and last names is random.

	A	B
1	Sorted Just by Last Name	
2		
3		
4	**Last Name**	**First Name**
5	Emry	Barbara
6	Emry	Alonzo
7	Emry	Judy
8	Emry	Matthew
9	Fitzgerald	Liz
10	Fitzgerald	Dennis
11	Fitzgerald	Frank
12	Fitzgerald	Jackie
13	Henderson	Carolyn
14	Henderson	Richard
15	Henderson	Ann

When sorted just by last name, first names are out of order.

When sorted by last name and then by first name, first names are in order.

	A	B
1	Sorted by Last Name,	
2	then by First Name	
3		
4	**Last Name**	**First Name**
5	Emry	Alonzo
6	Emry	Barbara
7	Emry	Judy
8	Emry	Matthew
9	Fitzgerald	Dennis
10	Fitzgerald	Frank
11	Fitzgerald	Jackie
12	Fitzgerald	Liz
13	Henderson	Ann
14	Henderson	Carolyn
15	Henderson	Richard

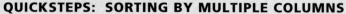

QUICKSTEPS: SORTING BY MULTIPLE COLUMNS

1. Select any cell in the list, pull down the **Data** menu, and click the **Sort** command to display the Sort dialog box and automatically select the list. (If the list isn't selected correctly, click the **Cancel** command button, select the list manually, and then repeat this step.)

2. Use any of the commands described in the box "Understanding the Sort Dialog Box."

3. Click the **OK** command button to sort the list based on the settings you have made in the Sort dialog box.

UNDERSTANDING THE SORT DIALOG BOX

When you pull down the **Data** menu and click the **Sort** command, the Sort dialog box is displayed. You use this dialog box to specify the Sort By columns and other options.

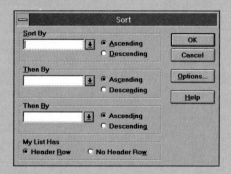

Sort By Section

The **Sort By** section specifies the column that will determine the main sort order.

Sort By drop-down arrow (⬇) displays the column labels from the list so you can select one by clicking it.

Ascending or **Descending** option buttons (◉) specify the sort order.

Then By Sections

There are two **Then By** sections that you can use to break ties. The first breaks ties in the **Sort By** sort order. The second breaks ties in the first **Then By** sort. Each section has drop-down arrows (⬇) and option buttons like those of the Sort By section.

My List Has Section

Header Row or **No Header Row** option buttons (◉) specify if the list you are sorting has a row of column labels. (Excel will guess the correct setting most of the time if the labels are formatted differently from the rest of the data in the list.)

Options Command Button

Options command button displays the Sort Options dialog box offering the following options:

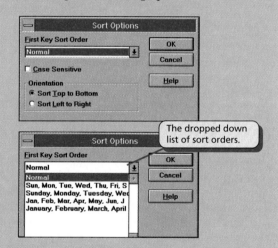

The dropped down list of sort orders.

First Key Sort Order drop-down arrow (⬇) displays a list of custom sort orders. Using these, you can sort by day of the week or month instead of alphabetically. (You can't use this option in the **Then By** boxes.)

Case Sensitive check box specifies if Excel should ignore the case of text characters when off (☐) or use it as the basis for the sort when on (☒).

Sort Top to Bottom or **Sort Left to Right** option buttons (◉) specify if the list is to be sorted by rows (the default setting) or by columns.

TUTORIAL

In this tutorial you sort a list by one or more columns and undo the sort.

Getting Started

1. Open the *salelst2.xls* workbook stored in the *tutorial* directory on the *Excel Student Resource Disk (Part 1)* and enter your name in cell A1. This is an expanded version of the list you have been entering. Notice how the list is now organized by salesperson's name in ascending alphabetical order.

Sorting The Database Using a Single Column

2. Select any cell in the *Salesperson* column (column A) of the list and first click the **Sort Descending** button on the toolbar and then click the **Sort Ascending** button.

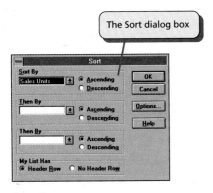

The Sort dialog box

Step 5

Sorted in descending order

	A	B	C	D
1	Type **Name: your name** into cell A1 and press **Enter**			
2	Filename: salelst2			
3	15-Nov-94			
4				
5	Salesperson	Country	Sales Units	Sales Dollars
6	Moreau	USA	289	7,225
7	Moreau	Spain	134	3,350
8	Moreau	Panama	120	3,000
9	Moreau	Australia	100	2,500
10	Moreau	Asia	90	2,250
11	Kendall			500
12	Kendall			50
13	Kendall			75
14	Kendall	A		00
15	Henderson	USA	25	625
16	Henderson	Mexico	35	875
17	Henderson	France	130	3,250
18	Henderson	Canada	200	5,000
19	Henderson	Asia	225	5,625
20	Fitzgerald	USA	35	875
21	Fitzgerald	Ireland	12	300
22	Fitzgerald	England	140	3,500
23	Fitzgerald	Canada	289	7,225
24	Fitzgerald	Australia	134	3,350
25	Fitzgerald	Asia	500	12,500
26	Emry	USA	75	1,875
27	Emry	Poland	225	5,625
28	Emry	Canada	25	625
29	Emry	Australia	200	5,000
30	Emry	Asia	130	3,250

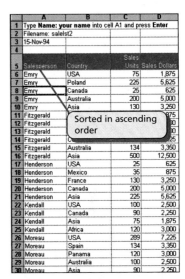

Sorted in ascending order

	A	B	C	D
1	Type **Name: your name** into cell A1 and press **Enter**			
2	Filename: salelst2			
3	15-Nov-94			
4				
5	Salesperson	Country	Sales Units	Sales Dollars
6	Emry	USA	75	1,875
7	Emry	Poland	225	5,625
8	Emry	Canada	25	625
9	Emry	Australia	200	5,000
10	Emry	Asia	130	3,250
11	Fitzgerald			875
12	Fitzgerald			0
13	Fitzgerald			0
14	Fitzgerald	C		25
15	Fitzgerald	Australia	134	3,350
16	Fitzgerald	Asia	500	12,500
17	Henderson	USA	25	625
18	Henderson	Mexico	35	875
19	Henderson	France	130	3,250
20	Henderson	Canada	200	5,000
21	Henderson	Asia	225	5,625
22	Kendall	USA	100	2,500
23	Kendall	Canada	90	2,250
24	Kendall	Asia	75	1,875
25	Kendall	Africa	120	3,000
26	Moreau	USA	289	7,225
27	Moreau	Spain	134	3,350
28	Moreau	Panama	120	3,000
29	Moreau	Australia	100	2,500
30	Moreau	Asia	90	2,250

3. Select any cell in the *Country* column (column B) of the list and first click the **Sort Descending** button on the toolbar and then click the **Sort Ascending** button.

4. Select any cell in the *Sales Units* column (column C) of the list and first click the **Sort Descending** button on the toolbar and then click the **Sort Ascending** button on the toolbar.

Sorting the Database Using Multiple Columns

5. Select any cell in the list, pull down the **Data** menu, and click the **Sort** command to display the Sort dialog box and highlight the entire list (see the top margin illustration).

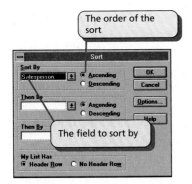

The order of the sort

The field to sort by

Step 6

6. Click the **Sort By** drop-down arrow (⬇), select the *Salesperson* field, and check that the **Ascending** option button is still on (◉) (see the middle margin illustration).

7. Click the **Then By** drop-down arrow (⬇), select the *Sales Units* field, and click the **Descending** option button to turn it on (◉) (see the bottom margin illustration).

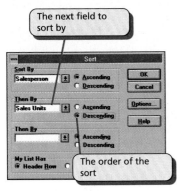

The next field to sort by

The order of the sort

Step 7

8. Click the **OK** command button to sort the list first by name of salesperson in ascending order and then by each salesperson's sales units in descending order (see the illustration on following page).

The list is sorted first by Salesperson...

...and then by units for each salesperson.

	A		Sales	
1	Type Name: your name			
2	Filename: salelst2			
3	15-Nov-94			
4				
5	Salesperson	Country	Units	Sales Dollars
6	Emry	Poland	225	5,625
7	Emry	Australia	200	5,000
8	Emry	Asia	130	3,250
9	Emry	USA	75	1,875
10	Emry	Canada	25	625
11	Fitzgerald	Asia	500	12,500
12	Fitzgerald	Canada	289	7,225
13	Fitzgerald	England	140	3,500
14	Fitzgerald	Australia	134	3,350
15	Fitzgerald	USA	35	875
16	Fitzgerald	Ireland	12	300
17	Henderson	Asia	225	5,625
18	Henderson	Canada	200	5,000
19	Henderson	France	130	3,250
20	Henderson	Mexico	35	875
21	Henderson	USA	25	625
22	Kendall	Africa	120	3,000
23	Kendall	USA	100	2,500
24	Kendall	Canada	90	2,250
25	Kendall	Asia	75	1,875
26	Moreau	USA	289	7,225
27	Moreau	Spain	134	3,350
28	Moreau	Panama	120	3,000
29	Moreau	Australia	100	2,500
30	Moreau	Asia	90	2,250

Step 8

TIP: SORTING PART OF A LIST

To sort only part of a list, select the cells to be sorted before choosing the **Sort** command. Excel will ask you to confirm the sort since this will rearrange parts of records and could substantially affect their content. If you proceed with the sort and don't like the results, immediately click the **Undo** button on the toolbar.

Undoing a Sort

9. Select any cell in the *Salesperson* column (column A) of the list and click the **Sort Descending** button on the toolbar.

10. Click the **Undo** button on the toolbar to return the list to its previous order.

PAUSING FOR PRACTICE

Continue sorting the list until you have mastered the concepts involved and can predict the outcome of any sort before you perform it.

Finishing Up

11. Click the **Print** button on the toolbar to print the sheet.

12. Close the workbook without saving your changes.

6-4. FINDING RECORDS USING THE DATA FORM

With short lists you can quickly find a record by looking at the list on the worksheet, or you can scroll through records on the data form by clicking the **Find Prev** or **Find Next** command or using the scroll bar. However, with longer lists, the fastest way to locate records is by using comparison criteria. Comparison criteria can be either text or a number. For example, you can enter a comparison criterion such as *Computer* or *100* to locate records that have those entries in the specified field. You can also use comparison operators such as > (greater than) or < (less than) to find records whose value in the field is greater than or less than the one you specify in the comparison criteria. For example, the comparison criterion *>100* will locate records that have numbers greater than 100 in the specified field. The comparison criterion *>F* will locate entries that begin with any letter from G to Z.

QUICKSTEPS: FINDING RECORDS USING A DATA FORM

1. Select any cell in the list, pull down the **Data** menu, and click the **Form** command to display the data form.

2. Click the **Criteria** command button to display the Criteria dialog box. (The dialog box changes slightly so you can enter comparison criteria that Excel will use to search the list and identify records. The changes are minor—*Criteria* is displayed instead of the record number indicator, and the **Delete** and **Criteria** command buttons change to **Clear** and **Form**.)

3. Enter your comparison criteria in one or more of the edit boxes, and then click the **Form** command button to return to the data form.

4. Click the **Find Next** or **Find Prev** buttons to locate records that match the criteria. Only those that do will be listed in the form where you can edit or delete them.

5. To change or remove the criteria, click the **Criteria** button again. Then enter a new criterion, or, to gain access to all records, click the **Clear** command button.

6. When finished, click the **Close** command button to close the data form.

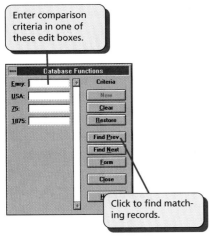

Enter comparison criteria in one of these edit boxes.

Click to find matching records.

A Criteria dialog box

FINDING EXACT MATCHES

To find records that contain a specific value in a field, pull down the **Data** menu and click the **Form** command to display the data form. Click the **Criteria** command button to display the Criteria dialog box, and type the text or number you want to match in the field's edit box. For example, to find any records with the number 1000 in the *Quantity* field, just enter **1000** in the *Quantity* edit box on the form. To find records with CA in the State field, enter **CA** in the *State* edit box. After entering your criteria, click the **Find Next** command button. What happens next depends on whether or not a match is found. If a match is found, the dialog box switches back to the data form and the first record on the list that matches your criteria is displayed in the form. You can click the **Find Prev** or **Find Next** command buttons to display others. (They only move between records that match the criteria.)

FINDING RANGES OF MATCHES

There are many times when you are not looking for an exact match, but rather for records that are above or below a certain value. For example, you may want to find all salespeople whose sales were below $10,000 or those above $50,000 for the month. Or you may want to find all products that have prices above $100 or below $200. To make searches of this kind, you use *comparison operators* that compare data in the specified field against a text or number value that you specify.

UNDERSTANDING COMPARISON OPERATORS

You use comparison operators in criteria to look for ranges of records. For example, you could specify one of the following numeric criteria to search the *Quantity* field or the text criteria to search the *Company* field. If you enter the criteria shown in the *Criteria* column, you'll display records show in the *Result* column:

Number Criteria	Result
=1000	numbers equal to 1000 (this is the same as entering the number by itself)
>1000	numbers greater than 1000
<1000	numbers less than 1000
>=1000	numbers greater than or equal to 1000
<=1000	numbers less than or equal to 1000
<>1000	numbers not equal to 1000

Text Criteria	Result
Gen	text that begins with the letters *Gen*
>*Gen*	text that begins with letters alphabetically later than *Gen*, for example, *Geo*
<*Gen*	text that begins with letters alphabetically earlier than *Gen*, for example, *Gem*
>=*Gen*	text that begins with letters alphabetically later than *Gen* or beginning with *Gen*
<=*Gen*	text that begins with letters alphabetically earlier than *Gen* or beginning with *Gen*
<>*Gen*	text that does not begin with the letters *Gen*
=*Gen*	*Gen* only, and not *General*, *Generic*, *Genetic*, and so on

---

USING WILDCARDS

You can use the wildcard symbols when entering text criteria.

▶ The * (asterisk) substitutes for any characters from the position of the asterisk to the end of the text. For example, the criterion **J* Watson** would find any records for Watson with a first name that began with the letter J.

When you enter text as a criterion, Excel will find all records with text in the field that begins with the characters you enter. For example, searching for *Head* will find both *Head* and *Headache*. Normally this saves you a great deal of time since you only have to type enough characters to uniquely identify what you are searching for. However, you can also find exact matches. To do so, enter the criterion in the form *=text* where *text* stands for the text you want to match exactly. For example, to find just *Head* and not *Headache*, enter the criterion as *=Head*.

▶ The ? (question mark) stands for any single character in the same position as the question mark. For example, **h?t** would find *hut, hat, hit-man, Hitachi, hot,* and *hit*.

To use the asterisk or question mark in your text criteria without having them act as wildcards, precede them with a tilde character (~). For example to find *True?*, enter the criterion as **True~?**.

TUTORIAL

In this tutorial you display a list using a data form and then find data in the list. You find exact matches and use comparison operators to find ranges of matches.

Getting Started

1. Open the *salelst2.xls* workbook stored in the *tutorial* directory on the *Excel Student Resource Disk (Part 1)*.

Finding Exact Matches

2. Select any cell in the list (it must have a column label), then pull down the **Data** menu and click the **Form** command to display the data form. Data from the first record in the list will be displayed in the form. The title of the dialog box is taken from the name of the worksheet as displayed on the sheet tab.

3. Click the **Criteria** command button to display the Criteria dialog box (see the top margin illustration).

4. Type **Fitzgerald** in the **Salesperson** edit box and click the **Find Next** command button to display the first record that meets the criterion (see the bottom margin illustration).

5. Continue clicking the **Find Next** and **Find Prev** command buttons to display each of the other records that meets the criterion.

Using Comparison Operators

6. Click the **Criteria** command button to display the Criteria dialog box.

7. Click the **Clear** command button to clear the current criterion.

8. Type **<150** in the **Sales Units** edit box and click the **Find Next** or **Find Prev** command button to display the first or last record that meets the criterion.

9. Continue clicking the **Find Next** and **Find Prev** command buttons to display each of the other records that meets the criterion.

10. Click the **Criteria** command button to display the Criteria dialog box.

11. Click the **Clear** command button to clear the current criterion.

12. Type **>150** in the **Sales Units** edit box and click the **Find Next** or **Find Prev** command button to display the first record that meets the criterion—more than 150 units (see illustration on following page).

13. Continue clicking the **Find Next** and **Find Prev** command buttons to display each of the other records that meets the criterion—more than 150 units.

Step 3

Step 4

Step 17

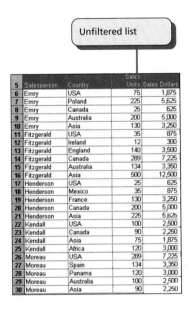

Unfiltered list

5	Salesperson	Country	Sales Units	Sales Dollars
6	Emry	USA	75	1,875
7	Emry	Poland	225	5,625
8	Emry	Canada	25	625
9	Emry	Australia	200	5,000
10	Emry	Asia	130	3,250
11	Fitzgerald	USA	35	875
12	Fitzgerald	Ireland	12	300
13	Fitzgerald	England	140	3,500
14	Fitzgerald	Canada	289	7,225
15	Fitzgerald	Australia	134	3,350
16	Fitzgerald	Asia	500	12,500
17	Henderson	USA	25	625
18	Henderson	Mexico	35	875
19	Henderson	France	130	3,250
20	Henderson	Canada	200	5,000
21	Henderson	Asia	225	5,625
22	Kendall	USA	100	2,500
23	Kendall	Canada	90	2,250
24	Kendall	Asia	75	1,875
25	Kendall	Africa	120	3,000
26	Moreau	USA	289	7,225
27	Moreau	Spain	134	3,350
28	Moreau	Panama	120	3,000
29	Moreau	Australia	100	2,500
30	Moreau	Asia	90	2,250

Filtered so just USA records are displayed

5	Salesperson	Country	Sales Units	Sales Dollars
6	Emry	USA	75	1,875
11	Fitzgerald	USA	35	875
17	Henderson	USA	25	625
22	Kendall	USA	100	2,500
26	Moreau	USA	289	7,225

Using Multiple Comparison Operators

14. Click the **Criteria** command button to display the Criteria dialog box.

15. Click the **Clear** command button to clear the current criterion.

16. Type **Emry** in the **Salesperson** edit box and <150 in the **Sales Units** edit box.

17. Click the **Find Next** or **Find Prev** command button to display the first or last record that meets both criteria. Continue clicking the **Find Next** and or **Find Prev** command buttons to display each of the other records that meets the criterion (see the top margin illustration).

Finishing Up

18. Click the **Close** command button to close the data form dialog box.

19. Close the workbook without saving your changes.

6-5. FILTERING RECORDS

There are times when only part of a list is of interest. For example, you may have a national membership list but only want to work with records for those members living in Lexington, Kentucky. In cases such as these, you can hide the records of all other people by filtering the list. A filter screens all of the records and only lets those that match the criteria pass through to the screen. Filtering does not rearrange the list as sorting does. Instead, it temporarily hides all records that do not match the criteria you specify.

To filter a list, you use Excel's AutoFilter command to look for exact matches or use comparison criteria just as you did to find records using the data form.

 QUICKSTEPS: FILTERING RECORDS WITH AUTOFILTER

1. Select any cell in the list.

2. Pull down the **Data** menu and click the **Filter** command to cascade the menu.

3. Click the **AutoFilter** command to add drop-down arrows (⊞) to the column label of each column in the list.

4. Click the drop-down arrow (⊞) for any column where you want to specify a criterion and select one of the filter criteria described in the box "Understanding AutoFilter Criteria." Immediately the program enters Filter mode, and records that do not match that criterion are hidden. (Repeat this step for other fields to filter the list even more.)

5. To display records again:
   ▸ Click any blue drop-down arrow (⊞) and click the *(All)* criterion at the top of the list to select it and turn off the filter for that column; or
   ▸ Pull down the **Data** menu, click the **Filter** command to cascade the menu, and click the **Show All** command.

6. To turn off Filter mode, pull down the **Data** menu, click the **Filter** command to cascade the menu, and click the **AutoFilter** command to turn it off and remove the drop-down arrows (⊞) from each column label in the list.

UNDERSTANDING AUTOFILTER CRITERIA

When you are in Filter mode, you can click any of the drop-down arrows (⬇) to specify a filter criterion for that column. When you do so, you have the following choices:

(All) turns filtering off for the column (and displays all records in the list provided the same has been done to all fields in the list).

(Custom) displays the Custom AutoFilter dialog box. Using this box you can specify comparison criteria to display records that fall above or below a certain value or fall within a range. To do so, you use the drop-down arrows (⬇) to specify a comparison operator (=, <, >, >=, <=, or <>) and a value.

You can also use this dialog box to search for records that meet two or more criteria (an **And** criteria) or meet one of two or more criteria (an **Or** criteria). To do so, you click the **And** or **Or** option button (◉) and specify a second criterion.

▶ **And** criteria display only those records that match all of the criteria you specify. For example, if you enter >100 **And** <500, only records greater than 100 AND less than 500 are displayed. This is an ideal way to display only those records that fall within a range.

▶ **Or** criteria display all records that match one or more of the criteria you specify. For example, if you enter <100 **Or** >500, only records less than 100 OR greater than 500 are displayed. Or if you enter =**Ohio Or** =**California**, only records from those two states are listed. This is an ideal way to display only those records that fall below one value or above another or meet one of two criteria.

Unique entries listed in any cell in the column are displayed. You can click any one of them to display only those records that match the entry. Selecting one is like using the equal to (=) comparison operator.

(Blanks) displays all records with no entries in the field.

(NonBlanks) displays all records with entries in the field.

TIP: SELECTING CRITERIA FROM THE DROP-DOWN LISTS

When you are in Filter mode and click one of the drop-down arrows (⬇) near a column label, every unique entry in that column is listed. If the list is a small one, after clicking the drop-down arrow (⬇), type the first few letters of the item and the list will scroll to that point.

TIP: VISUAL CLUES WHEN FILTERING

When you filter a list, you may forget you've done so and assume that all of the records are displayed. To prevent this, Excel provides you with a number of visual clues that the list has been filtered and that the program is in Filter mode.

▶ The status bar indicates the number of records that match the criteria and the total number of records in the list.

▶ The drop-down arrow (⬇) for the field where the filter criteria have been entered is blue.

▶ The row numbers for the filtered list are blue.

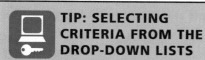

Step 3

TUTORIAL

In this tutorial you filter a list so only those records that match your criteria are displayed. You create filters with a single criterion and filters that have two criteria where both (AND) or either (OR) must be met.

Getting Started

1. Open the *salelst2.xls* workbook stored in the *tutorial* directory on the *Excel Student Resource Disk (Part 1)*.

Filtering Records That Meet a Single Criterion

2. Select any cell in the list, then pull down the **Data** menu and click the **Filter** command to cascade the menu.

3. Click the **AutoFilter** command to add drop-down arrows (⬇) to the column label of each column in the list (see the margin illustration).

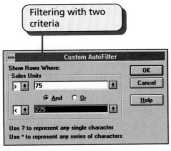

	A	B	C	D
1	Type **Name:** your name into cell A1 and press **Enter**			
2	Filename: salelst2			
3	15-Nov-94			
4				
5	Salesperson	Country	Sales Un	Sales Dolla
22	Kendall	USA	100	2,500
23	Kendall	Canada	90	2,250
24	Kendall	Asia	75	1,875
25	Kendall	Africa	120	3,000

Just records with *Kendall* in the field are displayed.

Step 4

4. Click the *Salesperson* drop-down arrow (⬇), and click *Kendall* to display just records with that name in the column (field). See the top margin illustration.

5. To display all records again, click the *Salesperson* drop-down arrow (⬇), and click *(All)* at the top of the list. (You may have to scroll the list to see it.)

6. Click the *Country* drop-down arrow (⬇), and click *Canada* to display just records with that country in the column.

7. To display all records again, click the *Country* drop-down arrow (⬇), and click *(All)*.

Filtering Records That Meet Two Criteria in Separate Fields (AND)

8. Click the *Salesperson* drop-down arrow (⬇), and click *Kendall* to display just records with that name in the column.

9. Click the *Country* drop-down arrow (⬇), and click *Canada* to display just records for Kendall in Canada.

10. To display all records again, pull down the **Data** menu, click the **Filter** command to cascade the menu, and click the **Show All** command.

Filtering Records That Meet Two Criteria in the Same Field (AND)

11. Click the *Sales Units* drop-down arrow (⬇), and click *(Custom...)* to display the Custom AutoFilter dialog box. The first box contains an equal sign (=), and the insertion point is flashing in the text box to its right.

12. Click the drop-down arrow (⬇) for the box containing the equal sign, and click the greater than operator (>) to select it.

13. Click the drop-down arrow (⬇) for the text box to the right, and click *75* to select it.

14. The **And** option button on the row between the two criteria should be on (◉). If it isn't on, click it.

15. Click the drop-down arrow (⬇) for the box below the one with the greater than sign, and click the less than operator (<), to select it.

16. Click the drop-down arrow (⬇) for the text box to its right, and click *225* to select it. (You will have to scroll the list to see it). See the middle margin illustration.

Filtering with two criteria

Custom AutoFilter

Show Rows Where:
Sales Units
[>] [75]   [OK]
                  [Cancel]
     ◉ **And**   ○ **Or**
[<] [225]   [Help]

Use **?** to represent any single character
Use ***** to represent any series of characters

Step 16

17. Click the **OK** command button to display all records with sales units of more than 75 or less than 225. Click in the *Sales Units* column and then click the **Sort Descending** button on the toolbar to sort the list (see the bottom margin illustration).

18. To turn off Filter mode, pull down the **Data** menu, click the **Filter** command to cascade the menu, and click the **AutoFilter** command to turn it off. This removes the drop-down arrows (⬇) from each column in the list and displays all records.

Finishing Up

19. Close the workbook without saving your changes.

	A	B	C	D
1	Type **Name:** your name into cell A1 and press **Enter**			
2	Filename: salelst2			
3	15-Nov-94			
4				
5	Salesperson	Country	Sales Un	Sales Dolla
9	Emry	Australia	200	5,000
10	Henderson	Canada	200	5,000
13	Fitzgerald	England	140	3,500
15	Fitzgerald	Australia	134	3,350
19	Moreau	Spain	134	3,350
20	Emry	Asia	130	3,250
22	Henderson	France	130	3,250
23	Kendall	Africa	120	3,000
25	Moreau	Panama	120	3,000
27	Kendall	USA	100	2,500
28	Moreau	Australia	100	2,500
29	Kendall	Canada	90	2,250
30	Moreau	Asia	90	2,250

Step 17

A descending sort of a multiple criteria filter

6-6. USING DATABASE FUNCTIONS

In PicTorial 4 we saw how to use functions. Excel has some special functions you can use to summarize data in lists. You use these functions, called *database functions*, when you want to summarize values that meet particular criteria. For instance, you can use the database function DSUM to total only sales from California and the database function DCOUNT to count the number of orders from Florida.

Let's look at an example based on the list we have been using in this PicTorial, *salelst2.xls*. In this list, sales are broken down by salesperson, country, sales units, and sales dollars. We can use the DSUM function to summarize any aspect of this data.

To use regular functions, you specify arguments. Database functions have similar requirements, and take the form FUNCTION NAME(*database,field,criteria*).

▶ The *database* is the address of the list you want checked, including the column labels. In our example, the database is the range A5:D30.

▶ The *field* is the address of the cell containing the column label of the data you want summarized. In our example, we will be summarizing sales dollars, and so we specify the field as the cell containing that column label, D5.

▶ To specify the criteria, you must create an area on the worksheet called a *criteria range* and enter into it the criteria to be used. The method in which you specify the criteria is important, and it is a little complicated.

In our example, we will use three separate criteria. We will summarize sales dollars by (1) salesperson, (2) country, and (3) salesperson by country. We will enter the criteria in three ranges, one of which overlaps the other two.

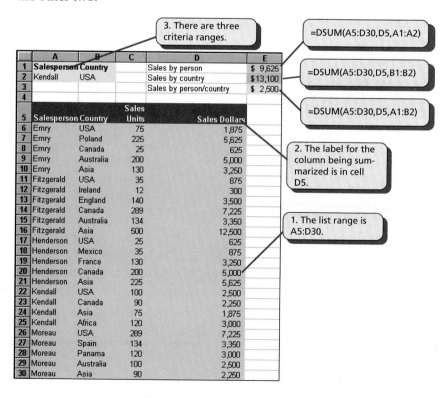

(1) The criteria range A1:A2 tells the function to sum all entries for Kendall.

(2) The criteria range B1:B2 tells the function to sum all entries for the USA.

(3) The criteria range A1:B2 tells the function to summarize all entries for Kendall in the USA.

Since rows of the list can be hidden during certain operations, we place the range above or below the list, not to its left or right. Note that each criteria range contains at least one column label (*Salesperson* or *Country*) and one criterion (*Kendall* or *USA*) that filters the records to be summarized. The criteria range's labels must match the column labels in the list exactly. To make them match exactly, use the Copy or Paste commands to copy the labels from the list to the criteria range.

The shape and content of the criteria range vary slightly depending on your goal. You can find records that meet all of your criteria, one of your criteria, or any number of your criteria.

To find records that match all of your criteria (an AND criterion), enter the criteria on the same row. For example, to find records for Kendall in the USA, enter both on the same row (see the top margin illustration).

To find records that match one of your criteria (an OR criterion), enter the criteria on different rows. For example, to find records for Kendall or records for the USA, enter them on different rows (see the middle margin illustration).

To find records that meet different criteria in the same column, use more than one of the column labels in the criteria range. For example, to find sales for Kendall or Henderson, enter the *Salesperson* column label for each (see the bottom margin illustration).

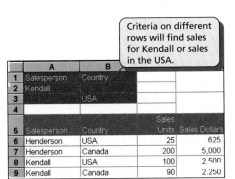

Both criteria on same row will find sales for Kendall in the USA.

An AND Criterion

Criteria on different rows will find sales for Kendall or sales in the USA.

An OR Criterion

TIP: NAMING RANGES

When using database functions, it is easier if you assign names to the database range so that you can refer to it in the functions by name rather than by cell addresses.

QUICKSTEPS: ENTERING DATABASE FUNCTIONS

1. Select the cell in which you want to enter the function, and then click the Function Wizard button on the toolbar.

2. Click *Database* in the **Function Category** list to select it and display database functions in the **Function Name** list.

3. Click the name of the desired function in the **Function Name** list to select it, and then click the **Next** command button to display the Function Wizard Step 2 of 2 dialog box.

4. Enter the database, field, and criteria in those text boxes, and then click the **OK** command button.

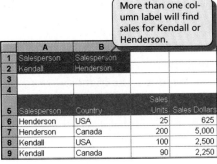

More than one column label will find sales for Kendall or Henderson.

Different Criterion

TUTORIAL

In this tutorial you use database functions to calculate the sales by a salesperson, the sales in a country, or the sales by a salesperson in a specific country. When finished, your list should look like the one in the figure "Using Database Functions."

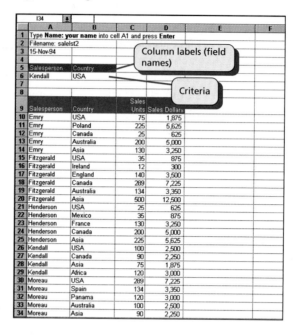

Using Database Functions

Getting Started

1. Open the *salelst2.xls* workbook stored in the *tutorial* directory on the *Excel Student Resource Disk (Part 1)*.

2. Select rows 5 through 8 using the row headings, click the right mouse button in the selected area to display a shortcut menu, and click **I**nsert to insert 4 blank rows above the list.

Entering a Criteria Range

3. Enter the labels for the criteria range by copying cells A9 and B9 (the column labels *Salesperson* and *Country*) and pasting them into cells A5 and B5.

4. Type the criteria *Kendall* into cell A6 and *USA* into cell B6.

Entering Database Functions

5. Select the range A9 through D34, click the Name box on the formula bar, type **Sales_List** to name the list, and press [Enter ←]. Then click anywhere on the worksheet to remove the highlight from the selected range.

6. Enter the headings and functions shown in the range E5 through F7 in the figure "The Database Functions" on the next page. Widen column E as necessary to fully display the descriptive labels for the functions, and format the function cells as currency with no decimal places. Notice how you identify the list by the name you assigned it rather than cell references. The numbers displayed in cells F5 through F7 are those for Kendall, for the USA, and Kendall's sales in the USA.

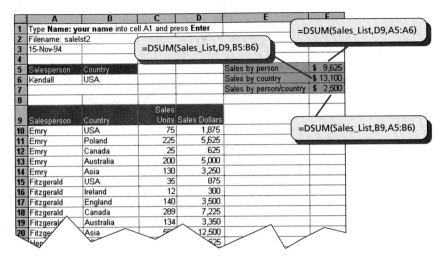

The Database Functions

Filtering Records That Meet One Criteria

7. Delete *Kendall* from cell A6. The *sales by person* are now displayed for all salespeople. The *sales by country* and *sales by person/country* are total USA sales.

8. Enter **Australia** in cell A7 in place of USA to calculate based on total Australian sales.

9. Type **Emry** into cell A6 to calculate based on total Emry's Australian sales.

Finishing Up

10. Save, print, and close the workbook.

6-7. CREATING AUTOMATIC SUBTOTALS

When you have a list containing identical entries in the same column, you can sort the list by that column to group identical entries together. You can then automatically subtotal other columns on the list based on those groupings. For example, you may have a list of sales by store, region, or country. Using Excel's Subtotals command, you can sort the list by any of these categories and then quickly add subtotals to compare them. This not only saves you time, but reduces the possibility of introducing errors.

QUICKSTEPS: CREATING AUTOMATIC SUBTOTALS

1. Sort the list using the field you want to group by as the Sort By column. (This is not the same column that you want to subtotal.)

2. Select any cell in the list, pull down the **Data** menu, and click the **Subtotals** command to display the Subtotal dialog box and automatically select the list. (If the list isn't selected correctly, click the **Cancel** command button, select the list manually, and then repeat this step.)

3. Enter responses into the dialog box as described in the box "Understanding the Subtotal Dialog Box."

4. Click the **OK** command button to add subtotals.

UNDERSTANDING THE SUBTOTAL DIALOG BOX

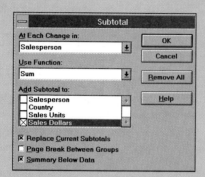

When you pull down the **Data** menu and click the **Subtotals** command, the Subtotal dialog box is displayed.

At Each Change In drop-down list displays a list of the columns in the list. Select the one that contains the grouping you want to subtotal.

Use Function drop-down list displays a list of subtotal functions you can specify. Your choices include:

▶ **Sum** totals the values in the subtotal group.

▶ **Count** counts the number of cells containing data in the subtotal group.

▶ **Average** averages the values in the subtotal group.

▶ **Max** finds the largest value in the subtotal group.

▶ **Min** finds the smallest value in the subtotal group.

▶ **Product** multiples all of the values in the subtotal group.

▶ **Count Nums** counts the number of records containing numeric data.

▶ **StdDev** estimates the standard deviation based on the subtotal group being a sample.

▶ **StdDevp** calculates the standard deviation based on the subtotal group being the entire population.

▶ **Var** estimates the variance based on the subtotal group being a sample.

▶ **Varp** calculates the variance based on the subtotal group being the entire population.

Add Subtotal to check boxes specify which columns will be subtotaled.

Replace Current Subtotals check box, when on (⊠), replaces all current subtotals with new ones that you specify. When off, current subtotals are retained and new ones added.

Page Break Between Groups check box, when on, prints each group starting on a new page.

Summary Data Below check box, when on, places the summary rows and grand total row below the associated data. When off, they are placed above the associated data.

Remove All command button removes all automatic subtotals from the list.

UNDERSTANDING OUTLINE SYMBOLS

When you use the Subtotals command, outline symbols are displayed at the left side of the worksheet. These symbols include the show detail symbols, the hide detail symbols, the outline level symbols, and the outline level

▶ *Row and column level symbols* (①, ②, ③) indicate the number of row and column levels in the outline. Click any one of these symbols to collapse or expand that level of the outline.

▶ *Show detail symbols* (⊞) indicate summary rows or columns with hidden detail rows or columns. Click the symbol to display the hidden detail.

▶ *Hide detail symbols* (⊟) indicate summary rows or columns with displayed detail rows or columns. Click the symbol to hide the detail data indicated by the column or row level bar.

▶ *Row and column level bars* appear when detail rows and columns are displayed. Click anywhere on these level bars to hide the detail rows or columns.

TUTORIAL

In this tutorial you create and remove automatic subtotals from a list. You also explore how you change the column used for determining which records are subtotaled.

Getting Started

1. Open the *salelst2.xls* workbook stored in the *tutorial* directory on the *Excel Student Resource Disk (Part 1)*.

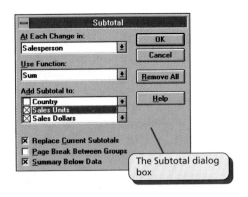

The Subtotal dialog box

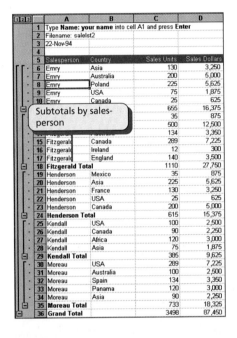

Subtotals by salesperson

	A	B	C	D
1	Type Name: your name into cell A1 and press Enter			
2	Filename: salelst2			
3	22-Nov-94			
4				
5	Salesperson	Country	Sales Units	Sales Dollars
6	Emry	Asia	130	3,250
7	Emry	Australia	200	5,000
8	Emry	Poland	225	5,625
9	Emry	USA	75	1,875
10	Emry	Canada	25	625
			655	16,375
			35	875
			500	12,500
			134	3,350
15	Fitzgerald	Canada	289	7,225
16	Fitzgerald	Ireland	12	300
17	Fitzgerald	England	140	3,500
18	Fitzgerald Total		1110	27,750
19	Henderson	Mexico	35	875
20	Henderson	Asia	225	5,625
21	Henderson	France	130	3,250
22	Henderson	USA	25	625
23	Henderson	Canada	200	5,000
24	Henderson Total		615	15,375
25	Kendall	USA	100	2,500
26	Kendall	Canada	90	2,250
27	Kendall	Africa	120	3,000
28	Kendall	Asia	75	1,875
29	Kendall Total		385	9,625
30	Moreau	USA	289	7,225
31	Moreau	Australia	100	2,500
32	Moreau	Spain	134	3,350
33	Moreau	Panama	120	3,000
34	Moreau	Asia	90	2,250
35	Moreau Total		733	18,325
36	Grand Total		3498	87,450

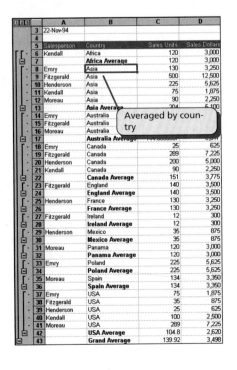

Averaged by country

	A	B	C	D
3	22-Nov-94			
4				
5	Salesperson	Country	Sales Units	Sales Dollars
6	Kendall	Africa	120	3,000
7		Africa Average	120	3,000
8	Emry	Asia	130	3,250
9	Fitzgerald	Asia	500	12,500
10	Henderson	Asia	225	5,625
11	Kendall	Asia	75	1,875
12	Moreau	Asia	90	2,250
13		Asia Average	204	5,100
14	Emry	Australia		
15	Fitzgerald	Australia		
16	Moreau	Australia		
17		Australia Average		
18	Emry	Canada	25	625
19	Fitzgerald	Canada	289	7,225
20	Henderson	Canada	200	5,000
21	Kendall	Canada	90	2,250
22		Canada Average	151	3,775
23	Fitzgerald	England	140	3,500
24		England Average	140	3,500
25	Henderson	France	130	3,250
26		France Average	130	3,250
27	Fitzgerald	Ireland	12	300
28		Ireland Average	12	300
29	Henderson	Mexico	35	875
30		Mexico Average	35	875
31	Moreau	Panama	120	3,000
32		Panama Average	120	3,000
33	Emry	Poland	225	5,625
34		Poland Average	225	5,625
35	Moreau	Spain	134	3,350
36		Spain Average	134	3,350
37	Emry	USA	75	1,875
38	Fitzgerald	USA	35	875
39	Henderson	USA	25	625
40	Kendall	USA	100	2,500
41	Moreau	USA	289	7,225
42		USA Average	104.8	2,620
43		Grand Average	139.92	3,498

Subtotals Based on Person

2. Click anywhere in column A of the list and then click the **Sort Ascending** button on the toolbar.

3. Select any cell in the list, pull down the **Data** menu and click the **Subtotals** command to display the Subtotal dialog box and automatically select the list. The dialog box specifies that subtotals be added for each salesperson, that they be sums, and that the sums are to be added to the sales dollars column.

4. Click the *Sales Units* check box in the **Add Subtotal to** list to turn it on (see the top margin illustration).

5. Click the **OK** command button to add subtotals. Notice how lines are inserted under each group of records with the same salesperson, and subtotals are added to the sales units and dollars columns. A grand total is displayed at the bottom of the list (see the middle margin illustration).

Removing Subtotals

6. Select any cell in the list, pull down the **Data** menu and click the **Subtotals** command to display the Subtotal dialog box and then click the **Remove All** command button.

Subtotals Based on Country

7. Click anywhere in column B of the list and then click the **Sort Ascending** button on the toolbar.

8. Select any cell in the list, pull down the **Data** menu and click the **Subtotals** command to display the Subtotal dialog box and automatically select the list.

9. In the **At Each Change in** section, click the drop-down arrow (⬇) to display the list of fields and click *Country* to select it.

10. In the **Use Function** section, click the drop-down arrow (⬇) to display the list of functions and click *Average* to select it.

Subtotals by country

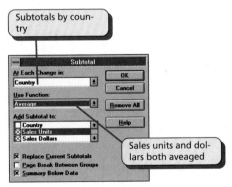

Sales units and dollars both aveaged

11. Click the **OK** command button to add subtotals based on the new settings. Notice how lines are inserted under each group of records with the same country and subtotals are added to the sales units and sales dollars column. The subtotals average the number of units and dollars sold in each country (see the bottom margin illustration).

Finishing Up

12. Click the **Print Preview** button on the toolbar to see if the worksheet will print on one page. If it won't, click the <u>S</u>etup button to display the Page Setup dialog box, on the Page tab click the <u>F</u>it to option button to turn it on, and then click the **OK** command button to return to the Print Preview window. Click the **Print** command button to print the worksheet.

13. Save and close the workbook.

PicTorial 6 Review Questions

 True-False

T F 1. All text in a column does not have to have the same format.

T F 2. You can sort on more than one field.

T F 3. You can edit records using the Data Form dialog box.

T F 4. You should have blank rows between column headings and records.

T F 5. You can have as many lists on a worksheet as you desire.

T F 6. It is recommended that column headings be formatted differently than the records below them.

T F 7. When using a number as text, insert a double quotation mark before the number.

T F 8. You cannot delete records using the Data Form dialog box.

T F 9. A list must have the same type of data in each field.

T F 10. You can find records using the Data Form dialog box.

 Multiple Choice

1. _____ are sets of related data.
   a. Fields
   b. Lists
   c. Records
   d. Cells

2. If using the criteria =**Gen**, the results would include _____.
   a. General
   b. Generic
   c. Gen
   d. All of the above

3. When entering numbers as text, type a(n) _____ as the first character.
   a. Parentheses
   b. Exclamation point

c. Quotation mark

d. Apostrophe

4. When sorting, the _____ key specifies the field on which the list is to be sorted.

   a. Initial

   b. Default

   c. Principal

   d. Primary

5. The _____ must be entered as the first row of a list.

   a. Fields

   b. Column headings

   c. Records

   d. Cells

6. To use the asterisk or question mark in a text criteria without having them act as wildcards, precede them with a(n) _____.

   a. Tilde

   b. Exclamation point

   c. Quotation mark

   d. Apostrophe

7. When using the Data Form, Edit boxes are labeled with a _____ name automatically taken from the list's column headings.

   a. Row

   b. Range

   c. File

   d. Field

8. _____ are columns of information that make up a record.

   a. Fields

   b. Lists

   c. Column headings

   d. Cells

9. When does Excel display the message **Cannot extend list or database**?

   a. When Excel recognizes that the disk is full

   b. When Excel recognizes the file is full

   c. When Excel finds data on the row beneath the last row of the list

   d. When Excel finds data on the row above the first row of the list

10. When using the Data Form, to move between edit boxes, press _____.

    a. Enter ←

    b. Tab ⇄

    c. Spacebar

    d. Ctrl + Enter ←

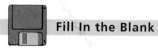

Fill In the Blank

Criteria

1. Another name for column labels is _field names_.

2. The fastest way to locate a record in a long list is to use _comparison criteria_

3. The term *database* is just another name for what Excel normally calls a(n) _list_.

4. When working with a list, you can display it using a special dialog box called the _data form_

5. When sorting in _Ascend_ order, text is organized from A to Z.

6. The row numbers for a filtered list are colored _blue_.

7. When sorting in _descending_ order, text is organized from Z to A.

8. When using AutoFilter, any records that do not match the criterion are _hidden_.

9. The _status bar_ indicates the number of records that match the criteria and the total number of records in the list.

10. When using AutoFilter, you can click any of the drop-down arrows to specify a filter criterion for that column. When you do so, you have the following choices: _all_, _custom_, _unique_, _blanks_, and _nonblanks_

Pictorial 6 Lab Activities

▶▶ COMPUTER-BASED TUTORIALS

We suggest you complete the following computer-based lessons to learn more about the features discussed in this PicTorial. To do so, pull down the **Help** menu and click the **Examples and Demos** command, click the *Topic* listed in the table "Suggested Examples and Demos to Complete" and then click the *Subtopic* listed in that same table. (If you need more help on using the system, see the "Computer-Based Tutorials" section at the end of PicTorial 1.)

Suggested Examples and Demos to Complete	
Topic	Subtopic
☐ Organizing Data in a List	Sorting a List
☐ Organizing Data in a List	Filtering a List Using AutoFilter
☐ Organizing Data in a List	Filtering Data Using Complex Criteria
☐ Organizing Data in a List	Adding Subtotals to a List

▶▶ QUICKSTEP DRILLS

6-1. The Anatomy of a List

An Excel list is organized into fields (columns) and records (rows). Each field is named on the first row or the list. In this drill you create a simple list from scratch. When finished, your model should look like the figure "The Address List."

	A	B	C	D	E	F	G	H
1	Type **Name: your name** into cell A1 and press **Enter**							
2	Filename: address							
3	16-Nov-94							
4								
5	LASTNAME	FIRSTNAME	STREET	CITY	STATE	ZIP	AREA	PHONE
6	Benjamin	Nancy	100 Elm Street	Cambridge	MA	01945	617	555-1000
7	Davis	John	300 Main Street	Alpine	NJ	07632	201	555-1001
8	Baxter	Michelle	48 Oak Avenue	San Francisco	CA	30255	415	555-1002
9	Jones	John	210001 3rd Street	Englewood Cliffs	NJ	07632	201	555-1003

The Address List

1. Open the *address.xls* workbook stored in the *drill* directory on the *Excel Student Resource Disk (Part 1)* and enter your name into cell A1.

2. Enter the column labels shown in the cells with the red background in the figure "The Address List." Format the column headings so they have a red background and white text.

3. Enter the records shown in the cells with the light yellow background in the figure "The Address List." (Remember to enter ZIP codes, area codes, and phone numbers as text by typing an apostrophe before typing each number. If you don't do this, ZIP codes beginning with a zero will not display the zero.)

4. Use the **Color** and **Font Color** buttons on the toolbar to format the column labels so they have a black background and bold white text.

5. Save, print, and close the workbook.

6-2. Entering and Editing Data Using a Data Form

In this drill you enter new records into an existing list using Excel's data form. When finished, your model should look like the figure "The Expanded Address List."

	A	B	C	D	E	F	G	H
1	Type **Name: your name** into cell A1 and press **Enter**							
2	Filename: address							
3	16-Nov-94							
4								
5	LASTNAME	FIRSTNAME	STREET	CITY	STATE	ZIP	AREA	PHONE
6	Benjamin	Nancy	100 Elm Street	Cambridge	MA	01945	617	555-1000
7	Davis	John	300 Main Street	Alpine	NJ	07632	201	555-1001
8	Baxter	Michelle	46 Oak Avenue	San Francisco	CA	30255	415	555-1002
9	Jones	John	210001 3rd Street	Englewood Cliffs	NJ	07632	201	555-1003
10	Kendall	Liz	176 Midville Road	Chicago	IL	60615	312	555-1004
11	June	Gary	75 Howdy Blvd.	Tenafly	NJ	07632	201	555-1005
12	Henderson	Carolyn	Beach Lane	Red Bank	NJ	07631	201	555-3001
13	Sen	Kunal	1250 N. Lake Shore	Chicago	IL	60615	312	555-1007
14	Foley	Kim	25 Elm Street	Salem	MA	01955	508	555-2001

The Expanded Address List

1. Open the *address.xls* workbook stored in the *drill* directory on the *Excel Student Resource Disk (Part 1)*.

2. Use the **Data**, **Form** command to display the list and enter the records shown in the cells with the light yellow background in the

figure "The Expanded Address List." (Remember to enter ZIP codes, area codes, and phone numbers as text by typing an apostrophe before typing each number. If you don't do this, ZIP codes beginning with a zero will not display the zero.)

3. Save, print, and close the workbook.

6-3. Performing Simple Sorts

Sorting a list is the fastest way to see how the contents of fields are related. For example, you can sort text, numbers, or dates so they range from a to z, smallest to largest, or earliest to latest. In this drill you practice sorting a list by a number of fields in ascending and descending orders.

1. Open the *bugs.xls* workbook stored in the *drill* directory on the *Excel Student Resource Disk (Part 1)* and enter your name into cell A1.

2. Sort the list first in ascending and then descending order by date. What were the dates of the first and last films?

3. Sort the list first in ascending and then descending order by title.

4. Sort the list first in ascending and then descending order by director's last name.

5. Sort the list by director's last name subsorted by date—both in ascending order.

6. Print the sheet, then close the workbook without saving your changes.

6-4. Understanding Criteria—Finding Records

When you have a large list, it can be difficult to find the record you want. To simplify the process you can use the data form's **Criteria** button to find a specific record. In this drill you find specific films based on dates, directors, and titles.

1. Open the *bugs.xls* workbook stored in the *drill* directory on the *Excel Student Resource Disk (Part 1)*.

2. Use the **Data**, **Form** command to display the data form for the list.

3. Use the **Criteria** command button to find all films released after *1-Jan-60*.

4. Use the **Criteria** command button to find all films directed by *Frank Tashlin*.

5. Use the **Criteria** command button to find the film titled *The Wacky Wabbit*.

6. Close the workbook without saving your changes.

6-5. Filtering Records

Instead of finding records, you can filter them so that only the records you want to see are displayed. In this drill you practice filtering the list of Bugs Bunny films.

1. Open the *bugs.xls* workbook stored in the *drill* directory on the *Excel Student Resource Disk (Part 1)*.

2. Use the **Data**, **Filter**, **AutoFilter** commands to add drop-down arrows (▼) to the column label of each column in the list.

3. Click the drop-down arrow (▼) on the *Director, Last* field and filter the list so only films directed by *Jones* are displayed.

4. Click the drop-down arrow (▼) on the *Director, Last* field and filter the list so only films directed by *Freleng* are displayed. Use the **Data**, **Filter**, **Show All** commands to show all records.

5. Click the drop-down arrow (▼) on the *Release* field, select *(Custom...)* and filter the list so only films made on or before *1-Jan-43* are displayed.

6. Click the drop-down arrow (▼) on the *Release* field, select *(Custom...)* and filter the list so only films made between *1-Jan-43* and *1-Jan-45* are displayed.

7. Click the drop-down arrow (▼) on the *Director, Last* and filter the list so only films directed by *Jones* are displayed. Then click the drop-down arrow (▼) on the *Release* field, select *(Custom...) and* filter the list so only films made by *Jones* on or before *1-Jan-46* are displayed.

8. Close the workbook without saving your changes.

6-6. Using Database Functions

In this drill you enter a database function that counts the number of films directed by the director that you enter in the criteria range. When finished, your model should look like the figure "The Bugs Database Function" shown in part.

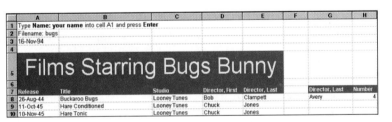

The Bugs Database Function

1. Open the *bugs.xls* workbook stored in the *drill* directory on the *Excel Student Resource Disk (Part 1)* and enter your name in cell A1.

2. Enter a database function that counts the number of films made by any specific director. The function should be entered into cell H8 as =DCOUNTA(A7:E176,E7,G7:G8).

3. Save the revised workbook, then print the page of the sheet with the database function on it.

4. Use the new function to find out how many films each were produced by *Jones*, *Avery*, *Freleng*, and *Clampett*. To do so, enter each of those names into cell G8 one after another.

5. Close the workbook.

6-7. Creating Automatic Subtotals

In this drill you use Excel's Subtotals command to count the number of films directed by each of the Warner Brothers directors. When finished, your model should look like the figure "The Bugs Database Function" shown in part.

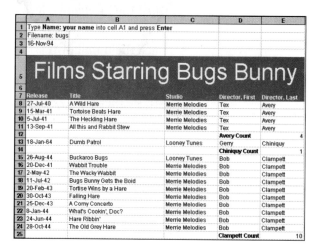

	A	B	C	D	E
1	Type **Name: your name** into cell A1 and press **Enter**				
2	Filename: bugs				
3	16-Nov-94				
4					
5	Films Starring Bugs Bunny				
6					
7	Release	Title	Studio	Director, First	Director, Last
8	27-Jul-40	A Wild Hare	Merrie Melodies	Tex	Avery
9	15-Mar-41	Tortoise Beats Hare	Merrie Melodies	Tex	Avery
10	5-Jul-41	The Heckling Hare	Merrie Melodies	Tex	Avery
11	13-Sep-41	All this and Rabbit Stew	Merrie Melodies	Tex	Avery
12				Avery Count	4
13	18-Jan-64	Dumb Patrol	Looney Tunes	Gerry	Chiniquy
14				Chiniquy Count	1
15	26-Aug-44	Buckaroo Bugs	Looney Tunes	Bob	Clampett
16	20-Dec-41	Wabbit Trouble	Merrie Melodies	Bob	Clampett
17	2-May-42	The Wacky Wabbit	Merrie Melodies	Bob	Clampett
18	11-Jul-42	Bugs Bunny Gets the Boid	Merrie Melodies	Bob	Clampett
19	20-Feb-43	Tortise Wins by a Hare	Merrie Melodies	Bob	Clampett
20	30-Oct-43	Falling Hare	Merrie Melodies	Bob	Clampett
21	25-Dec-43	A Corny Concerto	Merrie Melodies	Bob	Clampett
22	8-Jan-44	What's Cookin', Doc?	Merrie Melodies	Bob	Clampett
23	24-Jun-44	Hare Ribbin'	Merrie Melodies	Bob	Clampett
24	28-Oct-44	The Old Grey Hare	Merrie Melodies	Bob	Clampett
25				Clampett Count	10

Films Counted by Director

1. Open the *bugs.xls* workbook stored in the *drill* directory on the *Excel Student Resource Disk (Part 1)*.

2. Sort by the director's last name in ascending order.

3. Use the **Sub**totals command on the **Data** menu to count the number of films by each director. To do so, specify *Director, Last* as the field in the **At Each Change In** text box and select *Count* as the function from the **Use Function** list. Your results will look like those in the figure "Films Counted by Director."

4. Print the first page of the worksheet.

5. Sort by the *Studio* column in ascending order. When you do so, you will be warned that this will remove sorts and subtotals. Click the **OK** command button and the list is sorted.

6. Use the **Sub**totals command on the **Data** menu to count the number of films by each studio. To do so, change the field in the **At Each Change In** text box from *Director, Last* to *Studio*.

7. Close the workbook.

▶▶ SKILL-BUILDING EXERCISES

6-1. Querying the Textbook Costs Database

One of the most widely used procedures in computing is using comparison operators to limit searches. In this drill you use comparison operators to locate specific groups of records in a small list.

1. Open the *textbook.xls* workbook stored in the *exercise* directory on the *Excel Student Resource Disk (Part 2)* and enter your name.

2. Use the **Data**, **Filter**, **AutoFilter** commands to add drop-down arrows (⬇) to the column label of each column in the list. Use the drop-down arrow (⬇) on the % column to filter the list as follows:

   ▶ Click the drop-down arrow (⬇) on the % column and select (Custom..) to filter the list so only records with entries greater than 10% are displayed.

> ▸ Click the drop-down arrow (⬇) on the % column and select (Custom..) to filter the list so only records with entries less than 10% are displayed.

> ▸ Click the drop-down arrow (⬇) on the % column and select (Custom..) to filter the list so only records with entries less than or equal to 10.5% are displayed.

> ▸ Click the drop-down arrow (⬇) on the % column and select (Custom..) to filter the list so only records with entries greater than or equal to 10.5% are displayed.

3. Make a printout and then close the workbook without saving your changes.

6-2. Exploring the Congressional Database

When lists begin to get large, you can't tell much about them at a glance. However, using database procedures, you can analyze a list to see what organized information it contains. In this drill you analyze a relatively large database listing the members of the 103rd Congress of the United States. When finished, your model should look like the figure "The Congressional Database."

	A	B	C	D	E	F	G	H
1	Type **Name: your name** into cell A1 and press **Enter**						Party	State
2	Filename: congress						D	CA
3	16-Nov							
4							Count	30
5			103 Congress					
6			House of Representatives					
7								
8	Party ⬇	State ⬇	Name ⬇	Phone ⬇	Fax ⬇			
9	R	AK	Young, Donald	1-202-225-5765	1-202-225-5765			
10	R	AL	Bachus, Spencer	1-202-225-4921	na			
11	D	AL	Bevill, Thomas	1-202-225-4876	1-202-225-0842			
12	D	AL	Browder, Glen	1-202-225-3261	1-202-225-9020			
13	R	AL	Callahan, H. L.	1-202-225-4931	1-202-225-0562			
14	D	AL	Cramer Jr, Robert E.	1-202-225-4801	na			

The Congressional Database

1. Open the *congress.xls* workbook stored in the *exercise* directory on the *Excel Student Resource Disk (Part 2)* and enter your name into cell A1.

2. Use the **Data**, **Filter**, **AutoFilter** commands to add drop-down arrows (⬇) to the column label of each column in the list. Use the drop-down arrow (⬇) on the % column to filter the list as follows:

   ▸ Filter the list so only members from California (CA) are listed.

   ▸ Filter the list so only members from your own state are listed.

   ▸ Filter the list so only Democrats from your own state are listed.

   ▸ Filter the list so only Republicans from your own state are listed.

3. Use the **Data**, **Filter**, **Show All** commands to show all records.

4. Sort the list in ascending order by state, then use the **Data**, **Subtotals** command to count the number of members in each state.

5. Sort the list in ascending order by party, then use the **Data**, **Subtotals** command to count the number of members by party.

6. Use the **Data**, **Subtotals** command to remove subtotals from the list. Then use the **Data**, **Filter** command to turn off AutoFilter.

Party	State	Count
D		_____
R		_____
I		_____
D	CA	_____
R	CA	_____
D	NY	_____
R	NY	_____
D	FL	_____

7. Enter the criteria range in cells shown in cells G1:H2 in the figure "The Congressional Database."

8. Select the following ranges and use the Name box on the formula bar to assign them the indicated names.

   ▶ Assign the name Table to the range A8:E450.

   ▶ Assign the name Party to cell A8.

   ▶ Assign the name Criteria to the range G1:H2.

9. Type **Count** in cell G4 and enter the function **=DCOUNTA(Table,Party,Criteria)** in cell H4 to count the number of members from any specified state as shown in the figure "The Congressional Database."

10. Use the database functions to find answers to the following questions:

11. Make a printout of the first page and then close the workbook without saving your changes.

▶▶ REAL-WORLD PROJECTS

6-1. **Customer Analysis**

Analyzing customer purchase patterns is a common practice in the retail business. Computers are used to see who buys what and who spends the most. This way, special promotions can be targeted at the right people. In this project, you open *charges.xls* stored in the *project* directory of the *Excel Student Resource Disk*. This workbook contains a list like the one shown in the figure "Analysis of Customer Charges." You add the correct database functions to analyze the list. These functions should give the total charges, the average charges, and the number of charges for any customer you specify.

	A	B	C	D
1	Type **Name: your name** into cell A1 and press **Enter**			
2	Filename: charges			
3	16-Nov-94			
4				
5	First Name	Last Name	Amount	
6	Martha	Smith	$8	
7	Allen	Smith	$10	
8	Avery	James	$12	
9	Zoro	Smith	$12	
10	John	Smith	$14	
11	Martha	Smith	$19	
12	Bob	James	$23	
13	John	James	$23	
14	Barbara	Smith	$25	
15	Zelda	James	$32	
16	John	Smith	$35	
17	Martha	Smith	$42	
18	Yaz	Smith	$75	
19	Raymond	Smith	$80	
20	John	Smith	$95	
21				
22	First Name	Last Name		
23	John	Smith		
24				
25				
26	Customer Analysis			
27	Sum	144		
28	Average	48		
29	Count	3		

Analysis of Customer Charges

APPENDIX

INTRODUCING WINDOWS 3.1

After completing this PicTorial, you will be able to:

▸ Start your computer system and load Windows

▸ Name and describe the parts of a window

▸ Point with the mouse

▸ Click, double-click, and drag with the mouse

▸ Minimize, maximize, and restore windows

▸ Exit Windows and turn off your equipment

The microcomputer is a versatile machine. With it you can calculate a budget for this year's educational expenses, plot a graph of the results, and, finding that you won't have enough money, write a letter to your boss asking for a raise. To perform each of these tasks on the computer, you load an *application program* specific to it. For example, WordPerfect® and Microsoft® Word are word processing application programs used to enter, edit, and format memos, letters, reports, and other documents. Excel and Lotus® 1-2-3® are spreadsheet application programs used to work with numbers and make calculations.

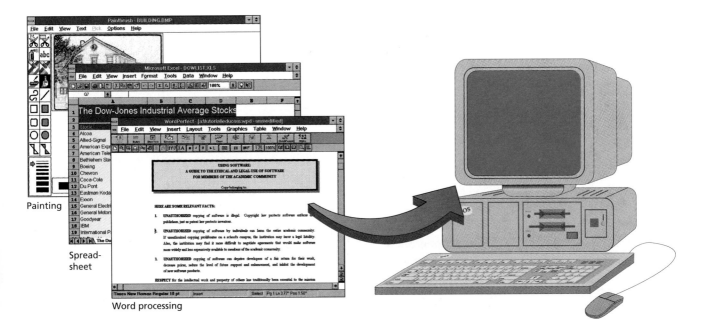

Painting

Spread-sheet

Word processing

To change from one application to another you switch from one application program to another. In this sense, the computer is like an actor, and the application programs are like scripts. When the actor changes scripts, he or she can perform a different role. By changing application programs, you can make your computer perform different applications. Being *computer literate* means that you understand how to use application programs to perform useful work.

Windows is designed to make it easy to work with application programs. Unlike earlier systems where the screen displayed just a command prompt (such as C:\>) and where you had to type all of the commands, Windows' *Graphical User Interface* (also called a GUI—pronounced "goo-ee") allows you to choose commands from pull-down menus and run more than one application program at a time, each in its own window. Using Windows you can run a spreadsheet in one window and a word processor in another. Windows also gives a common look to most programs that are developed to take advantage of its features. Standard commands are used to load programs; call up help; save, retrieve, and print files; enter and edit data; and quit applications. This makes it easier to learn new programs because many of your existing skills are transferable.

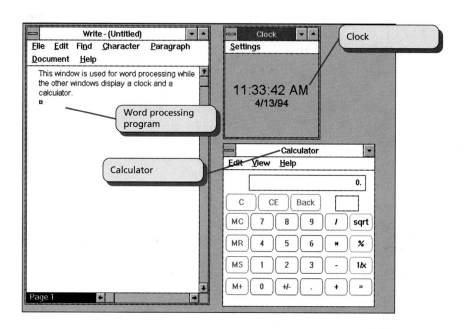

Windows comes with several built-in application programs and accessories, including a word processor, a calculator, and a clock—as shown in the illustration. The most important application program built into Windows is *Program Manager*. Program Manager is important because, unlike most other applications, it remains in the computer's memory from the time you load Windows until you quit. Program Manager's sole task is to start or *launch* all other Windows application programs such as word processors, spreadsheets, and database managers. When you exit an application that you launched from Program Manager, you always return to Program Manager.

This PicTorial gives you enough information about Program Manager to enable you to manipulate the screen and start your application programs. To learn more about Windows 3.1, you might like to read a companion volume in this series, *Windows 3.1 by PicTorial*.

A-1. LOADING WINDOWS

Before you can use Windows, you must load the computer's disk operating system, referred to as *DOS*. This is called *booting the system*. (The term *booting* comes from the expression "pulling yourself up by your bootstraps.") You boot the system by turning on your computer.

TUTORIAL

1. Before you turn on your computer, check to see whether there is a disk in floppy drive A. If there is, eject it or open the drive door. (Ask how to do this if you don't know.) When you turn on a computer, it looks to the *startup drive* for the operating system files that it needs to start up. On a hard disk system like the one you are using, the startup drive is hard drive C, but the computer still looks to floppy drive A first. If there is a disk in that drive when you turn on the computer, you could have a problem loading Windows.

2. Now boot the system by turning on the computer and the display monitor. If you can't find the on/off switches, ask someone where they are.

    When you turn on the computer, it may seem to be inactive for a few moments. In fact, it is running a diagnostic program to be sure the system is operating correctly. What then happens and what you do next depends on how your system is set up. Windows may load automatically, or one of the other outcomes illustrated in the figure "Things That Can Happen When You Boot a System" may occur.

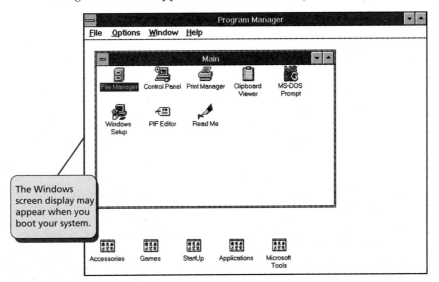

The Windows screen display may appear when you boot your system.

THINGS THAT CAN HAPPEN WHEN YOU BOOT A SYSTEM

A menu designed specifically for your computer lab may appear. If it does, you can usually type a number and press Enter ↵ to load Windows.

The screen may be blank. If it is, turn on the display monitor or adjust its brightness and contrast.

The DOS command prompt may appear. If this happens, type WIN and press Enter ↵.

An error message may read "Non-System disk or disk error." Remove the disk in drive A and follow the instructions on the screen.

3. If Windows does not load automatically, follow the directions that apply to the result you get.

TIP: ARE WE TIMING EGGS HERE, OR WHAT?

When you first load Windows, and at other times when you are using it, an hourglass will appear on the screen. This is Windows' way of telling you it's busy and that you should wait before expecting it to do anything else.

A-2. EXPLORING THE WINDOWS SCREEN

When Windows is first installed on a computer system, it is set to open with a screen that looks like the illustration shown here. But Windows can be customized, and your screen may not look like this. To follow the discussion on the next few pages, you may need to make some adjustments in your screen. Ask someone how to do this for you, or do it yourself following the instructions in the Tip box "Setting the Windows Opening Screen."

TIP: SETTING THE WINDOWS OPENING SCREEN

▶ If the area labeled "Program Manager window" in the illustration fills your whole screen, hold down Alt and press Spacebar. Release both keys and then press R. The Program Manager window should become smaller, revealing the area labeled "Desktop" in the illustration.

▶ If the area labeled "Main window" in the illustration does not appear on your screen, look for the word **Main** in the Program Manager window. Hold down Ctrl and repeatedly press Tab↹ until a highlight appears over the word **Main**. Now release Ctrl and press Enter↵. The Main window should appear.

Now your screen should resemble the one in the illustration.

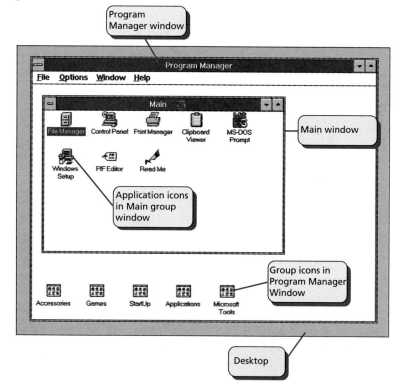

First, notice the boxlike area with a title bar at its top labeled *Program Manager*. This is a *window*. Inside this first window is another window with a title bar labeled *Main*. When working with Windows, it's common to see one window inside another.

Inside the Main window are graphical symbols called *icons*. Each icon has a descriptive label, and its design also gives you a visual clue to what it does. In fact, the term *icon* means "a picture, image, or other representation." Well-designed icons accurately represent their assigned function and are easy to remember. For example, the File Manager icon looks like a file cabinet because you use this application to manage the files on your disks.

Below the Main window are a series of small labeled boxes, also called icons. Your screen may display icons in this area that are labeled *Accessories*, *Games*, *StartUp*, and *Applications* and perhaps *Microsoft Tools*.

Notice that the windows and icons occupy only part of the screen. Around them (and beneath them) is an area called the *desktop*. This desktop is simply the space on the screen available for the display of Windows' various elements. You can add items to this electronic desktop, move items about on it, or take them away from it just as you can on the top of a real desk. In fact, some systems may display one or more icons on the desktop (and not in other windows) when you start Windows. For example, you may see an icon labeled *Vsafe Manager*. This application continually scans the system for signs of viruses that may damage data. If your desktop displays icons, you might ask what they are for.

TIP: DIFFERENT KINDS OF WINDOWS

As you work with Windows, you will find that there are different kinds of windows and icons. They all work the same, but they are referred to by different names. For example, since Program Manager is an application, its window and icon are referred to as an *application window* and an *application icon*. When Program Manager is displayed as a window, it may contain other windows that are called *group windows* because they contain groups of application icons. When you close one of these group windows to an icon, it is called a *group icon*. Group windows are simply a way to keep related application icons together so the desktop is organized.

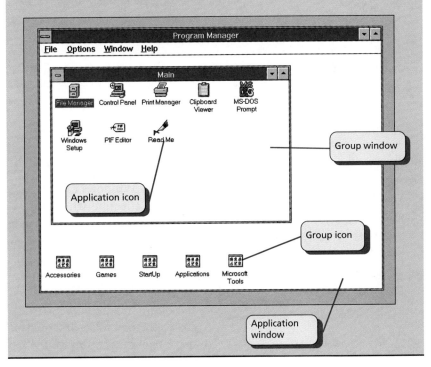

A-3. EXPLORING PROGRAM MANAGER

Windows gets its name because it displays application programs and documents in boxes called windows. All of these windows have many of the same features.

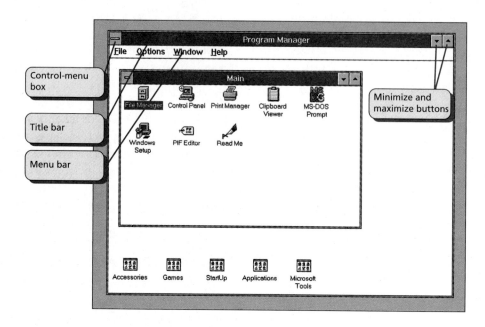

At the top of each window is a *title bar* that lists the name of the application program running in the window or otherwise describes the window's contents.

Every window displays up- and down-pointing arrowheads to the right of the title bar. These are called the Minimize (▼) and Maximize (▲) buttons. As you'll soon see, they are used to change the size of the window.

The upper-left corner of every window displays a *Control-menu box* that displays a Control menu when you click it with the mouse. We shall see that the Control-menu box can also be used to close an open window.

A *menu bar* immediately below the title bar displays the names of menus. These menus list commands that you execute to operate your program.

A-4. EXPLORING YOUR MOUSE

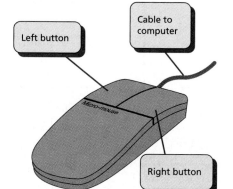

Although Windows can be operated from the keyboard, it is designed to be most effective when used with a pointing device such as a *mouse*. Using a mouse, you can execute commands, specify options, display help, or indicate where you want to type in data. Mice can vary considerably in design, but the most common mouse has two buttons and is connected to the computer by a thin cable.

Turn your mouse over and you may see part of a ball protruding through its bottom (not all mice use balls). Moving the mouse across the table surface makes this ball rotate and send electrical signals to the computer through the cable. These signals move the *mouse pointer* on the screen so its movement mimics the mouse's. The mouse pointer changes shape depending on what it is pointing to and what function it is ready to perform (see the upper margin

Mouse Pointer Shapes

Normal

Pointing to
left or right
window border

Pointing to
window corner

Pointing to
top or bottom
window border

Rest your index
finger on the
left button.

Grip the sides of
the mouse with
your thumb and
ring finger.

illustration). For example, when it is a single-headed arrow, you can click menu names, commands, icons, or buttons. When it is a two-headed arrow, you can drag a window's border to make the window wider or deeper.

TUTORIAL

1. With the mouse cable facing away from you, grip the mouse with your thumb and ring finger (see the lower margin illustration).

2. Move the mouse about the desk and watch the mouse pointer move about the screen. This is called *pointing*. If you haven't used a mouse before, you'll see that you need practice to make the mouse pointer move in a predictable fashion. If you run out of room on the desk or mouse pad when moving the mouse, lift it and place it in a new position and then continue moving it. When you lift the mouse off the desk or mouse pad, the mouse pointer remains fixed on the screen.

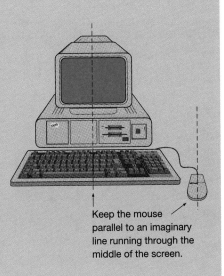

COMMON WRONG TURNS: MOVING THE MOUSE POINTER

When first using a mouse, most people cannot control the mouse pointer on the screen. It seems to move in unpredictable directions. To gain control, hold the mouse exactly perpendicular to the front of the screen. Now when you move it left or right, the pointer on the screen moves left or right on the screen. When you move the mouse forward or backward, the pointer moves up or down on the screen. If you hold the mouse at an angle other than perpendicular to the front of the screen, it's harder to predict the direction in which the pointer will move.

Keep the mouse
parallel to an imaginary
line running through the
middle of the screen.

3. Point to each side of the Program Manager window, and you'll see the pointer change shape.

4. Point to each corner of the Program Manager window, and you'll see the pointer take other shapes.

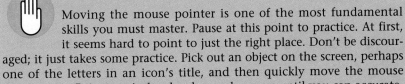

PAUSING FOR PRACTICE

Moving the mouse pointer is one of the most fundamental skills you must master. Pause at this point to practice. At first, it seems hard to point to just the right place. Don't be discouraged; it just takes some practice. Pick out an object on the screen, perhaps one of the letters in an icon's title, and then quickly move the mouse pointer to it. Point to window borders and corners until you can accurately make the pointer change shape. Continue practicing until you can move it to any point you want on the first try.

A-5. CLICKING, DOUBLE-CLICKING, AND DRAGGING

Moving the mouse pointer around the screen isn't enough to operate Windows. You must also know how and when to click the mouse buttons. Depending on the situation, you either click once or you click twice in quick succession—called double-clicking. The first question a new user always asks is "When do I click and when do I double-click?" Generally, you click once to select an item and double-click to execute an action. In other words, clicking an item tells Windows you want to use it. Double-clicking starts an application or executes a command.

The Windows desktop can display more than one window at a time, and sometimes one window can hide another one. You therefore need to know how to drag a window or icon around the screen with the mouse, to reveal the window you are interested in.

> ### TIP: USE THE LEFT BUTTON
>
> Since the left mouse button is the one used most frequently in Windows and Windows applications, the terms *click* and *double-click* in this text refer to the left button. Some application programs do use the right button, so when you need to click or double-click the right button, that button will be specified. (If you are left-handed and have reversed the functions of the mouse buttons, you'll have to remember to reverse the buttons described in this text—press the right button when no button is specified and the left button when we say the right.)

> ### QUICKSTEPS: CLICKING, DOUBLE-CLICKING, AND DRAGGING
>
> ▶ *Clicking* is quickly pressing and then releasing a mouse button—usually the left one. The finger action is similar to that of typing a character on the keyboard. (Windows has a command that swaps the functions of the left and right buttons on the mouse. If you are left-handed and having trouble, ask for help.)
>
> ▶ *Double-clicking* is quickly pressing a button twice in succession. Double-clicking takes practice.
>
> ▶ *Dragging* is pointing to an object, holding down the left mouse button, and moving the mouse to position the object. When you have dragged it to where you want it, you release the mouse button. To cancel a move once you have begun it, you press [Esc] before releasing the mouse button.

TUTORIAL

Clicking and Double-Clicking

1. With the mouse cable facing away from you, grip the mouse with your thumb and ring finger so that your index finger rests on the left mouse button (see the upper margin illustration).

2. Look closely at the title bar labeled *Main* (the smaller of the two windows on the screen), and you'll see two arrowheads, called buttons, to the right of the title (see the lower margin illustration). The Minimize button (▼) points down and the Maximize button (▲) points up. Move the mouse until the mouse pointer is pointing to the Main window's Minimize button (▼).

3. Click (the left button) once, and the Main window changes to an icon. It now looks just like the other icons at the bottom of the Program Manager window, but it is labeled *Main* just as the window was.

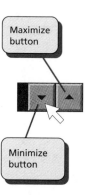

Maximize button

Minimize button

COMMON WRONG TURNS: DOUBLE-CLICKING

The first time most people use a mouse, the chances are good that they'll make one of two mistakes. Either they don't click the second click fast enough or they move the mouse with the button held down and thereby drag something on the screen. If you encounter these problems, first relax. The mouse moves because you are putting too much force into your action. Just grip the mouse lightly and then lightly click with your index finger. The second click must closely follow the first. If when double-clicking an icon you pause too long between clicks, a menu (called the Control menu) will be displayed above the icon. If this happens, point anywhere but at the icon or menu and click once to close the menu. Just try again until the window opens.

PAUSING FOR PRACTICE

Clicking and double-clicking are fundamental skills in Windows. Pause here and continue practicing these skills by repeating this Tutorial section until they are second nature. When you are finished, leave the Main group window open.

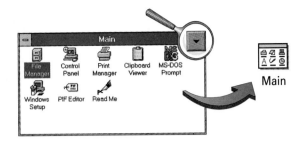

4. Double-click the Main icon to open it up into a window. (If you have problems doing this, see the box "Common Wrong Turns: Double-Clicking.")

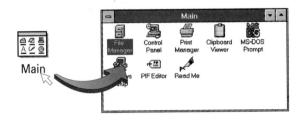

Dragging Windows and Icons

5. Point to Program Manager's title bar.

6. Hold down the left mouse button.

7. Drag the window to where you want it. As you are dragging the window, its outline is displayed.

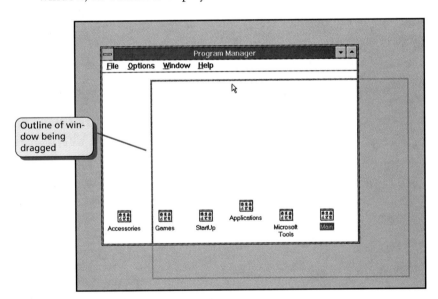

8. Release the left button.

9. If the Main group window is open, click its Minimize button to reduce it to an icon. Now point to the Main icon and hold down the left mouse button.

10. Drag the icon to where you want it and then release the mouse button.

11. Point to the Main icon again, hold down the left mouse button, and drag the icon to a new position but press [Esc] to cancel the

PAUSING FOR PRACTICE

Practice dragging windows and icons about the desktop until you feel comfortable with the procedure. Practice pressing [Esc] in the middle of dragging a group icon to cancel the move.

move before you release the mouse button. (This works with group icons but not with application icons.)

TIP: USING THE WINDOWS TUTORIAL TO LEARN ABOUT YOUR MOUSE

You can use Windows' built-in tutorial to learn more about using the mouse.

1. Point to the word **Help** on Program Manager's menu bar and click. A menu is pulled down.

2. Point to the **Windows Tutorial** command on the menu and click to execute the command.

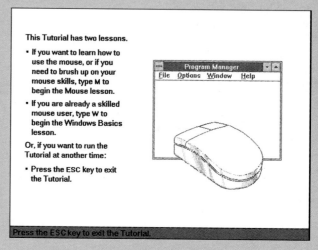

3. Press [M] to begin the mouse lesson.

4. Press [Enter ↵] to continue, and then follow the instructions that appear on the screen. You can press [Esc] at any point to end the tutorial.

A-6. MINIMIZING, MAXIMIZING, AND RESTORING WINDOWS

A window can be any one of three sizes: maximized so it fills the entire screen or the window that contains it, minimized to an icon, or restored to its original size to occupy only a part of the screen. To change sizes, you use the Maximize, Minimize, and Restore buttons located in the upper-right corner of each window (see the margin illustration).

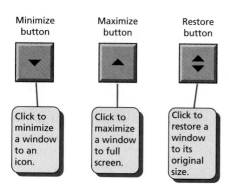

▶ Clicking the Minimize button (▼) minimizes the window to an icon. (Double-clicking an icon opens it up into a window of the same size it was before it was minimized.)

▶ Clicking the Maximize button (▲) expands the window to fill the screen or the window that contains it. Once you have clicked the Maximize button, it is replaced by the *Restore button*, which has both an up and a down arrowhead.

▶ Clicking the Restore button (↕) returns the window to its original size.

TUTORIAL

1. Click Program Manager's Maximize button to enlarge the window to full screen.

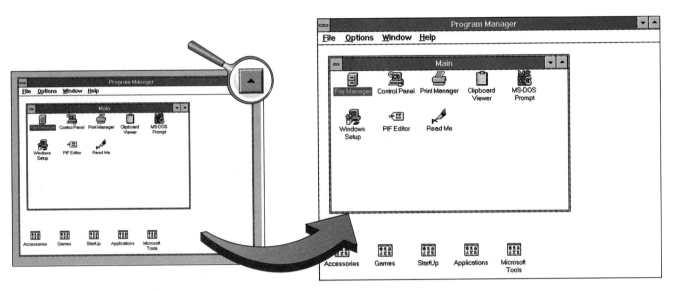

2. Click Program Manager's Restore button to restore the window to its original size.

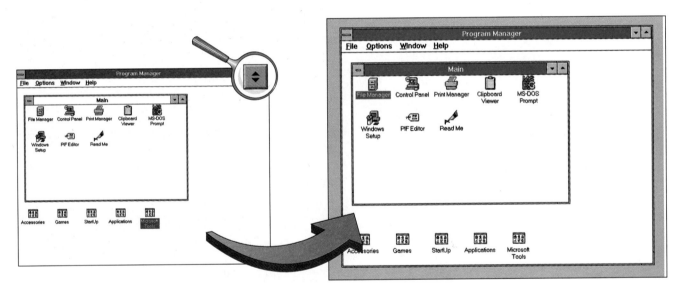

3. Click Program Manager's Minimize button to reduce the window to an icon.

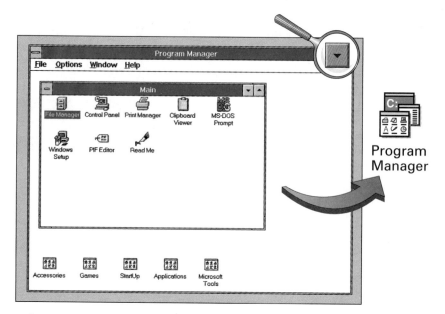

4. Double-click Program Manager's icon to open it back up into a window.

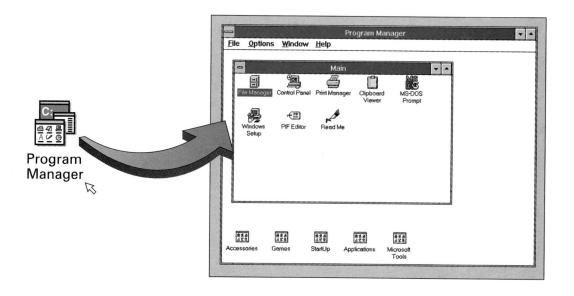

A-7. USING CONTROL MENUS

Every window has a Control-menu box in its upper-left corner. You can click this box to display a menu that performs such procedures as minimizing, maximizing, and restoring windows. (You display an icon's Control menu by clicking the icon.)

Double-clicking the Control-menu box also provides you with a shortcut to closing an open window. This procedure has different results depending on where you use it. For example, if you double-click Program Manager's Control-menu box, it ends your Windows session. If you double-click an application's Control-menu box, it closes the application. If you double-click a group window's Control-menu box, it minimizes it to an icon.

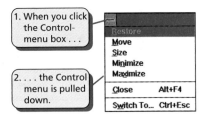

1. When you click the Control-menu box . . .

2. . . . the Control menu is pulled down.

The Control menu

TUTORIAL

1. Click Program Manager's Control-menu box located in the upper-left corner of its window to pull down the Control menu (see the upper margin illustration).

2. Click the **Minimize** command on the Control menu to reduce Program Manager to an icon.

3. Click Program Manager's icon to display its Control menu.

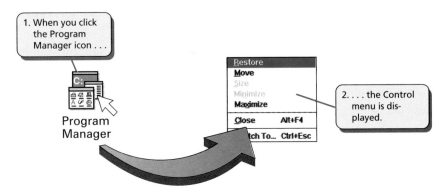

1. When you click the Program Manager icon . . .

Program Manager

2. . . . the Control menu is displayed.

4. Click the Control menu's **Restore** command to restore Program Manager to its original size.

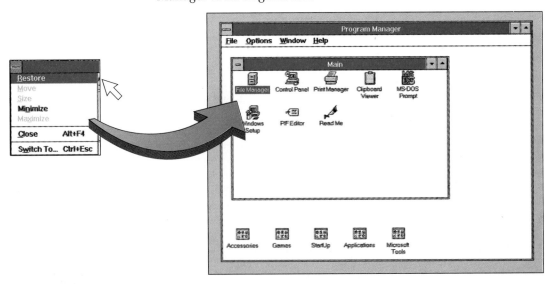

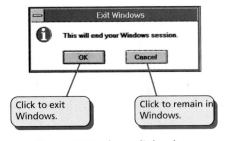

Click to exit Windows.

Click to remain in Windows.

The Exit Windows dialog box

5. Double-click Program Manager's Control-menu box to display a dialog box warning you that this will end your Windows session (see the lower margin illustration).

6. Click the **Cancel** command button to cancel the command. If you had clicked the **OK** command button, you would have exited the Windows program.

A-8. EXITING WINDOWS

When you have finished for the day, you should always exit Windows to return to the operating system. Windows frequently creates temporary files on the disk. When you exit correctly, these files are closed and all data is stored where it should be.

After exiting Windows, always do the following:

1. Remove any disks from the floppy disk drives. This will prevent their loss, increase security, and ensure that no one mistakenly erases them. (It also prevents the disk drives' read/write heads from leaving indentations in the disks' surfaces.) Make sure you take your own disks with you.

2. Turn off the computer or use the display monitor's controls to dim the screen so that an image will not be burned into its phosphor surface. (Windows has a built-in *screen saver* that you can turn on to prevent the screen from being damaged when the computer is left on for long periods of time with Windows running, but it is not available after you have exited Windows.)

TIP: EXITING WHEN YOU HAVEN'T SAVED YOUR WORK

If you try to exit Windows without first saving your work in an open application, you are prompted to save it and are offered the choices **Yes**, **No**, and **Cancel**. Click the **Yes** command button to save the file and the **No** command button to abandon it. To cancel the exit command and return to where you were, click the **Cancel** command button.

Point to the **File** menu name and click to pull down the menu.

File	Options	Window	H
New...			
Open	Enter		
Move...	F7		
Copy...	F8		
Delete	Del		
Properties...	Alt+Enter		
Run...			
Exit Windows...			

The File menu

TUTORIAL

1. If Program Manager is displayed as an icon, double-click it to open it up into a window. Click **File** on Program Manager's menu bar to pull down the menu (see the margin illustration).

COMMON WRONG TURNS: CLICKING COMMANDS

Many first-time users have trouble choosing commands because they don't point to the right place before clicking. The point of the mouse pointer must be over one of the letters in the command when you click. If it is above or below a letter, even by a little bit, you may execute the wrong command or the menu may disappear.

Point to the **Exit Windows** command and click to exit the program

File Options Window H
New...
Open   Enter
Move...   F7
Copy...   F8
Delete   Del
Properties...   Alt+Enter

Run...

Exit Windows...

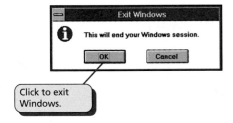

Exit Windows

This will end your Windows session.

OK   Cancel

Click to exit Windows.

2. Click the **Exit Windows** command on the menu (see the top margin illustration). A dialog box appears telling you that this will end your Windows session (see the bottom margin illustration).

3. Click the **OK** command button to exit or click the **Cancel** button to return to where you were if you want to continue working.

TIP: USING THE WINDOWS TUTORIAL TO LEARN MORE ABOUT WINDOWS

You can use Windows' built-in tutorial to learn more about using Windows. You run this tutorial from Windows Program Manager.

1. Point to Program Manager's **Help** menu and click to pull down the menu.

2. Point to the **Windows Tutorial** command and click to execute the command.

3. Press W to begin the Windows Basics lesson.

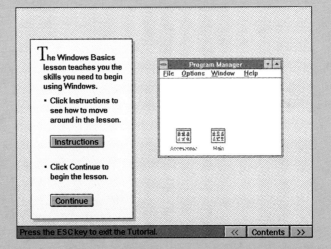

4. Follow the instructions that appear on the screen. Click the **Instructions** command button for advice on how to use the tutorial.

5. You can press Esc at any point to end the tutorial. To resume later, or to jump to another topic, click the **Contents** command button at the bottom of the screen. Then click the button in front of the topic you want to learn about.
